INTIMATE GRAMMARS

Intimate Grammars

An Ethnography of Navajo Poetry

ANTHONY K. WEBSTER

THE UNIVERSITY OF
ARIZONA PRESS

TUCSON

The University of Arizona Press
www.uapress.arizona.edu

Printed in the United States of America
21   20   19   18   17   16   7   6   5   4   3   2

ISBN-13: 978-0-8165-3153-0 (cloth)
ISBN-13: 978-0-8165-3419-7 (paper)

Cover design by David Drummond

Publication of this book is made possible in part by the proceeds of a permanent endowment
created with the assistance of a Challenge Grant from the National Endowment for the
Humanities, a federal agency.

Library of Congress Cataloguing-in-Publication Data
Webster, Anthony K., 1969– author.
  Intimate grammars : an ethnography of Navajo poetry / Anthony K. Webster.
    pages cm
  Includes bibliographical references and index.
  ISBN 978-0-8165-3153-0 (cloth : alk. paper)
  1. Navajo poetry—History and criticism. 2. Anthropological linguistics. I. Title.
  PM2008.5.W33 2015
  897.2'61009—dc23
                                    2014040047

♾ This paper meets the requirements of ANSI/NISO Z39.48-1992 (Permanence of Paper).

Contents

Preface and Acknowledgments

Thus all understanding is always at the same time a not-understanding,
all concurrence in thought and feeling at the same time divergence.
—WILHELM VON HUMBOLDT, *ON LANGUAGE*

The importance of poetry for Navajos can be suggested by noting that on April 24, 2013, Luci Tapahonso became the Navajo Nation's first poet laureate. I am unaware of any other Native American community having such a post. Its establishment asserts the prominence of Navajo poets and poetry and their equivalence to (and separateness from) the poetic traditions connected with the United States poet laureate and the poet laureate of the United Kingdom (on which the Navajo poet laureate's post is clearly modeled). Joel Sherzer (1990), writing about the Kuna of Panama, noted that "no Kuna verbal artist has ever won a Nobel prize. And none will." Sherzer argues that this is the case because Westerners "lack knowledge of and appreciation for" Kuna verbal artistry and because of a general devaluing of the verbal when compared to the written (13). There may come a day when a Navajo poet becomes U.S. poet laureate, but in creating a poet laureate of the Navajo Nation, Navajos have asserted the value and legitimacy of Navajo poets irrespective of the dominant society's aesthetic tastes and political leanings. Another poet, Rex Lee Jim, is—as of this writing in 2014—the vice president of the Navajo Nation. While Tapahonso and Jim are easily the most famous Navajo poets writing today, there are dozens of other Navajo poets that I have met over the years, and new poets continue to emerge (Sherwin Bitsui, personal communication, 2013).

This book attempts to combine an ethnography of speaking with a concern with ethnopoetics and to attend to some of the social work that some Navajos are attempting to engage in through their poetry. In short, this book is an extended exercise in listening. It is based on both ethnographic and linguistic research on and around the Navajo Nation as well as at poetry performances a fair distance from the American Southwest (i.e., in Pennsylvania and Illinois). In 2000 and2001 I lived on the Navajo Nation, first in Chinle, Arizona, and then in Lukachukai, Arizona. Here I did research on the emergence of contemporary written Navajo poetry that could be performed orally. Since then I have returned to the Navajo Nation for periods of fieldwork during the summers of 2007 to 2012. I have lived primarily near Shiprock, New Mexico, at the home of Blackhorse Mitchell. I have also traveled out to the Navajo Nation and its surrounds for various art openings and poetry performances at other times of the year. In 2014, I returned to the Navajo Nation to discuss the present book with Navajo poets and get their sense about the project. The response was positive. In my work with the Native American Heritage Month planning committee and as an associate professor in anthropology at Southern Illinois University at Carbondale (SIUC), I was also able to bring a number of Navajo poets, scholars, and filmmakers to Carbondale for performances, screenings, and lectures. Some of what they said at those events makes up parts of this book.

Research on the Navajo Nation could not have been done without permits from the Historic Preservation Office of the Navajo Nation. I especially thank Ron Maldonado for guiding me through the permit process. I also want to thank all the Navajos (poets and nonpoets) who have taken the time to talk with me over the years about a variety of topics. More than consultants, they have been my intellectual collaborators. Thanks to Ford Ashley, Tacey Atsitty, Esther Belin, Bert Benally, Zoey Benally, Sherwin Bitsui, Starrla Curley, Jennifer Denetdale, Tina Deschenie, Gloria Emerson, Larry Emerson, Nia Francisco, Karen Halona, Irene Hamilton, Cliff Jack, Rex Lee Jim, Hershman John, Damien Jones, Larry King, Bennie Klain, Aurelia Mitchell, Blackhorse Mitchell, Irvin Morris, Lorraine Nakai, the late Alyse Neundorf, Ellavina Perkins, Ed Singer, Luci Tapahonso, Wesley Thomas, Laura Tohe, Orlando White, and Venaya Yazzie. And thanks as well to those Navajos who wished to remain anonymous. I have been very fortunate to have kept company with such wonderful people. I also want to thank Sonja Horoshko, Bill Riddle, and Michael Thompson for their support and conversation while I've been out on and around the Navajo Nation. The debt this book owes to Blackhorse Mitchell cannot be overstated. I thank him for his patience and good humor and his generosity.

I've benefited from congenial places to work both at SIUC and at the University of Texas at Austin. I want to thank my colleagues at SIUC for enlivening my time there and for pushing my thinking in a myriad of new and interesting ways. Thanks especially to C. Andrew Hofling, Janet Fuller,

Jonathan Hill, David Sutton, Roberto Barrios, Gray Whaley, and Jo Nast. I was fortunate to have encountered and had the opportunity to get to know a delightful cadre of graduate students and now former graduate students at SIUC. They very much stimulated my thinking. Thanks to Dr. Aslihan Akkaya, Dr. Juan Rodríguez, Laura Warren, Morgan Siewert, Yuki Tanaka, Kamden Summers, Jiaying Liu, Monrico Brown, and Amanda Chahalis. About two-thirds of the way through the completion of this book, I left SIUC and returned to the University of Texas at Austin. It has been a wonderful and stimulating experience to return to my alma mater as faculty.

I've also greatly benefited from a lively network of scholars and friends in things Navajo, Athabaskan, linguistic-anthropological, and anthropological. Thanks to Rusty Barrett, Dick Bauman, Jeff Berglund, the late David Brugge, Erin Debenport, Ted Fernald, Margaret Field, Charlotte Frisbie, Thorsten Huth, Elizabeth Keating, Ward Keeler, Alex King, Lisa King, Paul Kockelman, Paul Kroskrity, Wesley Leonard, Paul Manning, Kim Marshall, Joyce McDonough, Barbra Meek, Eleanor Nevins, Janis Nuckolls, Sean O'Neill, Leighton Peterson, Willem de Reuse, Keren Rice, Scott Rushforth, David Samuels, Gwen Saul, Joel Sherzer, Mark Sicoli, Polly Strong, Dan Suslak, Siri Tuttle, Peter Wogan, Tony Woodbury, and Paul Zolbrod. Thanks too to Allyson Carter and the rest of the exceptional people at the University of Arizona Press and to the two reviewers of the book manuscript. Thanks to David Hill for boldly making this book a bit more readable.

Funding for this research has been provided at various times by the Wenner-Gren Foundation, the Phillips Fund of the American Philosophical Society, the Jacobs Fund from the Whatcom Museum, an Andrew Mellon postdoctoral fellowship at the Center for the Americas, Wesleyan University, a faculty seed grant from SIUC, and the University of Texas at Austin. I thank them very much. Earlier versions of some of the ideas taken up in this book have been published elsewhere. An earlier version of chapter 1 was published in the *Journal of Anthropological Research*. A different version of chapter 2 was published in the *Journal of Linguistic Anthropology*. Likewise, radically different versions of chapter 3 and chapter 4 were published respectively in the *American Indian Culture and Research Journal* and *Semiotica*. A very different version too of chapter 5 was published in the *Journal of Folklore Research*. The poem by Eugene Claw in chapter 3 is used with permission of the *Navajo Times*. The poetry by Blackhorse Mitchell is used with his permission.

I've been lucky to have the support of friends and family. They have made my days more enjoyable and more meaningful. I thank them all. My late father was a member of the Izaak Walton League and I remember spending much time with him at the League chapter at Cedar Creek in Indiana. Years later, older, I would read Walton's *The Compleat Angler* and take to heart Walton's final line (see the conclusion of this book). My mother was a lover of words and a one-time poet as well. My mother and father—both now deceased—remain a presence in my thinking. They linger in these pages. So too does my delightful aunt Helen Robinson, a retired art teacher, who it has been a joy to get to know better these last several years. Sadly, she was not able to see this book to completion. As Indiana native and American Impressionist painter T. C. Steele's headstone acknowledges: "Beauty outlives everything." Finally, anthropology is a strange business and can be trying on the families and spouses of anthropologists. Most of my summers have been spent on the Navajo Nation. And many of my days have been filled with the verbal ramblings that became this book. I thank my wife Aimee Hosemann for being so patient and so understanding. This book is for her.

INTIMATE GRAMMARS

Introduction

One way to think of the society in which one would like to live is to think of the kinds of voices it would have.
—DELL HYMES (1996A: 64), "REPORT FROM AN UNDERDEVELOPED
   COUNTRY: TOWARD LINGUISTIC COMPETENCE IN THE UNITED STATES"

Here is a bit of discourse from an October evening in 2006 in Carbondale, Illinois. The speaker is Navajo poet Laura Tohe and the event in question is to celebrate Southern Illinois University's Indigenous Peoples' Day. Lines are segmented according to breath-pause structure (Molina and Evers 1998).*

This a a poem that I wrote
long time ago when I was
first starting to write
a:h
and this is
about
Gallup Ceremonial
which is an event that takes place yearly in Gallup, New Mexico
a:h a lot of Indians and tourists come to the:
look at Native culture
and every year they have a
parade that goes through downtown Gallup

---

* Throughout this book, I have used line breaks to indicate breath-pause structure for speech I recorded. I do this not to argue that Navajos always speak in poetic lines, but rather to suggest something of the cadence and rhythm of the speakers, that is, to highlight something of the individual's "voice" (see Blommaert 2006). Here and in other transcripts, I use vowel doubling when a vowel is phonologically long (as in *saad*), but a colon when the length is phonetic (*a:h*).

I was [cough]
use to go there a lot with my family
and a so this poem is about that
and it's in two voices

"The Gallup Ceremonial Poem"

Midwesterner at the Gallup Ceremonial [clears throat]

"Look Mabel why don't you be more like that Indian couple
the old man is walking in front of the old woman
leading the way
now that is real tradition there"
upon hearing this a Navajo woman says,
"you're right
that is tradition
Navajo women have been walking behind their husbands since
time
immemorial"

Midwesterner
"Now I call that a tradition worth keeping"

Navajo woman
"Yes, Navajo women have been doing that
but they tell the men which way to go"
[laughter]

What are we to make of this poem by Tohe? The poem is predicated on
Midwestern tourists' misrecognition of Navajo semiotic practice (namely,
the way Navajo women follow Navajo men). Or more basically, it is predicated on Midwestern tourists' understanding of Navajo practices as rein-
forcing dominant white middle-class values. But, as the poem indicates,
this is a misrecognition and, indeed, Navajo values do not align with the
imagined Midwestern values of male dominance. In fact, the poem inverts
the relationship and it is Navajo women who direct Navajo men.

Considering "The Gallup Ceremonial Poem" as an abstract poem decon-
textualized from its immediate performance context, so far so good. But
what if we think of this stretch of discourse as embedded within a context
and see it and its introduction as a form of social action?

First we might note the way that Tohe already must contextualize the poem. She cannot assume that the audience—here students, faculty, staff, and community members at a Midwestern university—has the same stock of knowledge that she or other Navajos or people who live in Gallup might bring to this poem. She must explain what the Gallup Ceremonial is and who is likely to be in attendance. She does this succinctly and does not dwell on the ongoing debate among Navajos about the exploitative nature of the Gallup Ceremonial; though there is a telling moment, when she describes what the tourists and other Indians do as "look at Native culture." Tourists do not participate in Native culture, they look at it. And, as the poem suggests, it is in that looking that they see Native culture on their—tourists'—terms and not on Navajo terms. So we can note that Tohe has given an abbreviated bit of background knowledge so that the audience can understand the poem. Much as, it seems clear, the Navajo woman in the poem provides context about Navajo women following Navajo men to the Midwestern tourists so that they might recognize what is going on.

But this only gets us half the distance, I think. We might ask not just what this poem is about, but also why this poem at this event? The poem is read fairly early on in the evening. It was the very first poem that Tohe read that night. Might we not see Tohe's performance of this poem as placing non-Navajo misrecognition of Navajo practices at the forefront, challenging the audience to suspend their preconceived (and likely wrong) assumptions about Navajos. Like with much speech play, the overt humor may obscure the undercurrent of seriousness and critique (see K. Basso 1979; Sherzer 2002). This is poetry as intercultural critique. It is also a cautionary tale, meant to remind the audience that they do not know as much about Navajos as they may think and that knowledge will come from more than mere superficial observation, it will only come from full engagement. Her performing this poem challenges the certainty of the expectations of the audience. While funny, the poem has a serious message: you don't know nearly as much as you think you do about Navajos. Pay attention. Suspend your expectations. Listen.

∾

This book is an ethnography of contemporary Navajo poets and poetry. As such, it has its roots firmly planted in the linguistic-anthropological traditions of the ethnography of speaking, ethnopoetics, and a discourse-centered approach to language and culture (Hymes 1974, 1981, 2003; Bauman 1984; Bauman and Sherzer [1974] 1989; Sherzer 1983, 1987, 1990; Sherzer and

Woodbury 1987; Urban 1991). The focus of several of the chapters is on the actual words of Navajo poets, both in their poetry and in conversations. Conversations have been transcribed and presented and poems have been analyzed based on an awareness of Navajo ethnopoetics. The ethnography of speaking sought to understand speech—or communicative practice— as a cultural phenomenon in need of description and analysis. It treated languages as forms of social action and did not reduce them to abstract systems. Languages are cultural. A discourse-centered approach to language and culture forces us to focus on actual instances of discourse and not to reduce either language or culture to mere abstractions. They are emergent and contingent. I take ethnopoetics to be an attempt to understand local aesthetic and poetic practices within a wider field of meaningful communicative practice. And like language and culture, these practices too are emergent and contingent. My discussion of Navajo interlingual puns in chapter 5 should, I hope, make this clear (see also Webster 2010a).

This book is also, as it must be, about misrecognition. As Navajo historian Jennifer Denetdale (2007: 19) has noted, "Navajos continue to be understood within Western frameworks, thereby contributing to the ongoing distortion of the realities of Native lives, cultures . . . histories"—and, I would add, languages and poetry. Navajo poets are confronted with outside expectations. These expectations concern who they are and what kinds of languages they can and cannot control or use. One Navajo poet told me he often feels that many people who come to hear him read come for an "exotic" experience. He, as a human being, is incidental to that experience. In a previous work (Webster 2009), I argued that Navajo poetry was a kind of reckoning and a form of storytelling (*hane'*). In this book, I want to pursue different questions and think about issues of misrecognition and expectations. My goal is to analyze the ways that Navajo poets confront and challenge forms of misrecognition based on dominant expectations about Navajos and Navajo ways of being through their poetry. In simpler terms, I want to understand the kinds of social work that Navajo poets engage in through their poetry. Or said again, what they might be trying to say in and through their poetry.

There is also the question of "fame" or "renown" for Navajo poets. This is a complicated issue because many Navajos have told me that one should not call undue attention to oneself. Rather, people should recognize the work that a poet does without the poet having to constantly proclaim that work. They contrast this with what they view as the dominant society and celebrities and how people often seem overly dedicated to proclaiming how great they are. Stated simply, one should not brag about one's accomplishments.

As a couple Navajo consultants discussed with me, "fame" in Navajo is best understood as *shaa 'áhwiinidzin* 'know where I stand' (*shaa* 'about me', *'áhwiini-* 'in that manner', *-dzin* 'to know'). People should know where you stand from the work that you have done, not from you constantly telling them what you have done. One way that Navajo poets mitigate a focus on them as individuals is to traditionalize their poetry and place it within the voice of tradition (Webster 2012b). But this question of proper comportment is an issue that many poets feel deeply; many feel uncomfortable talking about their accomplishments, lest it be thought "bragging." They worry that such actions will be seen by other Navajos as displaying arrogance, hubris, and a lack of self-control (that is, acting in an ugly manner—see chapter 5). This book, I hope, is in the service of recognizing and acknowledging the artistry and social work of contemporary Navajo poets and their poetry.

This book is also part of a larger trend in linguistic anthropology of attending to the diversity of speech practices and the lived realities of Native peoples (see Webster and Peterson 2011). Recent linguistic-anthropological work among Indigenous communities by Erin Debenport (2011, 2012), Eleanor Nevins (2013), David Samuels (2004a), Barbra Meek (2010), Leighton C. Peterson (2011, 2013), Shaylih Muehlmann (2013), Paja Faudree (2013), Bernard Perley (2011), Justin Richland (2007), Mindy Morgan (2009), Wesley Leonard (2011), Dan Suslak (2011), me (Webster 2009), and Paul Kroskrity (2012a) have challenged assumptions about static and timeless Native languages and communities. Whether it be the Tewa soap operas described by Debenport (2011), the texting of Miami described by Leonard, or the use of Maliseet in graphic novels described by Perley, we need to explore the full range of languages in use. We need ethnography. It is through ethnography, I would contend, that we can recognize what Perley calls "emergent vitalities," the new ways that people delight in languages in use. Poetry—in a variety of languages and registers—is an emerging vitality for many Navajos.

Understanding Navajo poetry as a form of social action, then, entails looking closely at the context in which this poetry is created and performed. Part of that context, and the focus of chapter 1, is the inequality that exists between linguistic varieties and the felt attachments that adhere to certain stigmatized linguistic varieties in response to those inequalities. I term this phenomenon, following the work of Michael Herzfeld (1997) and Elizabeth Povinelli (2006), "intimate grammars." I take intimate grammars to be emotionally saturated uses of language that run the risk of negative evaluation by outsiders or nonoutsiders but are deeply and expressively feelingful for individuals. I look at intimate grammars by way of discussing something of the heteroglossia that daily confronts Navajos on and around the Navajo Nation (located in the American Southwest).

There is, as I discuss in chapter 2, a potent image that haunts much discussion concerning the Navajo language. This image is that of the boarding-school experience. In chapter 2, I examine that image and how it plays out in Laura Tohe's *No Parole Today*. In this chapter, I argue that Tohe dramatizes language use and creates an affective bond between speakers and the languages that they use. Rather than explicitly stating that Navajo should be the language of social intimacy for Navajos, Tohe dramatizes such relationships. Such implicit metadiscourses gain added import when understood within the larger social fields of the Navajo Nation and current beliefs, feelings, and values about the Navajo language. This chapter lays out the groundwork for how languages come to be feelingfully recognized and how concomitantly they can also be misrecognized.

If the Navajo language was at times stigmatized and dismissed in the boarding-school context, the Navajo English that emerged in the boarding schools was misrecognized as deficient English. This denial of Navajo English as a feelingfully expressive and satisfying way of speaking and writing is the topic of chapter 3. Here I focus on the work of Navajo author Blackhorse Mitchell, his 1967 book *Miracle Hill*, and his complicated relationship with his Anglo teacher T. D. Allen. Allen and many reviewers of the book consistently misrecognized Mitchell's use of Navajo English as mistakes. Mitchell, in an interview that I did with him, reasserts his voice and his language when he performs the poem "The Drifting Lonely Seed" for me. As the chapter further discusses, Mitchell was not the only Navajo poet whose work was misrecognized.

In chapter 4, I continue with the work of Blackhorse Mitchell and examine a performance of his poem "The Beauty of Navajoland" in Pennsylvania in 2004 as well as a series of more recent discussions I have had with him about this poem. The poem concerns an Anglo tourist misrecognizing what is really happening on the Navajo Nation. Instead of seeing the "ugliness" on the Navajo Nation, the tourist only sees the "beauty" of the Navajo Nation. I also discuss how I originally misrecognized Mitchell's use of the term *ugly* as a strange aesthetic judgment because I had treated it as if it were the same as in my variety of English. It was only later that I realized that *ugly* as Mitchell used it was a Navajo English form that had a different semantic meaning and a different context. I had, in ways a bit too uncomfortable, fallen into the same linguistic trap that T. D. Allen had fallen into with her critique of Mitchell's use of Navajo English, discussed in the previous chapter. Centrally this chapter is about learning to listen.

In chapter 5, I look at a poem by Rex Lee Jim that relies on the use of an expressive feature of Navajo. The expressive feature is the insertion of a velar fricative (*-x-*). This expressive feature does not so much change the semantic meaning of the word as the attitudinal stance toward the word. Jim uses the expressive feature to connect the poem with the concept of *hóchxǫ'* 'ugly'. This connection is based on punning and, indeed, an understanding of punning practices among Navajos suggests ways of attending to this poem that might reduce cases of misrecognition. Three kinds of misrecognition come into play here. First, linguists and anthropological linguists, because of a bias toward semantic and referential meaning and against expressive meanings, have sometimes been inclined to ignore such features because they were not deemed important. Second, because Jim writes the -x- into the words of the poem, some Navajo readers have misrecognized it as spelling mistakes and not as a creative achievement. Third, the poem is about not recognizing what one is doing to oneself. Like "The Beauty of Navajoland" by Mitchell, Jim is trying to alert Navajos to what they are doing so that they might begin to change. In Navajo terms, a state of *hóchxǫ'* 'ugliness' might be restored to *hózhǫ́* 'beauty'.

Later in the evening, long after Tohe had read her poem about the Midwestern tourists misrecognizing Navajo social facts according to their normative expectations, one of the audience members in attendance asked Tohe about the ancient Navajo writing system that had been shown on the television series *The X-Files*. The audience member was not asking about the ways that *The X-Files* had exoticized or othered Navajos and what Tohe thought of such representations, but rather if Tohe had firsthand experience with those ancient texts or knew anything about them. It was not the first time nor would it be the last time I heard such a question asked of a Navajo poet. Tohe's response was to direct the audience member to talk with me, since I was an "expert" on Navajo writing. Question avoided. But the reality seems inescapable that Navajos live in a world where outside expectations predominate. It also suggests that the art of listening, which many Navajos see as essential to the acquisition of knowledge, is an important skill to be cultivated so that forms of misrecognition and dominant expectations that result in ongoing structures of social inequality might be lessened. This book is an attempt to engage in a bit of listening and to hear, partially, never completely, what some Navajo poets have been saying.

CHAPTER ONE

Intimacies of Grammar

Then she said, "Wooshíí, wooshíí," and a radiant river
of baby laughter filled the hooghan.
—LUCI TAPAHONSO, *OLD SALT WOMAN*

In this chapter I survey the ethnolinguistic contours embedded in and consti-
tutive of a conception of the Navajo Nation, and look at the ways individuals
engage with languages. I conceive of the Navajo Nation as a politically
and socioculturally constituting locality that—through a variety of semiotic practices—radiates outward across various media (from face-to-face
interactions to books of poetry to social media on the Internet). By "the
ways individuals engage with languages," I mean the ways that individuals emotionally invest linguistic forms with "feeling tones" (Sapir 1921:
40). These felt attachments to linguistic forms do not occur in a vacuum,
of course, and here I am specifically interested in the ways that linguistic
forms come to be icons of identity, icons that are deeply felt, but that can
be evaluated negatively by outsiders. Taking Elizabeth Povinelli's (2006)
provocative term *intimate grammars* as a starting point, I want to combine it
with Michael Herzfeld's (1997) concern with "cultural intimacy" and investigate the ways that certain stigmatized ways of speaking can be expressions of an intimate grammar, an emotionally saturated use of language
that runs the risk of negative evaluation by outsiders (or nonoutsiders), yet
is deeply and expressively feelingful for individuals.* As Bonnie Urciuoli
(1996: 178–79) notes, the languages of "non-white 'races'" in the United
States are always "objects of scrutiny." Here, for example, one thinks of

---

* For useful discussions and applications of intimate grammars see Suslak 2010; Kroskrity
2011; Meek 2014.

Ana Celia Zentella's (2002, 2003) work on "Spanglish" and the pleasure that some bilingual speakers and writers take in the play across languages, including in poetry, even in the face of stigmatization and discrimination. As Zentella (2003: 61) states, uses of Spanglish "are part of the linguistic glue that binds Latin@s from distinct communities to each other." The fact is that even under scrutiny, individuals build affective bonds with linguistic forms, with languages.

In a provocative piece on the social inequalities of languages, Dell Hymes (1996a: 26) argues that "in actuality language is in large part what users have made of it. Navajo is what it is partly because it is a human language, partly because it is the language of Navajo[s]." My focus in this book will be on the ways that Navajo poets make sense of their languages, which include: Navajo English, a distinctive English dialect spoken and written by many Navajos on and around the Navajo Nation in the American Southwest and beyond; Navlish, a code-mixed variety spoken and written by many Navajos in the American Southwest and beyond; and Navajo, a Southern Athabaskan language also spoken and written in the American Southwest and beyond. Note that in actual practice there is no strict division between Navajo, Navajo English, and Navlish. I will engage a variety of ethnographic fragments concerning Navajo poets' affective relations to linguistic forms and the ways these forms are either scrutinized or imagined as objects of scrutiny. In each case, I argue that language is to be understood as an intimate grammar, a grammar that is potentially (if not actually) devalued by others (be they Navajo or non-Navajo). Rather than understanding language as something that is shared equally, I argue that individuals invest linguistic forms with felt attachments. These attachments accrue over time and make the uses of such intimate grammars iconic (see Friedrich 1979). This book is also part of the broader project of ethnography of poetry and poetic practices (see Caton 1990; Cavanaugh 2009).

Linguistic and language insecurities are a complex issue for many minority groups, and this is certainly true of Native Americans and Navajos as well (see Schaengold 2003; Field 2009; see also Kroskrity and Field 2009; Peterson and Webster 2011; Kroskrity 2012b). *Language insecurities* I take to be insecurities about the languages one speaks (or writes), for example, Navajo or English or Navajo English. *Linguistic insecurities* are, then, insecurities about the linguistic forms used in speaking (or writing), such as pluralization, tense markings, and pronunciations. Obviously, the two overlap a fair amount and there is not a sharp division. Young Navajos (and older Navajos too) are often negatively evaluated for their English-language skills or for their Navajo-language skills. These negative evaluations can come either from dominant outside institutions or from fellow Navajos. Navajos are quite aware that their speech can be and often is negatively evaluated as deficient. There is history here. Many Navajos are quite aware that the Navajo language has been the object of the dominant society's scorn and that it was also targeted for suppression and/or eradication. Older Navajos still tell of their experiences with boarding school, where speaking Navajo was either forbidden or devalued. Some Navajos have internalized Western educational notions of "correct" and "incorrect" grammar (see Platero 2001). Younger Navajos have experienced criticism for their use of Navajo, Navlish, or Navajo English, either from other Navajos or from outsiders. As Clay Slate, Martha Jackson, and Tony Goldtooth (1989: 12) note, "language shame is a problem for Navajo adolescents, many of whom will deny even understanding the language in most settings" (see also Lee 2007; Field 2009). Speaking, for many Navajos, is a tension-filled site, where they always run the risk of negative evaluation for their choices and uses of linguistic forms that are always objects of scrutiny.

Navajo poets face similar issues when they choose a language to write in or to perform in. That is, Navajo poets also run the risk of negative evaluations for the languages they use. These negative evaluations can again come from outside dominant standard-language ideologies (L. Milroy 2000) or from Navajos who have internalized certain standard-language ideologies (Field 2009). Yet, in spite of such risks, Navajo poets write and perform Navajo poetry in a variety of languages and linguistic forms. These poets are often quite aware of the risks such poetry represents, that it can and will be stereotyped as "Indian" or deficient or, as one Navajo consultant explained to me, "wrong." As Esther Belin once explained to me, concerning her then-new book of poetry (1999), her book was evidence not just that she could write English but that she could succeed at writing poetry in English. On the other hand, I have heard non-Navajos negatively evaluate the use of Navajo English in the poetry of Luci Tapahonso, where it is a stylistic device.

Many Navajo poets are also aware that some non-Navajos have expectations of what should and should not be written by Navajo poets. Minimal displays of Navajo are acceptable indexes of ethnic identity, but code-mixed forms such as Navlish or Navajo English violate a predominant standard-language ideology, under which linguistic difference is understood as linguistic deficit (see Lippi-Green 1997; L. Milroy 2000). While Navajo poetry is a relatively secured domain for the use of Navajo (see Woodbury 1998; Webster 2009), outside of such demarcated ethnically appropriate and "safe" domains, Navajo is still a language that is often devalued or stigmatized by many non-Navajos. This is especially true in the Navajo Nation's border towns. Certainly, following Urciuoli (1996), poetry is a nonthreatening domain where the Navajo language might be deemed "aesthetically" pleasing by a non-Navajo dominant society that seems reactionary with regard to language use in "the workplace." Indeed, conflicts do arise when Navajo is used in "the workplace" (see Zachary 2005). Dominant views of subordinate expressive forms as mere ethnic markers trivialize linguistic practices (see Zentella 2002: 323 on the "*chiquita*-fication" of Spanish). As Urciuoli (1996: 35) has noted, many displays of ethnic difference (including the use of languages other than English) revolve around dominant attempts at "ethnification" in which difference is sanctioned by making it "cultural, neat, and safe." But even in such "safe" moments, cannot an emotional bond between languages and language users perdure?

Cultural Intimacy and Intimate Grammars

A number of linguistic anthropologists have critiqued the Saussurean view of the arbitrariness of the sign (see Friedrich 1979, 1986; Feld 1988; Becker 1995; Farnell 1995; Nuckolls 1996; Samuels 2004a; Leavitt 2011). Following C. S. Peirce (1956), they have argued for an understanding of expressive forms as engaging in iconicity. Briefly, the Peircean trichotomy of signs involves: (1) *symbols*, the relatively arbitrary signs that represent something to someone; (2) *indexes*, those signs that "point" to social personas, places, contexts, and so on; and (3) *icons*, those signs that bear some "resemblance" to what they represent. All signs are to various degrees symbolic, indexical, and iconic simultaneously. As Brenda Farnell (1995) points out, there has been a Western bias against iconicity because it has been naïvely understood as more "primitive" or "basic." Both Roman Jakobson (1960) and Dell Hymes (1960) have argued for the intertwining of sound and meaning (especially in poetry) and against any naïve view of language or reference as "arbitrary." Paul Friedrich (1979), Steven Feld (1988), and David Samuels (2004b) have begun to sketch out something of the emotional or felt connection to linguistic and expressive forms. Such connections are saturated with iconicity, because the forms feel as if they resemble what they are expressing.

Edward Sapir (1921, 1925, 1929b), as Friedrich (1979: 39) notes, was less taken with the equation of "convention" and "arbitrariness" than a number of his contemporaries. Sapir was concerned with "expressive symbolism," symbolism that was psychologically salient and felt (1929b). For Sapir, words had "feeling tones" (1921: 39–41). These feeling tones were built up by individuals over time through uses, both their own uses and those of others. Such feelings, I would argue, are the iconicity of language, the felt attachments to language and linguistic forms that makes the use of such forms feel "consubstantial" and nonarbitrary (Friedrich 1979: 40). As Sapir, in the wake of World War I, notes, "would we be so ready to die for 'liberty,' to struggle for 'ideals,' if the words themselves were not ringing within us?" (1921: 17). This is what Samuels (2004a: 11) dubs "feelingful iconicity" or "an emotional attachment to aesthetic forms" or as Feld (1988: 132) puts it, echoing Friedrich (1986), "the emotionally satisfying dimensions" of aesthetic forms.

Given that linguistic forms gain felt attachments that make their uses feel nonarbitrary and consubstantial, that individuals invest linguistic forms with feelings, we might term the feelingful aspects of language, following Povinelli (2006) after a fashion, "intimate grammars." Povinelli is, more generally, arguing for an "intimate pragmatics"; here she wishes to combine metapragmatics with a more "psychoanalytically inspired account of subjectivity and desire" (193). My goal is less ambitious. Where I find resonance with Povinelli's work is in the ways that gender deictics—'he' or 'she'—can be evaluated as violating normative expectations (194). As she argues:

> Conservative language critics of feminist language projects sense but misdiagnose this metapragmatic function of grammar whey they accuse feminists or queer activists of incoherency or worse. . . . In English the refusal to abide by normative rules of pronominal usage only *seems* to render the semantics of an average conversation, well, queer—ill-informed, dysfunctional insofar as it is contra-normative, if not anti-normative. (195)

Yet, and here is my point, speakers are aware of such potential negative evaluations and, in spite of them, they persist in their use of "contranormative" linguistic forms. These uses, which run the risk of external critique, are displays of intimate grammars.

Here I find resonance with Herzfeld's (1997) concern with "cultural intimacy." By "cultural intimacy," Herzfeld means the "aspects of cultural identity that are considered a source of external embarrassment but that nevertheless provide insiders with their assurance of common sociality" (3). A part of this cultural intimacy is iconicity. As Herzfeld notes, "iconicity seems natural and is therefore an effective way of creating self-evidence" (27). Intimate grammars are a kind of cultural intimacy. By using linguistic forms that are felt to be iconic but are known to be externally devalued or sanctioned, individuals display a sense of intimate grammar. As Judith Irvine and Susan Gal (2000: 37) explain it, "linguistic features that index social groups or activities appear to be iconic representations of them, as if a linguistic feature somehow depicted or displayed a social group's inherent nature or essence." Such linguistic forms do not just index identity, they are feelingfully iconic of identity, an identity that is often positioned in contrast to "significant others." Here I follow David Sutton's (2008) work on Greek islanders' ways of imagining themselves in relation to outsiders, European or Athenian, Turk or American. The term *significant others* (85) should remind us of the intimacy that is often evoked in the processes of othering. The significant others for many Navajos are mainstream Anglo-American society, or what some Navajos refer to as "white society" or the "dominant society."

For example, a familiar critique of Navajo English is the use of the regular plural marking *-s* on *sheep*, that is, *sheeps* (see T. D. Allen 1967: xi; see also Bartelt 2001: 94). This, of course, violates mainstream language standards and can be and is understood as a mistake, a lack of understanding of the English language. This was the position that T. D. Allen took in her introduction to Blackhorse Mitchell's (1967; see now 2004) semiautobiographical book *Miracle Hill*. Yet in a number of conversations that I have had with Mitchell over the years he has explicitly stated that *sheeps* is not a mistake. Let me also stress, as Mitchell has to me, that he does not consider *sheep* to be a mistake. Instead, he prefers *sheeps* for aesthetic and practical reasons. He has a felt attachment to the form. It both sounds "better" and "makes more sense" to him than using *sheep* for the plural. Mitchell is also quite aware that his use of *sheeps* will be negatively evaluated as a mistake by external, Anglo-American mainstream language standards. For Mitchell, then, plural marking on *sheep* is an intimate grammar.

Navajos and Navajo Poetry

The Navajo Nation, covering parts of Arizona, New Mexico, and Utah, is roughly the size of West Virginia. According to the 2000 U.S. Census, there are nearly 300,000 people who identify as Navajo. Further, 178,014 people identified themselves on the census as speakers of Navajo, with roughly 120,000 of those identifying themselves as residents of the Navajo Nation. Rough numbers, then, give an impression that the Navajo language is widely spoken (in fact, it is spoken in every state in the U.S.) by a significant number of people. However, as Navajo scholars such as Tiffany Lee (2007) and AnCita Benally (Benally and Viri 2005) point out, the Navajo language is a threatened language. It is threatened in the sense that young Navajos are not learning it at a rate that will ensure its continued use. Also, despite a number of efforts over the years, literacy in Navajo is still rather limited (see McLaughlin 1992; Spolsky 2002). Both Navlish and Navajo English (to be discussed below) are also spoken on and around the Navajo Nation.

As I discuss in more detail in chapter 3, in 1933 a short eight-line poem was published in *Indians at Work*, a U.S. government publication (Hirschfelder and Singer 1992). The poem was composed by a collection of Navajo students at Tohatchi School in New Mexico (on the Navajo Nation). This poem, "If I Were a Pony," was one of the first published poems by Navajos and it concerned the desire the students had to be free of the school (like the aforementioned pony). The poem was written in English. Other poetry in English would follow. Much of it would be written in boarding schools and about the boarding-school experience. In the early 1960s, for example, Blackhorse Mitchell would write poetry that expressed his frustrations with the boarding school and his desire to be free from the boarding school (see chapter 3). For Mitchell, poetry was one way to find a voice in the boarding-school environment. Much of the critique of the boarding school would go unnoticed by Mitchell's teachers. Indeed, the Bureau of Indian Affairs schools would encourage the writing of poetry by young Navajos as a way to teach them English. Gloria Emerson (1971, 1972) would publish politically engaged poetry in English in the overtly political journal the *Indian Historian*. During the 1970s more and more Navajos began to write poetry. In 1977, Nia Francisco published a poem in Navajo in the journal *College English*. In the 1980s and 1990s even more poetry was published by Navajos; it appeared in major literary journals as well as through university presses. By the mid to late 1980s individually authored books of Navajo poetry were appearing.

Today there are a number of recognized Navajo poets. They include Navajo poet laureate Luci Tapahonso, Rex Lee Jim, Gloria Emerson, Blackhorse Mitchell, Esther Belin, Sherwin Bitsui, Hershman John, Orlando White, Venaya Yazzie, and Laura Tohe. Many of these poets have had their poetry published by major university presses. For example, Tohe's (2005) most recent book of poetry and prose was published by the University of Arizona Press. *No Parole Today* (Tohe 1999) was published by West End Press in Albuquerque but was distributed by the University of New Mexico Press. Tohe's most recent book was available for purchase at 'Ahwééh/ Gohwééh in the summers of 2007 and 2008. 'Ahwééh/Gohwééh (Coffee/ Coffee) was a coffee shop in Shiprock, New Mexico (on the Navajo Nation) run by Gloria Emerson that sold a number of books of poetry by Navajo authors and also sponsored poetry readings and the like. Unfortunately, and bespeaking the realities of running a business on the reservation, the coffee shop has since closed. A recent trend has been for Navajo poets to self-publish chapbooks of poetry. This includes, for example, publishing digital chapbooks that can be purchased and downloaded (see Ashley 2013). More than one Navajo poet has told me about a poetry manuscript that was rejected for not being "Navajo" enough. Navajo poets write and perform in a variety of languages. Predominantly they write in English, but Navajo poets also write in such stigmatized languages as Navajo English, Navlish, and, indeed, Navajo. Many Navajo poets perform their poetry for Navajo audiences on the Navajo Nation (see Webster 2009).

Navajo English

I want to begin by taking a closer look at the work of Navajo poet (among other things) Blackhorse Mitchell and his use of Navajo English. I will return to this topic in later chapters. First, I should say something about Navajo English. Navajo English is a distinctive local way of speaking and writing English that differs from an imagined "standard English" in a myriad of ways (see Leap 1993a, b; Bartelt 1981, 1983, 2001). These differences are phonological, syntactic, morphological, semantic, and discourse-related. As I noted above, plural marking on some irregular nouns, such as *sheep*, occurs. There is no gender distinction on pronouns in Navajo English. Pronouns that mainstream English speakers would understand as marking 'male' or 'female' are used interchangeably for, as far as I have been able to discern, no rhetorical effect. On the other hand, Navajo English speakers often use what are considered tense markings as aspect markers. As Guillermo Bartelt (1981: 382) notes, "much of the idiosyncratic tense usage found in Navajo English is a result of the use of English tenses as a vehicle for the expression of Navajo aspects and modes. Specifically, the English present tense seems to be used for the transfer of the Navajo usitative [habitual] mode, imperfective mode, and continuative aspect." Some of the distinctiveness of Navajo English is thus likely to be transfer from Navajo, while other features, such as plural markings on irregular nouns, are likely the process of regularization (see Bartelt 1981, 2001).

Like other nonmainstream uses of English, Navajo English is often negatively evaluated as mistakes or errors in using English (Leap 1993a; Lippi-Green 1997; Platero 2001; Meek 2011). The use of Navajo English is often seen, by external standards (sometimes internalized by Navajos as well), as a failure (Harvey 1974, 1976). It is true, as Susan Penfield (1982: 24) notes, that "on many reservations, where Indian English is the dominant linguistic code, it carries a sense of tribal identity with it that was once associated with the native language. That is, there is a positive social reinforcement within the Indian community for speaking English in a tribally specific way." Penfield's observation applies in certain respects to the Navajo community. As Esther Belin once explained to me, "English is a Diné language." However, it is also the case, as Lionel Wee (2005) notes, that intralanguage diversity—of which Navajo English is an example—is often stigmatized and devalued both by outsiders and even within communities. Take, as a brief example, an exchange that occurred on the *Navajo Times* Facebook page in April 2011. The *Navajo Times* asked its readership how they thought current Navajo Nation president Ben Shelly and vice president Rex Lee Jim were doing. One respondent posted the following (in each of the following examples I have followed the formatting in the original, including spelling, capitalization, and ellipsis points):*

AN EMBARRASSMENT TO THE NAVAJO PEOPLE! KNOWLEDGE OF THE ENGLISH LANGUAGE IS IMPORTANT TO PEOPLE OUTSIDE THE NATION. IF THEY CANNOT GRASP OR SPEAK PROPER ENGLISH, IT REFLECTS ON THE NATION AS A WHOLE! (Posted April 13, 2011)

This was then followed the same day by another respondent posting:

I have also been horrified at the language Ben Shelley uses. Such horrible grammar . . . I do not know how he is where he is today. He is a complete embarrassment to the Navajo people. . . .

Both of these respondents identified themselves as Navajos. Other self-identified Navajos challenged this position concerning President Shelly's English-language abilities. For example, one respondent that day posted the following in response:

WHAT DOES A MAN'S GRAMMAR WHO IS FROM THE REZ MATTER, SHELLY IS NOT AN EMBARASSMENT, THATS RIDICULOUS . . . I DONT HEAR YOU BEING EMBARRASSED BY ARNOLD SWARTZENAGERS ACCENT, BECAUSE THATS ALL IT IS . . . AN ACCENT. SOME PEOPLE KIDS TRY TO OUT DO ONE

---

* I should note that in my experience, especially with older Navajos, the use of all caps does not always indicate "emphasis" or "shouting" but rather is the regular way that some people write e-mails and the like. Reading the all caps here as emphatic may not be warranted. This remains a question to be investigated.

ANOTHER ON WHO CAN MASTERS WHITE MAN LANGUAGE BETTER THAN
THA NEXT . . . THATS AN EMBARASSMENT . . . AHO!!! (SORRY ABOUT THE
GRAMMAR BRO)

In this exchange we see the tensions inherent in an intimate grammar, in
language as an object of scrutiny. For the first two respondents, the "embarrassment" is that President Shelly speaks in Navajo English; because his
English is different from the imagined monoglot "proper" English, it is
deficient (see Meek 2006, 2011). For the third respondent, the use of Navajo
English seems to localize President Shelly, suggesting that he is "from the
rez." Speaking like a "white man" becomes the "embarrassment" for the
third respondent. Navajo English is a site of ideological struggle among
Navajos (Kroskrity and Field 2009).

Navajo English is sometimes linked with the boarding-school experience
and this lends an emotional resonance to its expressive forms (see Harvey
1974). Indeed, AnCita Benally and Denis Viri (2005: 104) go so far as
to claim:

> Although the presence of Navajo English—especially in schools—carries
> a certain stigma in contrast to Standard English, Navajo English enjoys
> considerable celebration in the expressive arts, particularly in the literary
> works of such accomplished Navajo writers as Laura Tohe, [Nia] Fran-
> cisco, Luc[i] Tapah[o]nso and Rex [Lee] Jim.

Yet even a well-known poet like Luci Tapahonso, the poet laureate of
the Navajo Nation, who self-consciously uses Navajo English to develop
characterological images of, for example, her uncle, runs the risk of being
negatively evaluated by "mainstream" English speakers for using Navajo
English. I have heard non-Navajos negatively evaluate the Navajo English
that Tapahonso (1997: 97–99) uses in "Hills Brothers Coffee." When Tapahonso performs this poem before audiences or when one listens to her
reading it on the CD that is included in her most recent collection of poetry
(2008), the following stretch of quoted speech, where the speaker is her
uncle, is often opened up to negative outside evaluation:

> Oh, that's the coffee with the man in a dress
> like a church man.
> Ah-h, that's the one that does it for me.
> Very good coffee.
> (Tapahonso 1997: 98)

In a number of performances of this poem that I have recorded, performances before largely Navajo audiences, Tapahonso has explained that this poem is an expected poem for Navajo audiences. She makes this observation, for example, at a performance I recorded in Window Rock, Arizona, on July 18, 2001. This transcript's lines are based on breath-pause structure (see Molina and Evers 1998; audience response has been included in brackets, and a colon indicates vowel lengthening).

> I'm going to read
> uhm a number of some poems
> that you've probably heard before
> and that I've learned over the years
> that I have to read or
> somebody's gonna sco:ld me [laughter]
> so I'll start with "Hills Brothers Coffee"

In an interview with *LINEbreak*, Tapahonso (1995) has also explained that the complicated syntax of the quotations of her uncle—who was monolingual in Navajo—in this poem is an attempt to "keep the syntax the same" from Navajo into English. She has attempted to transfer Navajo syntax into English. However, it is also an attempt to evoke in English a felt connection with the patterned ways of speaking of her uncle. She is attempting to translate the syntax of her uncle into English, because that syntax is affectively feelingful for her. This poem is a fan favorite for some Navajos. Yet this very stretch of poetry has been characterized, by some non-Navajos that I have spoken with about it, as substandard English or deficient in some way.

Perhaps a more telling example involves Blackhorse Mitchell's work (I will discuss this example more fully in chapter 3). In 1967, the University of Oklahoma published Blackhorse Mitchell's *Miracle Hill*. The cover claims that the book was cowritten by Mitchell and T. D. Allen. Allen was Mitchell's teacher at the Institute of American Indian Arts in Santa Fe. She provides an introduction that apologizes for the putative language problems of the book and urges readers to "read loose" (T. D. Allen 1967: vii). Allen claims that Mitchell uses "confused tenses and genders" (xi) and that "the thing you, the reader, and ... Blackhorse ... Mitchell don't have in common is grammar. He has made the effort to meet you halfway. He has learned your vocabulary (with some fascinating use variations) and he has learned some bits and pieces of your linguistic patterns" (vii). In each case, Allen claims that Mitchell's work, because it does not align with an imagined standard, is a failure or a mistake. In each case, Mitchell's language skills are negatively evaluated. Yet, as I will argue in chapter 3, Mitchell is not passive in the ways that his language abilities are framed and his poetry does work that seems to counter Allen's presumed monolithic representational power.

Navlish in Navajo Poetry

Since at least the early 1900s, Navajo speakers have been combining Navajo affixes and clitics with English lexical items (see Bodo 1998: 82; see also Holm, Holm, and Spolsky 1971: 6). Today this way of speaking is sometimes called "talking bilingual" and sometimes "Navlish" (see Schaengold 2003; Webster 2008a; Field 2009). However, as Charlotte Schaengold (2003: 249) notes, younger Navajos tend not to use Navlish with older speakers, "for fear of being publicly corrected and shamed." This has to do with a general "elder purism" among some older Navajos (Field 2009: 45). Indeed, the use of Navlish in contemporary Navajo poetry is relatively limited (Webster 2009). However, Navlish can be found on signs on and around the Navajo Nation, on notes, on flyers, and in hymnals, and it can be heard in a variety of settings (see McLaughlin 1992; Schaengold 2003; Webster 2008a). It can be found on the Internet as well. The website *Talk in Navajo: Wherever U Are* (Teller, n.d.) has a number of examples of Navlish as well as a discussion of the reasons to include Navlish on a website promoting using Navajo. As the author of the website notes, "With exception to the elderly, no one speaks entirely in Navajo anymore. If you truly want to sound like a local, or to sound *jigháąn*, you have to word things mixing Navajo and English." The use of Navlish can and does create a degree of intimacy or localness between speakers. *Shibro* 'my bro' and *shibuddy* 'my buddy' are two affective Navlish expressions that some Navajos consider indexes of social intimacy. In these examples, the first-person possessive prefix *shi-* is attached to an English lexical item. Sometimes this social intimacy is misplaced. One Navajo consultant complained that another Navajo had addressed him in an e-mail as *shibuddy*. My consultant's complaint was not with the use of Navlish, but rather with the social intimacy it suggested between him and his correspondent. *Shibuddy* was too informal for the relationship he felt they had. *Nizhóníful*, which takes *nizhóní* 'it is beautiful' and combines it with the English adjectival suffix *-ful*, changes the process slightly. Here you have a Navajo content form combined with an English affix rather than the other way around. *Nizhóníful* has become much more common among Navajos of different ages and has been described to me as having both a playful and socially intimate quality to it.

Given that Navlish can index social intimacy but can also be critiqued as a nonstandard language by both Navajos and non-Navajos, the use of Navlish in poetry can be seen as a display of an intimate grammar. When Rutherford Ashley (2001: 350), Esther Belin (2002: 8), and Norla Chee (2001: 6) use Navlish in their poetry, they run the risk of being negatively evaluated either by Navajo purists or by mainstream non-Navajos who see any form of code-mixing between English and any other language as an affront to English (see Lippi-Green 1997; Zentella 2003; Haviland 2003; J. Hill 2008). And indeed, contemporary Navajo written poetry is not a particularly conducive site for locating examples of Navlish (Webster 2009). Unlike the Latin@ poetry described by Zentella (2003), where Spanglish is often used, in a survey that I did of over twenty Navajo books of poetry, I could find only three examples of Navlish (Webster 2009).

On the other hand, the use of *shiheart* 'my love' by Navajo comedian Vincent Craig is a well-known affective display, and many Navajos use it. *Shiheart* is found on roadside safety-announcement billboards on and around the Navajo Nation and Belin uses part of a newspaper headline with *Shi Heart* written on it in a recent painting titled *Oh, Shi Heart.* Craig in his comedy is particularly adept at tapping into the linguistic anxiety that many Navajos have. Indeed, Craig's (1998) album title *Yer' Jus' Somehow* plays on a nonmainstream use of *somehow*. Navajos who I know recognize that the way *somehow* is used in much Navajo English discourse is an example of nonmainstream English, and they enjoy playing with its use, thereby creating a "common sociality" (Herzfeld 1997: 3), an intimate grammar. Craig is also known for his use of Navlish. Below is a well-known example from Craig and it comes from a long ballad titled "Old Chi'zee," a track on *Yer' Jus' Somehow* (which, as its subtitle states, was "recorded live at San Juan College" in Farmington, New Mexico). The lines below come after Old Chi'zee (a Navajo rapscallion) makes his entrance at the rodeo and has impressed "the ladies." (The transcription is mine and is again based on breath-pause structure, with analysis and glossing added in italics.)

And he tipped his hat
he winked his eyes
and the ladies said
"o:h *shi:ha:t*" [laughter]
   1POSS-heart
   my heart

Some Navajos that I have spoken with enjoy and appreciate using *shi-heart*, just as they enjoy using *shibuddy* and *shilove*. Norla Chee's (2001: 6) use of *shí buddy* in one of her poems and Rutherford Ashley's (2001: 350) use of *shi' love* in one of his (these are the ways that Chee and Ashley write these forms) are displays of the felt connection that Navajos have to these intimate grammars. Indeed, Navajos I have known enjoy Navlishing English lexical items by adding Navajo possessive prefixes to them: *shi-heart* evokes *shipant*, which evokes *shihat* (see Webster 2008a: 526). While Navajo English and Navajo (see below) have found a home in contemporary Navajo poetry, the use of Navlish in Navajo poetry is still a relatively rare and risky assertion of an intimate grammar (Webster 2009). Navlish does occur in other expressive genres, like the comedic balladry of Vincent Craig.

Navajo and Intimate Grammars

Many Navajos I have spoken with over the years have pointed out that Navajo is a language under assault by the dominant society. This has often been framed in terms of the boarding schools, where Navajos were sometimes punished for using the Navajo language. For many Navajos an affective bond between Navajos and Navajo was fostered in Navajo students' resistance to the stultifying language policies of the boarding schools (see Tohe 1999). During my fieldwork on the Navajo Nation in 2000 and 2001, two incidents confirmed for many Navajo consultants that their language was still under assault. The first was Arizona's Proposition 203, which meant to severely limit bilingual education (see House 2002). A number of community meetings took place during the fall of 2000 and homemade signs in Navajo, Navlish, and English appeared on the Navajo Nation protesting the proposition. The proposition eventually passed. The second was a legal case in Page, Arizona, involving the Equal Employment Opportunity Commission and the banning of the use of Navajo by employees at a local restaurant (see Zachary 2005). This also sparked discussion on the Navajo Nation. Navajos that I spoke with saw this as an affront to the Navajo language and concomitantly to Navajos.

Over the years, a number of Navajo poets have told me about Navajo words that they are particularly fond of. One poet told me that she wrote poetry to "capture the beautiful words of her children." Not all these poets were fluent in Navajo, but each had a felt attachment to specific Navajo lexical items. Five examples are: *na'asts'ǫǫsí* 'mouse', *tsé'áwózí* 'pebble', *hahodínéestą́* 'it has been raining for a while and it won't stop', *she'awéé'* 'my baby', and *nihik'inizdidláád* 'luminescence is all around'. In the first two cases, the fondness came from the sound of the words. *Na'asts'ǫǫsí* and *tsé'áwózí* are aesthetically pleasing words for the two poets who talked about these words. The sound of *na'asts'ǫǫsí* called up the image of a mouse going about kissing. *Ts'ǫǫs* is an ideophone for both 'kissing' and 'sucking' (see Webster 2009). Gloria Emerson enjoys using *tsé'áwózí* as a clan name in the formulaic clan introductions that Navajos often give at public events (see House 2002; Webster 2009). *Tsé'áwózí* is not a Navajo clan name, but Emerson delights in the sound of the word. In the third word, on the other hand, the fondness came from the image evoked. The poet I spoke with about it found the image of *hahodínéestą́*, of being in the middle of a rainstorm in the desert, particularly aesthetically pleasing; this poet has documented a number of "beautiful" Navajo words over the years. In the fourth word, the poet's fondness came from the social relationship expressed by *she'awéé'* 'my baby'. For that poet, it was the fact that this is how you speak to a baby in Navajo that was important; in fact, I have heard other Navajos besides poets express a fondness for this expression. The final example is from Laura Tohe. Here is how she explained her "love" of the word *nihik'inizdidláád* to a predominantly non-Navajo audience in an auditorium on the campus of Southern Illinois University in Carbondale on October 9, 2006. For ease of reference I have numbered each line. Though the numbering starts at 1, the quote actually comes from toward the end of her poetry performance that night.

The Navajo language is very poetic	1
when I first started writing	2
I used to think about poems in Navajo	3
and then write	4
turn them into English	5
and I guess maybe in some ways I still do that	6
because like I said the language is very poetic	7
the way it looks at the world	8
the world in terms of dualities	9
and even that	10
there's this line in that poem about female rain	11
about how the luminescence is all around	12
it took a long time to try	13
to find an equivalent in English	14
because the word itself a:h	15

there's that one word	16
I love that word in Navajo	17
nihik'inizdidláád which	18
it's an action	19
you know in Navajo it's verb-based	20
and so *nihik'inizdidláád* means you know	21
this light	22
just	23
poured over us	24
or among us	25
and there's this relationship you have with the light	26
but in the English it seems a little flat	27
when you say luminescence all around	28
it's just like a reporting about what happened	29
and there's none of that	30
personal connection	31
to light	32

The word *nihik'inizdidláád* can be morphologically analyzed as follows: *nihi-* cessative or terminative prefix, *-k'i-* 'straight', *-niz-* 'faraway', *-di-* 'extending along a line', *-dláád* 'shine a light'. Tohe poetically glosses this as 'luminescence is all around'. But note that Tohe considers this glossing to be incomplete. It misses something. It "seems a little flat." Rather than evoking the moment, it is merely a report of what has happened. The relationship between language use and language form is missing in the English gloss. This relationship, as Tohe notes, is a "personal connection to light" that is evoked by *nihik'inizdidláád*. Part of that personal connection may arise from the homonymy, that is, the equivalence in sound despite difference in meaning, of *nihi-* the cessative or terminative prefix and the first-person-plural possessive prefix *nihi-* 'our' (e.g., *nihizaad* 'our language'). Structurally the terminative *nihi-* and *nihi-* 'our' do not align (the terminative prefix is attached to verbs, the possessive prefix attaches to nouns). However, as potentially evocative, the homonymy here adds a layer of resonance.

The homonymy between *nihi-* and *nihi-*, where the two senses reverberate off of each other, was something that other Navajos, including Navajo poets, often commented on. For example, Luci Tapahonso (2008: 18), in her most recent book *A Radiant Curve*, notes that "the word for mountain, *dził*, is very much like *dziil*, which means 'to be strong' or 'to possess strength.' Thus mountains serve as literal reminders that, like our ancestors, we can persevere in difficult situations." Such felt echoes motivate poetic expressions in Navajo (this issue is taken up in chapter 5). Indeed, many Navajo consultants I have worked with have enjoyed speculating on various homonyms and near homonyms, attempting to find semantic links between iconic forms. As Clyde Kluckhohn and Dorothea Leighton (1962: 260) noted, "homonymous words and syllables gives [*sic*] rise to the many puns in which the Navahos delight. For instance, *ha'át'ííshą níłį* means either 'what is flowing?' or 'what clan are you?' and The People [Navajos] tell stories with many embellishments about this question's being asked of a man who was standing beside a river" (see also Sapir 1932; Webster 2009).

Navajos are, however, quite aware that their use of Navajo off the Navajo Nation can be and often is negatively evaluated. Navajos I know who speak Navajo freely on the Navajo Nation are sometimes reluctant to do so in border towns such as Gallup, New Mexico, or Farmington, New Mexico. In Farmington, I have heard condescending remarks by non-Navajos about Navajo being "primitive" (among other things). Indeed, according to a recent headline in the *Navajo Times*, tracking the work of the Navajo Nation Human Rights Commission's investigation of Farmington, "NAVAJO MEN SAY THEY'RE NOT ALLOWED TO SPEAK NATIVE LANGUAGES AT WORK" (Yurth 2009: A1). Another recent *Navajo Times* headline, in the online edition, reports "DINÉ WORKER FIRED FOR SPEAKING NAVAJO" (K. Allen 2012). Such headlines reaffirm many Navajo concerns about discriminatory practices toward the Navajo language. These concerns are shared by other Native peoples besides Navajos, as Brenda Farnell (1995: 139) illustrates: "I soon learned that to speak Nakota in town was not acceptable. . . . I began to realize that for many people at Fort Belknap, the places where as an Indian one can feel comfortable exist as a series of islands." The use of Navajo or Nakota (or almost any Indigenous language) becomes an intimate grammar, because the very use of the language is often met with animosity or devaluing. This is certainly one of the legacies of the boarding-school experience for many Native Americans (see chapter 2).

Some Navajos see the Navajo language as an "object of shame," something that is premodern, backwards, and associated with reservation poverty—what is sometimes termed, in colloquial Navajo, *john/jáan* (glossed by one Navajo consultant as 'hick' and by another as 'hillbilly'). *John* can also be used for Navajos who speak Navajo English. Navajo scholar Tiffany Lee (2007: 22) cogently describes *john* this way:

> My opinion is that it [*john*] stems from the indoctrination of Western education, worldviews, and ways of life during colonization, carried through the boarding school era, and continues now. The policies of boarding

schools and the general attitude of mainstream America assigned an inferior status to Navajo people, culture, language, and worldview. The term
"john" is a manifestation of this type of thinking and influence.

Concern for critique is thus not always externally based (see Lee 2007;
Field 2009). One Navajo poet I knew, who used Navajo lexical items in
their poetry, was reluctant to read that poetry before a Navajo audience.
This poet, who considered themselves nonfluent in Navajo, was concerned
with a possible negative evaluation from a Navajo audience. Indeed, they
often checked their spelling of Navajo words against the spellings in Robert
Young and William Morgan's (1987) Navajo dictionary. Yet, and this is
crucial, this poet also expressed a deep appreciation and fondness for the
Navajo they used in their poetry, especially the way those words reminded
them of their maternal grandmother (who had spoken Navajo to them as a
child). Here the felt connection is based on the relationship—the feelingful
iconicity—between Navajo and one's grandparents. Other Navajo poets
also expressed a felt attachment to Navajo words that they associated with
their grandparents or other elders. One poet, as noted above, expressed a
felt attachment to the "beautiful words" her children used. Her poetry was
an attempt to evoke those "beautiful words" of her children. As Bakhtin
(1986) reminds us, our words are always also the words of others, and part
of the felt connection to linguistic form is a tying of words to people (be
they elders, grandparents, or children).

For many Navajos, certainly not all, there is a pleasure in the use of the
Navajo language. Navajos have told me that they "love" various Navajo
words or they enjoy the sounds of Navajo. This is not confined to the five
words above, it can also be seen in the pleasure that some Navajos take in
using ideophones, as this chapter's epigraph by Luci Tapahonso suggests,
or in the use of Navajo place-names (see Webster 2009; see also K. Basso
1996). Finally, both fluent and nonfluent Navajos have told me of their love
for certain Navajo words and their enjoyment in hearing the Navajo language.

Intimate Grammars

The term *intimate grammars*, as I have developed it here, is meant to remind
us that language is not purely an abstract system (see also Hymes 1996a;
Sherzer 1990; Tedlock 1983). There has been a trend in some circles of seeing language as wholly a window into the workings of the mind—grammar
as "a realm of the mind" (Harrison 2007: 236), language as only interesting

in what it refers to, language choices as merely the expression of various calculi to index social personas. Here I echo Keith Basso's (1991: 74) chastisement of those who would reduce languages and grammars "to a rigidly literalist view of language." Such views neglect the reality that people build felt attachments to language, that there can be an emotional attachment between individuals and their languages. For a discipline like linguistics, which based its notion of grammaticality on the intuitive judgments, the feelings, of speakers, this seems a curious oversight (see Hymes 1996a). When Blackhorse Mitchell uses *sheeps* he is well aware that such a usage will be negatively evaluated by external criteria. Adding the plural marking to *sheep* is not just applying a regularized rule (though that is a part of it). It is both asserting a voice and taking pleasure in language use. When Gloria Emerson says *tsé'áwózí*, one senses the pleasure she takes in the sounds of the word, and the way that word captures the feeling of expression. *Pebble* misses the felt attachment, the iconicity of sound and meaning, that *tsé'áwózí* captures for Emerson. Vincent Craig's *shiheart* is an aesthetically pleasing use of language for a number of Navajos. Yet in each case, the use of Navajo or Navajo English or Navlish can be, and often is, negatively evaluated by external criteria or ideologies of "standard languages" (L. Milroy 2000). Or it can be trivialized, in the case of Navajo, as a "safe" display of ethnic difference (see Urciuoli 1996; Webster 2009).

One can argue that intimate grammars are forms of resistance, a la James Scott (1990); there is something to be said for that view. However, by focusing exclusively on resistance, we miss the felt attachments to aesthetic forms, we miss the pleasure of *sheeps*. Likewise, a focus on indexicality is a partial truth. It misses the individual uses of languages for expressive and aesthetic satisfaction. People build attachments to languages. A focus solely on the calculi of indexicality misses the deep and perduring delight that speakers take in using languages, the smile my Navajo consultant had as she said *na'astsǫǫsí* or the laughter evoked by *shipant* 'my pants'.

There has been much recent concern over "endangered languages" and concern over the ways they are described (see Woodbury 1998; Nettle and Romaine 2000; J. Hill 2002; Harrison 2007; Muehlmann 2008; Evans 2010). While it may seem a given that linguistic anthropologists treat language as a form of social action, a trend nevertheless in much literature on endangered languages is to lament the loss of particular languages' words for things. Daniel Nettle and Suzanne Romaine (2000) title one of their chapters "Lost Words/Lost Worlds," and David Harrison's (2007) book is replete with examples of the loss of language as the loss of ecological knowledge. Such works strip language and grammar of the emotional attachments that speakers have to the uses of their languages and grammars. Such positions replicate a view of human emotions and aesthetics as not nearly as important as the science of encoding ecological knowledge. It sees languages as primarily about reference. It forgets the delight that speakers take in language form. As linguistic anthropologists we do a disservice to the speakers of languages if we neglect the feelings they have toward their languages.

Michelle Rosaldo (1972) long ago warned against any straightforward link between plant terms and plants among the Ilongot, against taking an overly literalist view of language. More recently, Anthony Woodbury (1998) has argued for understanding the aesthetic uses of language and the ways such uses are interwoven with a larger set of expressive activities, from storytelling to kin terms. Keith Basso's (1996) work on Western Apache place-names, David Samuels's (2004a) work on Western Apache puns, Brenda Farnell's (1995) work on Nakota and Plains Sign Talk, and Janis Nuckolls's (1996, 2010) work on ideophony among the Runa all remind us of the pleasure that language users take in using their languages. Jane Hill (2002) and Shaylih Muehlmann (2008: 34) remind us that discourses about endangered languages are often based on a view of language as a "closed system." That is, a concern with endangered languages sometimes reifies identities and languages and treats them as fixed (Muehlmann 2008; Woodbury 1998), arguing, in effect, that "authentic" Navajos speak "authentic" Navajo. Interlingual puns—of the kind described by Samuels (2004a) for Western Apache, Farnell (1995: 136) for Nakota, and Wallace Chafe (1998: 189) for Seneca, but early noted by W. W. Hill (1943: 18) for Navajos, and found today in *télii alizhgo* 'urinating donkey' for 'television'—remind us that, in the mouths of speakers, languages reverberate off each other, and in such reverberations one finds the delight in languages, the pleasure in the play across languages (see also K. Basso 1979; Webster 2009; on the potential danger of interlingual puns, see Haas 1951). Consider, for example, the story that a Navajo woman told me about her and her boarding-school classmates, during the morning recitation of the Pledge of Allegiance, punning on *justice* as *jástis* 'calf'. As we talked about the pun, she repeated it several times and clearly took pleasure in saying "and *jástis* for all, and *jástis* for all."* She said that such group punning "probably helped our survival in boarding school." Such interlingual punning can create the "common sociality" (Herzfeld 1997: 3) of intimate grammars.

---

* I originally misheard this as *'ajáádts'in* 'leg bone'. Another consultant noted that *'ajáádts'in* was also a good pun for *and justice*.

Hymes (1996a) has argued—contrary to a widely held mantra of linguistics—that all languages are not equal because speakers of languages are not politically, socially, or economically equal. A concern with intimate grammars is a concern with people and the varieties of linguistic forms they use and build attachments to, even in the face of stigmatization or negative evaluations. In this book I look not just at Navajo but also at Navlish and Navajo English. Navajo poets have built felt attachments to all three. As linguistic anthropologists, we should be concerned not just with named languages like Navajo but also with Navlish and Navajo English and the still other ways that Navajos, and others, express themselves (see Davis and Supalla 1995). Other multimodal expressive forms besides language are also intimate expressive forms. One thinks of the comedic skits of James and Ernie—two Navajo comedians who perform on and around the Navajo Nation—where they highlight Navajo lip pointing (see Bailey 1942; see also Enfield 2001). Navajos in the audience laugh at such displays of their intimate deictic grammar, knowing that lip pointing is something that outsiders sometimes stigmatize. Yet lip pointing is often both pleasurable and functional. As Navajos have noted, when you are carrying bags in both hands, pointing with your lips is simply easier. It is also something that Navajos see as distinguishing them from non-Navajos; it becomes iconic of being Navajo.

Throughout the rest of this book, I will not be overly concerned with the traditional ecological knowledge encoded in *sheeps* or *tsé'áwózí*, but rather with the aesthetic pleasure that Navajos take in the use of such intimate grammars, their unease about using them, and the moral force of using them. Language is more than mere reference. It is more than a communicative tool. It is also a set of poetic, aesthetic, and expressive forms that individual speakers build felt attachments to and through. Language is pleasurable and sensuous. This is because individuals create language through use, and such uses create felt attachments to linguistic forms. I will be grappling with languages as intimate companions. As Navajo poet Orlando White remarked to me in the summer of 2010, "languages are a companion, someone you travel with, you get to know." He then added, "I'm still trying to get to know English and what I can do with it."

However, for many minority populations, the use of their languages—in the full, multifaceted sense, to include mixed forms like Navlish and non-mainstream dialects like Navajo English—is often devalued and stigmatized (see Zentella 2002, 2003; Meek 2006; J. Hill 2008). When such intimate grammars are saturated with emotional attachments, they are iconic of identity and of expression. *Sheeps* is no longer merely a word for things, rather it is motivated by emotional and aesthetic considerations. It becomes iconic in that sense. The ramifications of language shift are not just that words for things are lost (the referentialist fear) but also that ways of being intimate with others and the world are lost (this is the iconism of language). As the following chapters in this book will show, grammars are not merely an abstract system. They are intimately and deeply felt expressions of voice, the "intuitive basis that underlies all linguistic expression" (Sapir 1921: 224). This book explores the intimate and felt attachments that Navajo poets have toward their languages and the ways such intimate and felt attachments are imagined through literary productions. In exploring such felt attachments, I argue, we can begin to understand something of the social work that contemporary Navajo poetry does for Navajos. It is to that work that I now turn.

CHAPTER TWO

Imagining Navajo in the Boarding School

On April 23, 2009, the *Navajo Times*, the paper of record for many Navajos, runs the headline TONGUE-TIED: NAVAJO MEN SAY THEY'RE NOT ALLOWED TO SPEAK NATIVE LANGUAGE AT WORK above the fold. The article goes on to state:

> But the men, who asked not to be identified in the newspaper for fear of retaliation, said the request [not to speak Navajo] feels like a violation of their rights and evokes the days when the BIA boarding school students had their mouths washed out with soap. (Yurth 2009: A1)

Here the image of the boarding school functions as part of an *explicit* metadiscourse on language policies, connecting the current experiences of language stigmatization with the efforts of the Bureau of Indian Affairs to suppress Navajo at boarding schools. Yet, as I will show, just as the boarding school itself was a complex site for the ideological struggle about language, the image of the boarding school, as an *implicit* metadiscourse, continues to haunt the contemporary discourse concerning the place of the Navajo language among contemporary Navajos.

To understand Navajos' contemporary metadiscourse about language, one must understand this haunting image of the boarding school that informs it: What kinds of metadiscourses about Navajo and the boarding schools circulate on the Navajo Nation? How, for example, are the Navajo language and the boarding-school experience imagined through literary works? And what is the social work of imaginative depictions of languages and concomitantly those who would use them? This chapter begins to engage these questions by investigating the ways that Navajo poet Laura Tohe's *No Parole Today* (1999) dramatizes language use in the boarding-school context and in so doing creates an emotionally salient metadiscourse about both languages and language users and the links between them. Yet, unlike the above quote from the *Navajo Times*, Tohe's characterological work in *No Parole Today* is often, though not always, an implicit metadiscourse on the role and value of languages (Agha 2003: 257). That is, there is no explicit statement in *No Parole Today* concerning the relative value of one language or another, but Tohe does present an image of Navajos using language to create affective bonds between Navajos. There are tensions in the ways that both Navajos and non-Navajos imagine the Navajo language. Other images of the Navajo language and Navajos as language users also circulate. These images, often externally rooted, devalue and stigmatize Navajos and the languages they use (see Webster 2010b).

In this chapter I look at three creative pieces by Tohe from *No Parole Today*. I supplement this with insights gained from my ethnographic and linguistic fieldwork on the Navajo Nation from 2000 to 2001 and during the summers of 2007 to 2012. The three pieces that form the focus of this chapter are:

1. The short story "So I Blow Smoke in Her Face" (Tohe 1999: 25–29)
2. The poem "The Names" (Tohe 1999: 4–5)
3. The poem "Sometimes Those Pueblo Men Can Sure Be Coyotes" (Tohe 1999: 16–17)

I focus on *No Parole Today* because it has the boarding-school experience as backdrop and much of it is a metadiscourse on the importance of language (specifically Navajo, or *Diné bizaad*) and language use. The boarding school is a particularly apt site for the investigation of such imagined dialogues because the boarding school was often explicitly about limiting the language options of Native Americans (Iverson 1998: 20) and is still, as we see in the *Navajo Times* article cited at the beginning of this chapter, a potent image of language oppression for many Navajos.

In this chapter, I argue that language works as an affective register (Irvine 1990) to display an emotional bond between languages and their users. To understand such affective displays, we need to situate them in a language-ideological framework because it is language ideologies that inform such language and affective associations (Kroskrity 2004). Building on Asif Agha's (2003) analysis of the social and ideological work of characterological images, I argue that metadiscourses dramatize registers and create iconic relations between speakers and languages. Such relations are mediated by affect, that is, the felt attachment that speakers have to their languages. To make this argument, I focus on a short story and two poems by Tohe and show how these metadiscourses variously create iconic relations between speakers and languages. In these Navajo literary works, the boarding-school experience works as a trope that gives these metadiscourses an intertextual linkage as a shared or potentially shared historical memory (see Hanks 1999). The use of Navajo (by Navajos) in Tohe's works acts as an index of social intimacy. Such social intimacy is informed by and informs the historical memory of the boarding-school experience. Note that not only does Tohe create an image of Navajo as an index of social intimacy between Navajo speakers, she also creates, through the iconic relation between speaker and language, a social intimacy between speaker and language; this is the intimacy of language ideologies.

Navajos and Boarding Schools

The topic of Native Americans and the boarding-school institutions has been much written about (see Greenfeld 2001; Lomawaima 1995; Adams 1997; Lomawaima and McCarty 2006; Trafzer, Keller, and Sisquoc 2006). My goal in this section is not to review the entire literature on boarding-school practices but to focus more narrowly on Navajo boarding-school experiences. In many ways, Navajo boarding-school experiences were both similar to and different from the larger Native American boarding-school trends (see Spicer 1962: 441–44). Let me also note at the outset that, as Alice Littlefield (2004: 327) has pointed out, the boarding school often presents an "apparent paradox": namely, "former students often expressed positive attitudes toward these schools and even protested when such schools were closed." Tohe's (1999) work, I would argue, presents a complex vision of the boarding school and of the ways speaking was and was not regimented.

Peter Iverson (1998) recounts some of the motivations behind the boarding-school system in the late 1800s. Iverson points out that "proponents of these distant boarding schools argued that such isolation was necessary to remove children from the harmful, counterproductive influences of their home communities" (19). Native American children were removed from their homes and boarded at distant schools. One of the "counterproductive influences" was the use of their ancestral language. Commissioner of Indian Affairs J. D. C. Atkins was particularly clear on this point. As Iverson explains:

In 1887 he [Atkins] emphasized the government "must remove the stumbling block of hereditary customs and manners, and of these language is one of the most important elements." He had made up his mind: "This language, which is good enough for a white man and a black man, ought to be good enough for the red man." (20)

In the initial phases of the boarding school, Navajo children, because of the geographic isolation of the Navajo Reservation, were less completely immersed in that system (Iverson 2002: 81–86). For example, the infamous Carlisle Institute in Carlisle, Pennsylvania, run by Richard Henry Pratt—who is the addressee of Laura Tohe's (1999: ix–xii) introductory letter—never had more than four dozen Navajos in attendance (Iverson 2002: 83). Manuelito, an important Navajo leader, sent both his sons and a nephew to Carlisle. All three died, one son at Carlisle and the other son and the nephew from tuberculosis back on the Navajo Reservation (see Iverson 2002: 83; Denetdale 2007: 82–83).

However, in the early twentieth century, boarding school for Navajo children began in earnest (Iverson 2002: 118). Even then, a number of schools were built on the reservation rather than off it. As Edward Spicer (1962: 223) notes, "Navajos were either uninterested in or directly antagonistic to the boarding school at Fort Defiance [on the Navajo Nation]." As Henry Shonerd (1990: 193) has noted, the "language policy for the Navajo . . . is best understood in light of an almost 400-year history of attempts to suppress language varieties indigenous to the culture," and the early boarding-school experiences were a part of that larger trend. It should, however, be noted that the attitude toward Navajo shifted in the 1930s, from active suppression to an attempt to support Navajo fluency and literacy (Spicer 1962: 456; Iverson 2002: 172–74). But then in the 1950s there was a renewed use of boarding schools for Navajos (Spicer 1962: 443; Iverson 2002: 193). This was the "Special Navajo Program" that sent thousands of Navajos to off-reservation boarding schools in places like Albuquerque; Riverside, California; Phoenix; and Chemawa, Oregon. On-reservation boarding schools were also continued from the previous era. Galena Dick describes her experiences at the on-reservation Chinle Boarding School (in Chinle, Arizona) during the 1950s in the following manner:

We were forced and pressured to learn English. We had to struggle. It was confusing and difficult. Students were punished and abused for speaking their native language. . . . If we were caught speaking Navajo, the matrons gave us chores like scrubbing and waxing the floors, or they slapped our hands with rulers. Some students had their mouths "washed" with yellow bar soap. . . . This shows that even for Navajo adults like the dorm matrons, school was not a place for Navajos to be Navajo. (Dick and McCarty 1997: 72–73)

Tellingly, Navajo matrons were complicit in the aggressive suppression of the use of Navajo. As Spicer (1962: 443) notes, "the major emphasis [was] on learning to speak, read, and write English."* As Robert Young (1970: 226) writes, "during the 1950s, major emphasis in the Navajo education program was placed once again on the learning of English and the study of conventional subjects." Federal policy and boarding-school policies toward Navajo and English were capricious.

It should be noted that some Navajos wanted an education in English (see for example Mitchell 2004; Iverson 2002: 196) and that some viewed going to the boarding schools in a positive light (see Iverson 2002: 195; Littlefield 2004). Some Navajos that I have spoken with about their boarding-school experience have stated that they were not punished for speaking Navajo. However, this is not to say that they did not feel their voice was silenced (see Webster 2010c). As I have argued elsewhere (Webster 2009), Tohe links the boarding-school experience with oppression and the nostalgia of youth at the same time. As Lomawaima (1995) argues and Tohe dramatizes, Native American students found a variety of ways to resist boarding-school regimes. The boarding school was a complex site and a variety of attitudes continue to inform discussions about the boarding-school experience. Tohe presents one vision of the Navajo boarding-school experience.

As Teresa McCarty (2002) has ably demonstrated, two of the persistent problems with the off-reservation boarding schools (and for that matter with on-reservation schools as well) were the lack of any encouragement for expressions of being Navajo and the lack of local control of the schools by Navajos. It is against this background that we need to understand the poems and narratives found in Tohe's (1999) *No Parole Today*. For many Navajos, going to boarding school was like going to prison. That is the analogy of Tohe's title. On the other hand, Tohe became aware of a second way of reading her title, as "no speaking today" (based on another meaning of *parole*,

---

* It is important to note that, as Gina Harvey (1974: 287) points out, the English that Navajos spoke in boarding school was not "standard English" but rather what Harvey terms "Dormitory English," an "alternative dialect." By 1974, as Harvey notes, "Dormitory English" was no longer confined solely to boarding schools, but could also be found in various parts of the Navajo Nation.

which comes from the French for 'speech' or 'word'), and she discussed that interpretation at a poetry performance in Window Rock, Arizona, on July 18, 2001. Here is the relevant excerpt. This is an explicit metadiscourse on the boarding school and language policy. (Line breaks indicate breath-pause structure, as in previous chapters.)

> A this book I wrote
> because I was in a boarding school
> uh on the reservation at Crystal
> uh where I lived for a while and then was sent to the Albuquerque Indian
>   School
> and lived there for
> four years
> a this
> title is called *No Parole Today* but I didn't know at the time that it's French
> uh word meaning no voice
> or no one to speak for you
> uh and for me that's what Indian schools were all about
> was was assimilation
> and it was also the taking away of our language

In the short story to be analyzed below, and in one of the poems, Navajo students at the boarding school do continue to speak Navajo. For Tohe, many of the affective dimensions of Navajo are relatable to the trauma of the boarding-school experience.

That the Navajo language is still a topic of concern for many Navajos also needs to be accounted for. Many Navajos that I have spoken with, but certainly not all, continue to see the Navajo language as a language under attack. Even Navajos who do not speak Navajo have sometimes told me that mainstream American society is attempting to suppress the Navajo language. During my fieldwork in 2000, the state of Arizona had a ballot initiative that meant to curtail the use of bilingual education in schools (see House 2002). I attended a number of public meetings led by Navajos about opposing the ballot initiative (see Webster 2009). Many Navajos linked the ballot initiative with the boarding-school experience. About the same time as the ballot initiative was passing, a legal case in Page, Arizona, involving the Equal Employment Opportunity Commission and the banning of Navajo at a local restaurant also sparked controversy on the Navajo Nation (see Zachary 2005). Again, Navajos that I spoke with saw this as an affront to the Navajo language and concomitantly to Navajos. Note also that the headline and attendant article I cited at the beginning of this chapter foreground the continued suppression of the Navajo language by outsiders (Yurth 2009). It also points to the way that contemporary concerns about language issues are often linked with images of the boarding-school experience. Couple this with concern on the part of many Navajos about the current language shift on the Navajo Nation (see Lee 2007) and one readily appreciates why many Navajos feel that Navajo is still under attack from outsiders (and nonoutsiders).

Not all Navajos valorize the Navajo language as especially useful (see Holm and Holm 1995; Lee 2007). For example, Navajo scholar Agnes Holm and Wayne Holm (1995: 155) described some of these attitudes as follows: "In most schools and communities, Navajo does not have the 'status' that English does. . . . Thus begins the vicious cycle whereby the use of Navajo in school comes to acquire low status, as Navajo is equated with rurality, poverty, and lack of 'cool.'" Holm and Holm go on to point out that Navajo becomes associated with "remedial" classes as well. As Field (2009: 44) notes:

> "Elder speaker purism" (regardless of religious affiliation) is linked to powerful feelings concerning Navajo identity and group solidarity and is in direct opposition to a variety of language ideologies on the part of younger Navajos, be it linguistic insecurity, an emergent identity as speakers of "Navlish," or a rejection of Navajo language entirely on the part of the very young.

McCarty, Romero-Little, and Zepeda (2008: 168) note that for some teenage Navajos, the Navajo language can be seen as "emblems of shame" or "useless." Some Navajo Christians also are ambivalent toward the Navajo language. As Bernard Spolsky (2002: 149) notes, some "Navajo Christian churches . . . oppose the teaching of Navajo in school for fear that it will bring with it the teaching of Navajo religious practices and beliefs." I have heard such arguments at Navajo-language conferences as well. On the other hand, a number of Navajos, both young and old, have explained to me that the use of Navajo terms is simply more affectively meaningful and feelingful than the use of English (see chapter 1). A language ideology that sees Navajo as more feelingful than English stands in contrast to and in tension with the more prominent Anglo-American language ideology of linguistic paranoia. It also stands in tension with Navajo language ideologies that would "reject" Navajo. It should be clear that the languages that Navajos speak are an ideologically contentious issue.

Creating Intimate Characterological Images

I believe we can understand Tohe's work as an implicit metapragmatic discourse on the intimacies, the affective relations, between speakers and the
languages they speak. That is, we can glimpse something of the ways felt
attachments between speakers (or potential speakers) and their languages
are imagined. Recent work by Agha on the ways Received Pronunciation
was imagined in metadiscourses in nineteenth-century England suggests
an avenue for understanding the metapragmatic work that Tohe is engaged
in. Among these nineteenth-century metadiscourses Agha (2003) singles
out penny weeklies, popular handbooks, and literary works as aiding in
the construction of a recognized register and the social values associated
with that register. These metadiscourses then "depict icons of personhood
linked to speech that invite forms of role alignment on the part of the reader"
(257). That is, metadiscourses that dramatize registers also create iconic
relations between speakers (as imagined in the literary works) and the very
languages, registers, dialects, etc. that they use.* These are "characterological images" (259), much like the images of Nootkas described by Edward
Sapir ([1915] 1985).

Sapir noted the creation of affective associations, both humorous and
disparaging, between linguistic forms and people through literary uses of
reported speech (see also Hastings and Manning 2004). He showed the
ways that Nootka speakers could create mocking characterizations of people
with physical defects through the uses of "consonantal play" (181) that are
sometimes linked with the voices of mythic characters. Mythic characters
speak in certain recognizable ways through the characterological images of

---

* It is important here to reiterate a point made by Agha: investigations like his are not arguments about mass media determining "individual views." Rather, the concern should be

> with the ways these representations expand the social domain of individuals acquainted
> with register stereotypes, and allow individuals, once aware of them, to respond to their
> characterological value in various ways, aligning their own self-images with them in
> some cases, transforming them in others through their own metasemiotic work. (242)

These metadiscourses, which create, by degrees, alignments of social value with languages and
language users, are often "implicit" (270). As we look at the examples from Tohe below, we
will not see explicit statements that align the use of Navajo by Navajos with affectively intimate
bonds; what we will encounter are value-laden characterological images (stereotypes, if you will)
that are built up by way of metapragmatic terms and by the ways languages are used. On that
point, Leighton C. Peterson (2011, 2013) has described the ways that Navajo filmmakers have
worked to create affective bonds between viewers and screen images of Navajo language in use.

"consonantal play," and those voices are then evoked through corresponding "consonantal play"—not quotations—in mocking terms of address or
reference (sometimes disparaging and sometimes affectionately done). Such
"consonantal play" then creates affective relations between language forms,
registers, and characterological images. As Judith Irvine (1990: 131) argues,
"such conventions, linguistically expressed, represent a cultural construction of available emotions, personalities, and so on that are linked to other
dimensions of culture and society." Irvine argues for an understanding of
"affective registers" (128). My argument extends the notion of register
from a language-internal focus to a realization that in certain multilingual
situations, the choice of language or languages can be seen as an affective
display. In such cases, languages can sometimes become affective registers
(see Webster 2006a).

A crucial part of such dramatizations, or characterological images, is
the ways that language use is represented or reported in them, that is, their
metapragmatics. The work of Voloshinov (1986) has been particularly
important in understanding the issues of direct and indirect reported speech.
As Voloshinov notes, "reported speech is speech within speech, utterance
within utterance, and at the same time also *speech about speech, utterance
about utterance*" (115; emphasis in original). Reported speech is, then,
a metadiscourse. Michael Silverstein (1985) has analyzed the ways that
verbs of speaking in Chinook model proper ways of speaking in narratives.
Following on the work of Silverstein, James Collins (1987) argues for an
understanding of Navajo metapragmatic terms in mythic narratives.* As
Collins notes, "metapragmatic forms are valuable because they provide
insight into the conceptual knowledge which the speakers of a language
bring to bear on understanding the use of that language" (72).†

---

* Collins treats all the narratives as of the same kind for his analysis. Thus he does not do a
breakdown of the genres or kinds of narratives in which various metapragmatic forms occur.
For example, he does not note that John Watchman, who told two Coyote narratives to Sapir
(Sapir and Hoijer 1942), did not use the verb stem -*zin* 'think' in either of those stories (see
Webster 2008b). As Sherzer (1989) has shown for Kuna narratives, various verb forms can
be indexes of different genres (see also Woodbury 1985; Kroskrity 1993). Collins's analysis
obscures such genre-specific uses of metapragmatic verb stems. Various metapragmatic forms
may also serve as indicators of individual voice or act as forms of traditionalization (see
Johnstone 1996; Hymes 2003; Blommaert 2006; on traditionalization see Bauman 1992;
Kroskrity 1993; Webster 2009).

† It should be noted that in Navajo, indirect reported speech does not occur, only direct
reported speech (Li 1986). In what follows, then, all reported speech that occurs using Navajo
metapragmatic terms is to be recognized as quoted speech.

Metapragmatic terms, or "reportive metapragmatics" (Dinwoodie 2007: 16), create certain expectations of reported content. The juxtaposition of certain received or "normative expectations" (Collins 1987: 72) with quoted material that misaligns with those expectations is often used for humorous purposes. Collins gives the following example (see also Silverstein 1985: 133):

"Shut up," he explained.

Here the content of the quoted form, the affective display, stands in contrast with the reportive metapragmatic term *explained* according to certain received expectations. This is an example of how metapragmatic forms can aid in the construction of characterological images (Agha 2003: 259). Their use works to create social voices and stances for imagined literary characters. We recognize characters as "playful" or "serious" by the metapragmatic terms used for them (say, *jokes* versus *explains*). Metapragmatic terms, then, allow for affective displays as well. They can indicate the affective demeanor that a speaker (here an imagined speaker in a literary work) has toward a hearer (here an imagined hearer in a literary work). When coupled with switches in language, metapragmatic terms can work toward the establishment of recognizable affective registers. The metadiscourses thus created have, of course, real-world consequences. Miyako Inoue (2006) has shown, for example, how a literary movement aided in the construction of what is now recognized as "Japanese women's speech." Japanese women in the early twentieth century began to align themselves with the quoted voices of women found in contemporary novels. These novels were metadiscourses on the social value of languages and those (women) that would speak them.

Related, I would argue, to Irvine's (1990: 128) concern with "other dimensions of culture and society" is the need to understand affective displays within a language-ideological framework (see also Silverstein 1979). As Kroskrity (2004: 498) argues, language ideologies are "beliefs, or feelings, about languages as used in their social world." They are, as Margaret Field (2009: 41) states, always multiple. They are also felt through and expressed through the agency of individuals (see Kroskrity 2009). Linguistic anthropologists would do well to attend to the feelings expressed through affective displays toward languages. John Haviland (2003: 771) describes a prominent Anglo-American language ideology as "linguistic paranoia." He explains, "there is a political loading to the use of non-English as threatening, insulting, and — much like its speakers themselves — insubordinate" (770). Note the recursiveness and iconization (Irvine and

Gal 2000) between languages and speakers. In this prominent language ideology of "linguistic paranoia," the use of a non-English language in an English-language context is understood as an affective display, in this case, an insult. The reverse, when subordinate people (e.g., Navajos) use their own non-English language or languages (e.g., Navajo or Navlish), can also sometimes be seen as an affective display, in this case, social intimacy or the like. Such distinctions are not, however, categorical or totalizing. It is certainly also the case that within any group there will be levels of hierarchy and that such code-switches can also work to alienate or marginalize. What is needed is to understand the language ideologies that inform such language and affective associations.

Laura Tohe and Navajo Poetry

Tohe's creative work does not occur in a vacuum, either with respect to broader discourses about the boarding school or with respect to the larger context of contemporary Navajo poetry. When I conducted ethnographic and linguistic research on the emergence of written contemporary poetry on the Navajo Nation from 2000 to 2001, I often began interviews by attempting to elicit Navajo terms for "poetry." The Navajo word most often suggested by Navajo poets and nonpoets was *hane'* (story, narrative). There is a sense to *hane'* that dictates that it must be publicly shared (see also Peterson 2006). Many Navajo poets mentioned as one central feature of contemporary Navajo poetry that it was meant to be shared. Another feature of poetry that many Navajos commented on was that it was also emotionally intense language (Webster 2009).

Tohe grew up on the Navajo Nation, but now lives off-reservation. She attended the Albuquerque Indian School, a point she often makes at her poetry performances (Webster 2009). Tohe and many of the other poets are part of a Navajo intelligentsia and are thus linked with larger Indigenous movements and literary cultural-ethnic renaissances (see, for example, Park 2007). Many including Tohe have performed their poetry for Indigenous groups outside the United States. Nevertheless, many, Tohe included, see their poetry as directed toward Navajos and especially younger college-age Navajos. Here the link with *hane'* is particularly important. As a "story," Navajo poetry needs to be publicly shared. Tohe once explained to me that boarding schools had tried to take the stories of Navajos away from them. Her poetry about the boarding school can be seen as a reassertion of the ability to tell stories. As a critique of the boarding school, her work thus links with a persistent theme in Navajo poetry. Tohe's poetry is also linkable with issues of Navajo nationalism and sovereignty (Webster 2009). The metadiscourses of Navajo and those that would use it can be understood within an argument that sees Tohe's work as contributing to an imagined Navajo-language community (see Webster 2009).

Many Navajo poets have had their poetry published by major university presses; some have published their own work or had it published by small-scale local presses. Tohe's most recent book of poetry and prose, *Tséyi'* (2005), was published by the University of Arizona Press and can be found at the Navajo Arts and Crafts Enterprise stores in Shiprock, New Mexico, and Window Rock, Arizona. It and *No Parole Today* (1999), which was published by West End Press in Albuquerque but distributed by the University of New Mexico Press, can both be purchased at the Navajo Nation Museum in Window Rock. Her first book of poetry was published in 1986 by Nosila Press in Omaha, Nebraska, and is largely out of circulation now. One way that *No Parole Today* circulates is from Navajo to Navajo. One Navajo woman that I know was reading *No Parole Today* in the summer of 2009 and planned to give a copy of it to her sister. Her sister had attended boarding school, whereas she had not. For her it was a literary work that documented something of the stories her sister had told her about the boarding-school experience. For her sister it seemed to validate her experiences at boarding school. This is, in fact, how books often circulate on the Navajo Nation. One Navajo may read a book and then give it to another Navajo. The collecting of books—so familiar to many middle-class readers—is not something that is normally found among Navajos. One Navajo author I knew actually lamented that Navajos did not buy, so much as share, books authored by Navajos.

The primary language that contemporary Navajo poetry is written in is English. This has to do with the fact that Navajo literacy is still rather limited. Indeed, some poets have actively begun to learn how to write in Navajo so that they can write poetry in Navajo. Tohe has been at the forefront of promoting the Navajo language in creative and literary works. During my initial fieldwork in 2000 and 2001, Tohe had begun to perform poems written entirely in Navajo and she had also published and performed poems that code-switched into Navajo. Tohe was also taking classes at Diné College in Tsaile, Arizona, to learn to write in Navajo. Like many Navajos, she could speak Navajo but not write it. Many of Tohe's poems are in English and it is often through English that she asserts a Navajo identity. Some Navajo poetry is written entirely in Navajo (down to the page numbers; see Jim 1995), but Tohe's poetry is often composed in both Navajo and English. In using both languages in her work, Tohe is able to create contrasting images of them. In writing in English, Tohe makes her poems more accessible to the larger, non-Navajo, English-speaking society, but also to many young Navajo readers, who are not literate in Navajo. Indeed, for many Navajos who are not literate in Navajo, poetry composed in Navajo is still largely only accessed as an oral phenomenon. Navajo poets who write in Navajo often perform their poems on KTNN, the Navajo radio station, or at public venues. Many Navajo poets perform their poetry for Navajo audiences on the Navajo Nation.

"So I Blow Smoke in Her Face"

In this section I look at the reportive metapragmatic devices used in the short story "So I Blow Smoke in Her Face" and the ways they create metadiscourses about languages and language users. As we will see, through the use of metapragmatic forms, Tohe constructs an image of the boarding school as a place where Navajos are silenced and humiliated, but also a place where at times they assert their own voices and challenge the boarding-school regimes. She accomplishes this characterological work through the creative deployment of both explicit metapragmatic terms and, interwoven with them, implicit characterological work.

Tohe creates an emergent contrast in the short story between the metapragmatic terms *tell* on the one hand and *tease* and *joke* on the other. What we see in the use of *tell* is a construction of language use as a monologic critique or directive. On the other hand, the uses of *tease* and *joke* create an affectively salient mark of social intimacy between Navajos. Indeed, *tell* is the linchpin of this narrative, because it is precisely the narrator Vida's thwarting of the dorm matron Mrs. Harry's attempt to "tell" Vida off that is the climax of this story. Tohe's repeated use of *tell*, contrasting with the more socially intimate uses of *tease* and *joke*, creates affective expectations as well as characterological associations with these metapragmatic terms.

"So I Blow Smoke in Her Face" (Tohe 1999: 25–29) concerns the interactions between the narrator Vida (a Navajo girl), her cousin Viv, Edgar (the object of the narrator's affection), and Mrs. Harry, one of the women in charge of the girls at the Albuquerque Indian School. The Navajo students are represented as positive and affable characters, ready icons of personhood for role alignment (Agha 2003). Importantly, neither Mrs. Harry nor Mrs. Chavez, another authority figure at the Indian School, is described as Navajo (contrast this with Galena Dick's memories of the Navajo matrons at Chinle

Boarding School, quoted above). In fact, Mrs. Harry is explicitly described as "a Heinz 57, an Indian who is from several different tribes" (28). Though the story is set in an off-reservation boarding school, it begins on the Navajo Nation with the narrator and Viv riding horses and spending time with their uncle. It then switches to events at the Albuquerque Indian School, then concludes back on the Navajo Nation. The opening and closing scenes thus contrast with the medial scene with respect to their setting.

The metapragmatic term *tease* occurs fairly early in the narrative. The first section of the story involves the narrator and her cousin (Viv) riding horses on the Navajo Nation. "My uncle teases me because my legs are bowed" (25). Shortly after, *tell* also occurs, without accompanying quoted speech. "Later, Uncle catches up and tells us we shouldn't tire the horses out like that" (26). Note that *tell* is used to critique, while *tease* is used in an affective way that suggests a degree of social intimacy between uncle and niece.

With the next section the story moves to Albuquerque, where the narrator and her cousin are now attending the Albuquerque Indian School. In a brief interlude, Vida and Viv are picked up by two "Chicanos" in "their low riders." They "cruise" Central Avenue (a major thoroughfare in Albuquerque) until the boys "get serious" (26). Tohe then uses the metapragmatic term *tell* twice. In both cases, there is no accompanying quoted speech.

> We drive down Fourth and I **tell** the driver to let us out. They don't want to but when I **tell** them we're government property and they could get in a lot of trouble, the door swings open. (27)

The action then switches to outside the window of Edgar, another student at the school. Here Viv and the narrator have snuck over to the boy's dormitory and are standing outside the "steel mesh" window of Edgar's room. This sequence begins with quoted speech, but not accompanied by a metapragmatic term: "'Shhhhd, Edgar'" (27). The use of *shhhhd* is a conventional way that many Navajos have explained to me of attracting the attention of other Navajos, especially those of the opposite sex. There are a number of Navajo jokes that focus on the use of this form. Notice that Tohe makes no attempt to lexicalize this form. That is, she does not attempt to make it into a word by adding a vowel. This form is sometimes represented in writing as *shiid* (see for example, W. Morgan 1949: 24).

Instead of Edgar coming to the window, Jasper, his cousin, does. This is followed by another use of quoted speech without an external metapragmatic term. There is a metapragmatic term embedded in the quoted speech, though: "Oh, hi Jasper. Edgar *hágo bidiní*" (27). The speaker is either Vida or Viv; it is unclear. *Hágo* means 'come here' and *bidiní* can be glossed as 'you tell him'. All together, the sentence can be glossed as 'You tell him, "Edgar, come here."' (Note, however, that the verb form is based on the stem *-ní* 'say' and not *-ne'* 'tell'.) This is an example of what Field (2001) has termed a "triadic directive," that is, a directive made through an intermediary. Field argues that triadic directives are the preferred form of directives among certain Navajos, who often, but not always, have a *yáhásin* or "bashful" relationship with each other (see also Aberle 1961: 158; Field 1998). Most of the examples that Field focuses on are examples of teacher-student interactions. Thus, a teacher will tell a student to say "tell her, 'be tough,'" with an embedded quoted form within the utterance (see Field 2001: 256). Here the speaker, a female student, tells Jasper what to say to Edgar. Jasper then leaves and returns with Edgar.

Edgar's entrance coincides with the use of a metapragmatic term with quoted speech. "Edgar smiles at me from behind the mesh cover and says 'cigarette-*ísh nee hólǫ́*?'" (27). Edgar's question can be glossed as 'Do you have a cigarette?' *Hólǫ́* (as it is sometimes written in dictionaries) means 'it exists'. *Nee* is the second-person pronoun *n(i)*- plus the postposition *-ee* (with). *Nee hólǫ́* is thus literally 'it exists with you'. The interrogative enclitic *-ísh* is attached to the English lexical item *cigarette*. This is an indirect request for a cigarette (see Field 1998). Vida replies by giving Edgar a cigarette. The attaching of the interrogative enclitic to the English lexical item is an example of what Charlotte Schaengold (2003) has termed "bilingual Navajo" and what some of my consultants have termed Navlish (sometimes also *Navglish* or *Navalish* or *Navdlish*) (see Webster 2009; see also Field 2009). Here an English lexical item takes on the morphology of Navajo affixes and clitics. Susan Foster et al. (1989: 16) provide another example, where an English lexical item takes the interrogative enclitic *-ísh*, "*Everydayísh nániłtééh doo?*" (Will you bring him/her every day?). From my experience, Navlish is not normally used in contemporary written poetry (Webster 2009). That it shows up in this short story, on the other hand, is of some interest. This is reminiscent of Bakhtin's (1981) assertion that it is in the discourse of the novel, not in poetic discourse, that heteroglossia is more readily on display.

Tohe then lets the reader in on something of the ethnography of speaking of the Albuquerque Indian School. There is an explicit metapragmatic explanation: "'Is it time for your bedcheck?' I tease. It's just an expression that we use to make a joke" (27). Tohe here uses the metapragmatic term *tease* and then explains the meaning of the quoted material as being a "joke."

Edgar then responds. "'I have dishpan hands,' he announces and puts his fingers through the mesh to show us." The use of *announce* allows the reader to understand that Edgar is not taking up the teasing that Vida has begun, but instead shifts the conversation to his "shriveled" fingers and "soft and pale" nails. After Viv and Vida have looked at the evidence for his claim, Edgar adds an explanation. "'I just got back from kitchen detail. They're so clean I could operate with them,' he jokes and stares at his hands" (27).

Viv responds immediately to his remark. "'*Hát'íílá naadeidą́ą́*? Was it bear meat again?' Viv asks. It's a joke . . .'" (27). The narrator then explains that various meat dishes served at the Albuquerque Indian School were called "bear meat" and "rubber meat." The fact that Viv repeats the question in English may suggest that Edgar's command of Navajo is limited. Certainly Edgar seems comfortable using the Navajo interrogative enclitic, but not all speakers of "bilingual Navajo" are bilingual in Navajo and English (see Schaengold 2003). On the other hand, Viv's repetition may be an example of what Guillermo Bartelt (1982) has described as "rhetorical redundancy" in Navajo English. In this case, the redundancy appears to be used for humorous effect: first the Navajo and then the English form—in either language, that meat is tough!

After a brief interlude, where the narrator reflects on the fact that she and Viv are breaking the rules to be at Edgar's window and compares seizing control of one's life to taking care of cattle, Edgar does indeed show his ability to speak Navajo. "'*Nihíma nicháa'ha'dooshkeeł*,' Edgar teases back" (28). Here Tohe does not provide an English gloss of Navajo. In not doing so, here and elsewhere in this story, she challenges a view of Navajo and English as referentially transparent (Haviland 2003: 768). Edgar's Navajo form can be glossed as 'our mother will catch you and scold you'. *Nicháa'ha'dooshkeeł* is 'will scold you', but one consultant I spoke with suggested that there was also a sense of "catching" suggested in the form. This may be a by-product of the use of the future tense. The phrase is based on the metapragmatic verb stem *-keed* 'scold, berate' (see Young and Morgan 1991: 276). The use of *nihíma* 'our mother' is a nonliteral use of a kinship term (this form can also be written as *nihimá*: *nihi-* 'our', *-má* 'mother'). It is applied to Mrs. Harry, the head matron, who is an "Indian" or, as the narrator says, "a Heinz 57, an Indian who's from several different tribes" (28). While Indian, she is not explicitly described as "Navajo."

Vida then responds. "'*'Éí laa*'. She's had it in for me ever since I got back late from Christmas vacation,' I say as I inhale." The Navajo form indicates agreement and acts as a form of conversational uptake. The narrator then switches to English. Edgar teases in Navajo, the narrator responds in Navajo and then switches into English.

The next two uses of metapragmatic terms concern indirect reports of things that Mrs. Harry "told" Vida to do. Note the parallelism of the two constructions as well, adding to the force of the directives.

She told me to mop up the water in the showers when it wasn't my detail.

She told me to sweep the porch after Edgar walked me back from the rec hall.

This last example is then followed directly by quoted speech and metapragmatic terms. The "she" is Mrs. Harry again. "'No sweeping, no TV,' she said. I said okay and went into my room."

Mrs. Chavez then enters the scene. Mrs. Chavez is the "girl's dorm attendant." After she spots Viv and Vida outside Edgar's window, we get the following: "She makes her rounds and tells us to get back to our dorm. 'Mrs. Harry wants to see you, Vida' she says and looks at me." Here the use of *tell* to describe Mrs. Chavez's speech act echoes with the uses of *tell* to describe the speech acts of Mrs. Harry. Vida responds then: "'Another month in the salt mines,' I say sarcastically." Tohe provides the adverb *sarcastically* as an affective display of Vida's stance toward Mrs. Chavez.

The next use of a metapragmatic term comes at the final confrontation between Mrs. Harry and Vida. Tohe uses the metalinguistic label *tell off* for the speech act that Mrs. Harry is about to engage in: "She's ready to tell me off, to shame and humiliate me again" (29). Mrs. Harry never gets the chance to "tell off" Vida. Instead, Vida blows smoke in her face. The use of *tell off* echoes with the six other uses of the metapragmatic term *tell*. In each case, an utterance is directed at the listener and is not meant to be opened up for response. With these uses of *tell* in "So I Blow Smoke in Her Face," Tohe creates an emergent image of *tell* as a monologic assertion, often in the form of critique or directives. To recap those six uses: the uncle "tells" Vida and Viv not to overwork the horses; when the Chicano boys get "serious," Vida first "tells" them to drop her and Viv off and then "tells" them that she and Viv are government property; Mrs. Harry "tells" Vida twice to do her chores as punishment; and Mrs. Chavez, when she catches Vida and Viv outside Edgar's window, "tells" them to get back to their dorm. The final "telling", however, by Mrs. Harry, is thwarted when Vida blows smoke in her face. Here we see the setting up of rhetorical expectation and its subsequent thwarting (see Burke 1968; Woodbury 1985; Hymes 2003).

On the Uses of Navajo and Teasing

Having discussed in some detail the metapragmatic forms used in Tohe's "So I Blow Smoke in Her Face," I turn now to the uses of Navajo within quoted speech in the story. Here I suggest that the use of Navajo and Navlish forms add to a characterological image but also that they are metadiscourses on the social value of Navajo and Navlish. These two processes are linked, I would argue, through the metapragmatic term *tease*. Before turning to that, I want to preface it with a few remarks on *dloh hodichí* or "teasing" and Navajos.

Early on in my fieldwork, I sat down with a Navajo poet consultant for an interview. As we began talking, I noted that I was the repeated object of what Navajos call in English "teasing." My Navajo consultant, who teased me a great deal himself, explained that in Navajo to be teased is a sign of affection and that it was a good thing that people felt comfortable teasing me. He added that had I not been teased so much, I should be concerned. Tohe, in a poetry performance October 9, 2006, in Carbondale, Illinois, also discussed the issue of Navajos teasing me while I did fieldwork. Below is an excerpt from that performance (see Webster 2009 for more on this performance; the colon indicates nonphonemic vowel lengthening):

Tony
uhm
he was on the Navajo reservation my reservation
for about a year and a half and
he was
everywhere that we went
and I
als
almost like my own personal stalker [laughter]
but
he was on the reservation so long that
we started to call him our in-law [laughter]
and we used to tea:se him that
maybe you would find a Navajo woman on the reservation [laughter]

This is, of course, not only a description of teasing me but also an example of teasing me. Tohe teases me here by noting that I was sometimes known as her "personal stalker" and that I was sometimes encouraged to "find a Navajo woman." Such examples of teasing are relatively common in my field recordings. They are an affective display, indicating a degree of social intimacy between myself and various Navajos that I have spent time with. Sometimes this teasing was in English and occasionally it was also in Navajo, especially when I mispronounced a Navajo word. Such teasing reminded me to be careful speaking Navajo. In "So I Blow Smoke in Her Face," Tohe uses the metapragmatic term *tease* to establish an affectionate relationship between Vida and her (maternal) uncle. This is the classic "joking relationship" between maternal uncles and their nieces and nephews (see Kluckhohn and Leighton 1962; Aberle 1961). Nicknames, as in Tohe's (1999: 25) example of Vida's uncle calling her "Wishbone," are an especially common form of teasing among many Navajos (see Kluckhohn and Leighton 1962: 115; Aberle 1961: 155). As Tohe once explained to me, "Navajos love to make up names for people."

Donna Deyhle (1992) and Tiffany Lee (2007) have both discussed teasing within an educational setting. As Deyhle notes, "teasing among Navajo was a traditional form of social control." According to Deyhle's consultants, Navajos would tease each other for looking down on things Navajo and for not speaking Navajo. Deyhle also points out that teasing was an expression of "cultural solidarity." The use of teasing, as Deyhle notes, is often given as an explanation for why Navajos fail in school settings.

Lee adds to this discussion of Navajos, education, and teasing. As Lee notes, "Navajo people, like many Native communities, have used teasing to teach the norms and morals of their society. But this was typically done through the Navajo language." Lee goes on to suggest that "perhaps those nuances that make teasing less severe when done in the Navajo language do not come across the same way in English. In any case, today's Navajo teenagers are much more sensitive to any teasing, and especially scolding, that they experience" (28). Some Navajos have told me that younger Navajos do not understand the social purposes of teasing. In Tohe's short story, Navajos tease each other in both English and Navajo. The important factors here seem to be that Edgar and Vida are Navajos, are students, and have an attraction between them. The teases are also directed at the Indian School and Mrs. Harry, and never at individual qualities of either Vida or Edgar.*

We have also already encountered the use of a Navajo form *nicháa-'ha'dooshkeeł* for "scold" in a teasing situation above, in the scene at

---

* The one example of negative teasing from *No Parole Today* that I will discuss—not explicitly identified as "teasing" by metapragmatic terms, however—arises from the mispronunciation of Tohe's name by the algebra teacher in "The Names," one of the poems to be discussed below. It seems of consequence that the metapragmatic label *tease* is not included in the poem.

Edgar's window. Tohe in fact uses the metapragmatic term *tease* in that
example. "Scold" is also a salient metalinguistic label on the Navajo Nation.
Examples of the use of the English word *scold* in joking situations can
be given. Here I provide an example by Navajo poet Luci Tapahonso at
a poetry performance in Window Rock, July 18, 2001 (we have seen this
example before, in the discussion of Tapahonso's "Hills Brothers Coffee"
in chapter 1). The audience was primarily Navajo, with an emphasis on
high-school-aged Navajos.

> I'm going to read
> uhm a number of some poems
> that you've probably heard before
> and that I've learned over the years
> that I have to read or
> somebody's gonna sco:ld me [laughter]

The laughter after Tapahonso says "sco:ld" (with an extended vowel here)
indicates that many of the Navajo in attendance understood this as a joke.
    Finally, Lee (2007: 20–21) adds an important bit of information con-
cerning the participants in teasing and interpretation of that teasing based
on who is doing it:

> Teasing experiences, for the most part, have not been easily dismissed by
> a number of the students interviewed. Particularly when the source of the
> teasing was an older relative or another adult, the experience made the
> students feel demeaned, embarrassed, and defensive.

Teasing is sometimes given as an explanation for why young Navajos do
not speak in Navajo (Deyhle 1992; Lee 2007). As Keith Basso (1979) long
ago noted concerning joking imitations of white people by Western Apaches
that have as their targets other Western Apaches, such forms of linguistic
play are always "humorous" and "dangerous" (see also Sherzer 2002). The
risk in teasing is that it is not interpreted as humorous but as the veiled insult
that always lurks in it.
    Let us now return to Tohe's short story and the uses of Navajo and Navlish
in it. The first use of Navajo in "So I Blow Smoke in Her Face" comes when
Vida (or Viv) uses a triadic directive at Edgar's window. As Field (2001)
has noted, this is a polite and appropriate way to give a directive in Navajo
(see Aberle 1961). Jasper is used as an intermediary to summon Edgar:
'You tell him, "Edgar, come here"' (Tohe 1999: 27). It is the embedded

metapragmatic term that signals this as a triadic directive. This is an implicit metadiscourse on proper ways of speaking.

The next use of Navajo follows when Edgar makes an indirect request for a cigarette from Vida. Here the use of the interrogative enclitic on the English lexical item creates a code-mixed form (Schaengold 2003; Webster 2009; Field 2009), which Navajos sometimes refer to as Navlish. Navlish is used by a number of Navajos, especially contemporary Navajos, in everyday conversations on and around the Navajo Nation. As discussed in chapter 1, the use of Navlish in contemporary Navajo discourse is often associated with affective displays of social intimacy and locality. For example, we saw how Navajo comedian Vincent Craig often uses *shiheart* (my love) in a number of his comedic skits. However, it is also often subject to criticism from Navajo-language purists. Tohe's use of Navlish here seems to signal a relaxed sociable moment between Edgar and Vida. It is not negatively evaluated by Tohe or by any of the characters in the story. Here Tohe challenges, implicitly, any "elder-speaker purism" by including in the story a code-mixed form that aids in a positive characterological image of "cool."

Tohe next uses Navajo when Viv jokes about the meat served at the Indian School. Tohe marks this use with the explanatory metapragmatic label "it's a joke," which follows the joke in Navajo and its repetition in English. This is then followed by Edgar "teasing" Vida in Navajo, "*Nihíma nicháa'ha'dooshkeeł*" (28). Tohe does not translate this reported speech into English. Again, the use of the Navajo kinship term *nihíma* 'our mother' in a nonliteral manner for Mrs. Harry, as if she were a mother who would "scold" her children, is done here for humorous effect. Vida responds in Navajo with an agreement uptake before switching to English. The use of Navajo (*nicháa'ha'dooshkeeł* 'will scold you') rather than English in this teasing example resonates with Lee's (2007: 28) contention that teasing in Navajo is "less severe" than teasing in English. Edgar's use of the metapragmatic term in Navajo seems to be part of the humor of the teasing. Certainly, Mrs. Harry was not going to "scold" Vida in Navajo (like, one expects, Vida's mother would have done). The language of the tease thus contrasts with the expected language of Mrs. Harry's scolding.

In the short story, Navajo and Navlish are only used by the Navajo students. They are used for indirect requests, triadic directives, and teasing and joking. Their use suggests proper ways of speaking, social intimacy, and solidarity. They are used dialogically. Here we see an emergent contrast with the uses of the metapragmatic term *tell*, discussed above, which seem to cluster around monologic directives, often in the form of reproaches. English can also be used for joking among the Navajo students, so we cannot say that only Navajo is used for moments of social intimacy; rather, that Navajo is only used for moments of social intimacy. The use of Navajo in this short story then acts as an affective display of social intimacy. It is not the only way that such social intimacy can be displayed, but in all cases it contrasts with the use of the metapragmatic term *tell*. This story is then, following Agha (2003: 257), a metadiscourse, an *implicit* metadiscourse, on the social value of using Navajo and Navlish. Tohe never explicitly states that Navajo and Navlish are the languages of social intimacy, rather she dramatizes this iconicity. To borrow from Moore (1993: 237), Navajo and Navlish become affective "emblems of value." Their use in the story by Tohe is also a way of imagining the boarding-school experience. Like the rural Japanese women who encountered "Japanese women's language" and a "modern" and "urban" lifestyle only through the images of the novel (Inoue 2006: 103), today's young Navajos' encounters with the boarding-school experience are, in part, through literary imaginings like Tohe's. This is the historical-memory work of such imaginings.

On Non-Navajos Speaking Navajo

I now turn to two poems by Tohe and the metapragmatic terms used in them and the uses of Navajo in them. I begin with "The Names" and then discuss "Sometimes Those Pueblo Men Can Sure Be Coyotes." Like the use of *tell off* in the short story to name a speech style, Tohe begins "The Names" (1999: 4–5) with a metapragmatic term for a named speech style. The poem dramatizes the calling of role by a non-Navajo teacher, her mispronunciation of Navajo names, and the students' muted response. The metapragmatic term *call roll* sets the stage for much of the following interaction in this poem. The teacher calls out various Navajo names and the students are forced to respond to the mispronounced form. There are no further metapragmatic terms used in this poem in association with quoted speech, though there are six zero quotatives (quotations not marked by any quotative) and two more metapragmatic terms.

Tohe does, however, describe something of the responses that various Navajo students give. In so doing, she provides characterological images of the students and something of their affective displays toward the teacher, displays that the teacher either ignores or is unaware of. "'Virginia Spears,' the Algebra teacher calls roll" (4). We are informed by the narrator (Tohe herself) that the girl's name is Virginia Speans. Speans replies: "'Here.' Soft voice / She never corrects the teachers." This is an affective display.

The characterization "soft voice" and the detail that Speans never corrects the teacher add affective poignancy to this moment. Tohe describes the quality of the voice to indicate Speans's affective stance. She does not use metapragmatic terms to do so. In fact she negates the metapragmatic term *corrects* here as well. Navajo children respond, they do not engage.

The pattern of describing the responses without using an explicit metapragmatic term for them continues throughout the poem. The teacher calls out the next name; though no explicit metapragmatic term is used here either, the teacher's voice is linked with the opening metapragmatic term *calls roll.* "Leonard T-sosie." Tsosie responds with silence and a raised hand. And then the next student: "Mary Lou Yazzy. Are you related to Thomas Yazzy?" This question is followed by a short exchange between Yazzie and the teacher. "Mary Lou with puzzled expression. 'No.'/ 'Oh, I thought you might be. He's quiet too.'" Tohe again describes Mary Lou's expressive features without using an explicit metapragmatic term. This is again an affective display. The "puzzled expression" comes from the fact, which Tohe notes, that Yazzie is a very common Navajo last name. I will return to this point in the next section.

Finally, the teacher gets to Tohe herself. "Laura Toe." The narrator can only sink into her chair and imagine the teasing that she will get on the school bus, "to dread hearing it on the bus tossed around." I would argue that *tossed* here is a metapragmatic term. This use of *tossed* links the teasing with the image of "kids playing keep-away."

The lack of metapragmatic terms for the Navajo children creates an image of them as targets of talk, not coparticipants in a dialogue. This is reinforced by the affective images that Tohe presents of the replies: "silent," "soft voice," "puzzled," and "sink." And it is firmly established with the negation of the metapragmatic term *correct* at the beginning of the poem. The Navajo students never speak Navajo in this poem. Unlike in the short story, where Vida resists Mrs. Harry's authority, in this poem the students do not overtly challenge the teacher. Instead, their silence can be seen as recognition that the teacher is an ambiguous and potentially dangerous interlocutor and therefore the best course of action is to remain silent. As Keith Basso (1991) notes for Western Apaches, silence is a communicative resource that is often used when an interaction is seen as unpredictable, uncertain, or ambiguous. Some Navajos, like Western Apaches, prefer to remain silent so that they can let the situation unfold (see also Webster 2012a). As with encounters with people who are drunk (K. Basso 1991: 97), Navajos prefer to remain silent in the face of such ambiguous and potentially dangerous interlocutors because to speak might only exacerbate the situation.

"Sometimes Those Pueblo Men Can Sure Be Coyotes" (Tohe 1999: 16–17) focuses on the adventures of two adolescent Navajo girls (Rena and the narrator) with Mr. Kayate, a Pueblo man. Mr. Kayate is the driver of the "G-car" (government car), as the girls "called it" (16), at the Indian School in Albuquerque. Puebloan peoples, historically, spoke a variety of Keresan and Kiowa-Tanoan languages, neither of which is related to Navajo (a Southern Athabaskan language). The incidents in this poem take place along Albuquerque's Central Avenue, like Vida and Viv's encounter with the Chicano boys in "So I Blow Smoke in Her Face." The girls telephone the Indian School to have a car sent to get them. The driver of that car is the Pueblo man Mr. Kayate, a "handsome" man. Here is where quoted speech begins:

> when one of us said
> > *Éí hastiin ayóo baa dzólní'* this man is very handsome
> > *Éí laa'* I agree

Tohe begins this exchange with the use of the metapragmatic term *said*. When the speaker shifts, there is no attendant metapragmatic term to signal the shift. The shift is accomplished through a zero quotative. The English glosses that Tohe adds are for the reader's benefit and are not to be understood as part of the actual quoted dialogue. This is made clear in the following line, "then we were making all kinds of comments about him in Diné." *Diné*, that is, *Diné bizaad* or the Navajo language, is understood, through the metapragmatics here, to be the language of the interaction. That is crucial, because in the written version the next examples of quoted speech are given in English: "saying those things that adolescent girls say / I wonder if he's married / of course, these handsome men always have a woman / how old do you think he is / do you think he has children." The use of the opening metapragmatic label "saying those things that adolescent girls say" places this dialogue within the speech style of "girl talk." Tohe clearly indicates that this is nonserious talk. The affective display here is of social intimacy between two girls. The use of Navajo, or at least the description of Navajo being used, seems to solidify that affective bond.

Once Mr. Kayate has taken the girls back to the Indian School he responds to their comments: "*A'héhee' at'ééke* he said thank you, girls" (17). That he responds in Navajo indicates that he has understood the entire conversation that the two girls have been engaging in. The metapragmatic term here, *said*, frames this as a form of quoted speech, but it does not seem to indicate anything about the speaker's affective stance. However, the title's linking of the Pueblo man with Coyote, a trickster in Navajo narratives (see Toelken and Scott 1981), seems to suggest a characterological image of Mr. Kayate. Notice too the potential pun between *Kayate* and *Coyote*. Even Mr. Kayate's name may evoke Coyote.

If "So I Blow Smoke in Her Face" presents a view of Navajo as the language of social intimacy, the two poems, on the other hand, challenge any simple alignment of Navajo with intimacy and solidarity. When we look at "The Names" we see that the algebra teacher repeatedly mispronounces Navajo names. Tohe gives metapragmatic descriptions of those mispronunciations: "'Leonard T-sosie.' / (His name is Tsosie.) Silent first letter as in ptomaine," and "Yazzie is a common Navajo name, like Smith or Jones. / She rhymes it with jazzy and snazzy" (Tohe 1999: 4). In each case, Tohe indicates the point of contrast between a Navajo pronunciation and a non-Navajo pronunciation. She then concludes by writing the Navajo names in the current Navajo practical orthography, indicating high tone and glottal stops.

> Tohe, from T'óhii means Towards Water.
> Tsosie. Ts'ósí means Slender.
> And Yazzie, from Yázhí, means Beloved Little One/Son.
> (5)

Such meanings are unavailable to the algebra teacher, much as the pronunciations also appear to be. What this poem highlights is the linguistic gulf between teacher and Navajo students.

Finally, the poem "Sometimes Those Pueblo Men Can Sure Be Coyotes" also uses Navajo. The use of Navajo by the two adolescent schoolgirls indexes social intimacy between them. However, the response in Navajo by the Pueblo man reminds readers that the use of Navajo can also be dangerous. That is, one must be careful with whom and in front of whom one uses Navajo. This is a metadiscourse on the careful use of Navajo in interactions. Note also that, by making Mr. Kayate a competent Navajo speaker, Tohe challenges any naïve view of Navajo as something only spoken by Navajos.

On the Affects of Navajo

The boarding school was a complicated speech environment. Languages were at times overtly suppressed and at other times only nominally allowed. Tohe's work is an attempt to creatively imagine that complicated speech environment. As Agha (2003: 255) notes, such literary images of languages "do not merely represent the realities of social life, they amplify and transform them into more memorable, figuratively rendered forms" (see also Bakhtin 1981: 295; Williams 1977: 46). These images are constructed by way of the metapragmatic terms used to describe speech and the languages used in that speech. Navajo students engage in affective displays, they tease and joke with one another. Maternal uncles may also tease. Non-Navajo teachers and dorm matrons, on the other hand, "call roll" and "tell" Navajo students what to do. Sometimes, like the trickster Coyote, non-Navajos are listening in on the intimate conversations of adolescent girls. Matrons, on the other hand, humiliate and shame Navajo students. While the boarding school is a place where Navajos are silenced, in Tohe's work it is also a place where Navajos can recognize and imagine a "Navajo" voice of resistance.

Tohe foregrounds the ways that the languages used also reveal telling affective relationships. When Navajo students use Navajo or Navlish, they use it in appropriate request making and indirect directives. They also use it when they tease and joke with each other. When non-Navajo teachers use Navajo they mispronounce the Navajo forms, embarrassing and shaming the Navajo students. When the Pueblo man uses Navajo he too embarrasses the young Navajo girls. When Navajo students use Navajo, they are displaying social intimacy and solidarity with each other. When non-Navajos use Navajo, they are embarrassing Navajo students through either their ignorance or their hidden knowledge of Navajo; they intrude into the secured domain of social intimacy created by Navajo students using Navajo. These are all implicit metadiscourses on languages and language users.

Note that in the published version of "Sometimes Those Pueblo Men Can Sure Be Coyotes," the use of only English to stand for what was said in Navajo suggests a "referential transparency" of semantic content between Navajo and English (see Haviland 2003: 768). The use of only English also gives the impression of Navajo as secondary to English (see Meek and Messing 2007). All of this changes, however, in the oral performances of this poem that I have documented. There Tohe gives the girls' speech in Navajo first throughout the exchange, and the English is at best secondary to the Navajo. Such differences between written and oral versions put into relief why we need to understand the ways such literary works are continually enacted and performed.

In "So I Blow Smoke in Her Face," the use of Navajo can be seen as an affective register. In both of the poems, such a straightforward analysis of the use of Navajo is challenged and modified. It is modified by specifying who the speakers of Navajo are, or rather by providing context and social situations in which such uses occur. In both cases, when Navajo is used by a non-Navajo, Navajo students are embarrassed. In both cases, those that use Navajo are not only non-Navajo but also have positions of authority. The short story is a metadiscourse on the emotional bond between Navajos and the Navajo language (including Navlish); the poems are cautions about the ways non-Navajos may (mis)use Navajo.

Some Navajos have told me that Navajo is a "dangerous language" and should be spoken with care. There are jokes that still circulate on the Navajo Nation concerning Indian Health Service doctors who were too eager to learn Navajo and spoke inappropriately to elder Navajo women as a result. On the other hand, Navajos have sometimes told me that the Navajo language is a more intimate language, a more feelingfully affective language, than English. Navajo poets have talked to me about their "love" of certain Navajo words. Other Navajos have told me about the delight they take in hearing Navajo spoken. All of these people's statements concerning the feelings they have about their language are part of their language ideologies as well. Some Navajos express, in such statements, a language ideology that sees an emotional bond between Navajos and the Navajo language. As Kroskrity (2004) reminds us, we, as linguistic anthropologists, need to attend to the feelings that speakers have about languages. These feelings can be positive, as in the examples of Navajo used by Navajos here discussed, or they can be negative, as Haviland's (2003) discussion of "linguistic paranoia" makes clear, or as in the uses of Navajo by non-Navajos in Tohe's work, or in the way some Navajos "reject" Navajo (Field 2009). In the Equal Employment Opportunity Commission "English-only" case in Page, one of the arguments made by the restaurant owner, echoing the linguistic paranoia described by Haviland, was that Navajos used Navajo to "insult" people and to say "crude" and "vulgar" things (Zachary 2005: 6). Tohe's short story presents a radically different image of Navajo. In it, English and its attendant metapragmatic term *tell* are used to "shame and humiliate," while Navajo is used as an affective display of social intimacy. The iconicity here is between Navajos and using Navajo for social intimacy.*

Lee (2007) and Deyhle (1992) have suggested that teasing may be one reason that young Navajos do not attempt to speak Navajo, that they become

---

* Significantly, Tohe does not link the Navajo language to Navajo ceremonialism in any of these works. As noted earlier, some Navajo Christians are resistant to Navajo-language instruction in schools because they believe that Navajo cannot be disentangled from Navajo philosophy/religion. Some Navajo poets do link the Navajo language with Navajo ceremonialism (Webster 2006a).

ashamed of speaking Navajo. As Lee aptly notes, "the policies of boarding schools and the general attitude of mainstream America assigned an inferior status to Navajo people, culture, language, and worldview" (22). The three literary works by Tohe discussed here, through implicit metadiscourses of characterological images, link Navajos speaking Navajo with positive social values and emotional attachments. Navajo readers are meant to identify with the Navajo students and the images of Navajo that they present. Instead of Navajo being seen as an emblem of shame (McCarty, Romero-Little, and Zepeda 2008), Tohe's work is one way that positive valuation of and emotional attachments to being Navajo and using the Navajo language are circulated. Navajo becomes an affective emblem of value (Moore 1993).* Language ideologies are intimate, emotionally salient, because they can be deeply felt. Tohe's literary works provide ways of imagining the intimacy, the affective resonance, between languages and language users.

Conclusion

Metadiscourses, literary or otherwise, always take place in real social contexts. As Agha (2003: 242) notes, "contemporary mass media depictions are themselves the products of individuals caught up in larger historical processes" (see also Williams 1977). As the boarding-school experience becomes further removed from the lived experiences of Navajos and other Native Americans, literary representations of boarding-school encounters take on greater resonance. This resonance is compounded as fewer and fewer Navajos learn Navajo. Understanding the kinds of social value, the metadiscourses about languages and language users, and the affectivity of languages that circulate through Navajo literary discourse becomes important for understanding how Navajos, especially college-age Navajos, can imagine themselves in the role of boarding-school students and (more generally) as users of Navajo. Through Tohe's work young Navajos can imagine

---

* This is not, however, to say that all of Tohe's poetry is an implicit metadiscourse on language and language users. There are explicit metadiscourses as well, echoing the *Navajo Times* article cited at the beginning of this chapter, including Tohe's story-poem "Our Tongues Slapped into Silence" (originally published in the *Journal of Navajo Education*), where Tohe unequivocally states, "utter one word in Diné and the government made sure our tongues were drowned in the murky water of assimilation" (Tohe 1999: 3). But, of course, Tohe does represent Navajo being spoken in the boarding-school context, by both Navajos and non-Navajos. Such explicit and implicit metadiscourses can and do work in tandem to create recognizable value-laden images of languages and language users.

the boarding school in particular ways, but they can also imagine ways of being Navajo and the Navajo language in particular ways. Tohe's work is an implicit metadiscourse on and dramatization of the ways that Navajos can be intimate with each other through Navajo. Such implicit metadiscourses resonate with a general notion that I have heard among Navajos, that people should be left to make their own decisions and interpretations (Webster 2009).

Finally, Tohe has explained to me on a variety of occasions that "poetry is performance." While I have not seen Tohe perform her short story, I do know that the two poems have circulated as both written and oral speech events. Tohe has performed both of these poems to largely college-age Navajo audiences at Diné College on the Navajo Nation. These are precisely the audiences that various Navajo and non-Navajo scholars have pointed to as having the most ambivalent attitudes toward the Navajo language and their own language abilities (see Lee 2007; Field 2009). Through such performances, these poems have still further become part of a complex set of implicit metadiscourses on the social values and emotional attachments associated with speaking Navajo and those who would speak it.

CHAPTER THREE

The Drifting Lonely Seed

But the linguist still runs his hands up the length of our tongues,
perplexed that we even have a tongue   at all.
—SHERWIN BITSUI (2003), *SHAPESHIFT*

Some poetry lingers; the words continue to echo long after the performance. Navajo poet Sherwin Bitsui's "Chrysalis" (2003: 64) is one such poem. I heard and recorded it numerous times during my fieldwork on the Navajo Nation during 2000 and 2001. Bitsui, like many Navajo poets, has a keen sense and ambivalence about linguists and anthropologists, about those who would document Navajos. Like many Navajo poets, Bitsui also has complicated emotions and felt attachments toward his languages. When Bitsui was in Carbondale, Illinois, for a poetry performance, he read a poem that notes that

> the beginning is always the argument
> arrangements, patterns
> who gets this portion of lamb
> who gets to speak English as a second language.
> (Bitsui 2003: 29)

Navajo poet Esther Belin (2007: 74) provocatively asks, "How do I know when my language is no longer English or Navajo?" The pivot in Belin's question, the complement to Bitsui's lines, is the first-person possessive and attendant noun, *my language*. As Belin has explained to me, it is time to consider English "a Diné language."

This chapter is about the ways that some critics (literary or otherwise) of Navajo poetry have been "perplexed" that Navajos can own "English." This chapter is also about the felt attachments that adhere to the uses of Englishes by Navajo poets—what I described in chapter 1, following both Povinelli (2006) and Herzfeld (1997) by degrees, as "intimate grammars." Philip Deloria (2004), in his insightful and provocative *Indians in Unexpected Places*, takes up the issue of expectations and anomalies in representations of Native Americans, as they relate to practice. Deloria asks us to investigate the "unexpectedness" of Native Americans, not so much for what it reveals about Native Americans as the ways Native Americans have been imagined. He singles out a number of such recurring tropes: "primitivism, technological incompetence, physical distance, and cultural difference—these have been the ways many Americans have imagined Indians" (4). This chapter attempts to glimpse something of the ways that Native American languages have been imagined as "unexpected." For some, the mere fact that Native Americans had languages was unexpected. That Native American languages—as traditionally understood—have been constructed as "primitive" should also not be surprising (see Hymes 1996a). But recent Indigenous efforts have attempted to valorize traditionally understood Native American languages and encourage the maintenance or awakening of them (see House 2002; Webster 2009; Kroskrity and Field 2009; Leonard 2011; Perley 2011).

Writing became one crucial area in which American Indians were seen as "technologically incompetent"; a host of evolutionary scenarios were used to deny that Native American inscriptive practices, from Lakhota winter counts to Tohono O'odham calendar sticks, were "true writing" (that is, like Western alphabetic writing). Native American inscriptive practices were (mis) judged by Western expectations, which then validated and licensed conquest and colonialism (see, for examples, Mignolo 1995; Collins and Blot 2003). Mindy Morgan (2009) describes writing practices on the Fort Belknap Reservation. Writing in English became the technology of civilization; English literacy was the ideological sign (symbolic, indexical, and iconic) in which were wrapped metasemiotic stereotypes of civilization. But note, if you will, just how much a phrase like "writing in English" may obscure. What does it mean to write or speak in "English"? That question is at the heart of the expectations about languages and Native Americans that we will explore.

American Indian Englishes have been the target of mockery and dismissal by dominant discourses. As Meek (2006, 2011) has shown, popular media—from *Peter Pan* to *Pocahontas*—have imagined American Indian Englishes in stereotypical ways, reproducing racist images of Native peoples (see also J. Hill 2008). What is less well understood, and what I dwell on here, is the ways that the Englishes (written and otherwise) Native Americans have used for expressive purposes have also been considered "primitive" and "incompetent." The way, for example, that reviewers of

Blackhorse Mitchell's *Miracle Hill: The Story of a Navajo Boy*, because it was written in Navajo English (a local way of speaking and writing), largely dismissed it as mere documentation or an incompetent attempt to write in some imagined "standard" English.

It is not just popular media that have participated in the marginalization and dismissal of local ways of speaking and writing that do not fit into an idealized image of bounded and discrete languages. As Lionel Wee (2005) has noted regarding Singlish (a Singapore English), recognition of interlanguage rights by linguists, educators, and governments has been much more common than recognition of marginalized intralanguage differences by them. While we may quibble with Wee's distinction between *intralanguage* and *interlanguage* (as I argue throughout this book, such dichotomous ways of seeing language miss the fuzziness of language boundaries), his point that "intralanguages" like Singlish and Navajo English are often stigmatized and marginalized by outsiders (scholars and nonscholars alike) and by their own speakers is very much worth keeping in mind. Many outsiders and many Navajos concede the importance of the Navajo language in Navajo cultural traditions but still consider Navajo English to be a deficient and dysfluent way of speaking and writing. As Jessica Ball and May Bernhardt (2008: 585) note, such misrecognizing of local ways of speaking as "true language deficits" have real consequences in educational settings (see also Lippi-Green 1997). This is a kind of Herderian conceit in which glottonymically nameable languages map onto ethnonymically nameable peoples (Bauman and Briggs 2003; Silverstein 2003). By *glottonymically nameable language*, I mean a lexical-grammatical code that has come to have a recognized "language name." One project of modernism is to name various "things" (here really sets of practices) so that they can be counted.

To put this more pointedly, although there has been a great deal of concern with documentation of Indigenous languages of late (a concern I share), documentation has often been narrowly understood to the exclusion of local spoken and written Englishes (or Spanishes or Frenches or the like). For example, a recent important set of articles in *Transforming Anthropology* compares African American English (AAE) with Native American languages (as traditionally understood). Arthur Spears and Leanne Hinton (2010: 12) state in the introduction to that issue that the "recognition of the right of Native Americans to maintain and promote their languages, and encouragement of the uses of Native American languages in the schools, is a complete reversal of the government philosophy . . . and is of course completely opposite to the attitudes toward the presence of AAE in the schools." However, this statement is only true if we ignore or erase the myriad of American Indian Englishes that currently are spoken and written by Native Americans. Here, echoing Belin, we might ask what it means to speak or write in a Navajo way. I argue that speaking and writing in a Navajo way, what some Navajos sometimes call *Dinék'ehjí yáłti'* (he/she is talking the Diné way), does not presuppose speaking something called "Navajo." This does not mean that I want to ignore Navajo, but rather that we must attend to all the myriad ways of speaking and writing that Navajos engage in. None should be dismissed a priori.

This chapter takes as its case study Blackhorse Mitchell's *Miracle Hill* and the ways that the book was framed by T. D. Allen and reviewed in the popular press. I then turn to a discussion that I had with Mitchell about his book, specifically the poem "The Drifting Lonely Seed" included in it, and show the ways that Mitchell rejects the characterization of his work by Allen. In particular, I describe how Mitchell performs the poem in Navajo English during our conversation. This, too, is a poem that echoes for me and for Mitchell. I begin by locating Mitchell's work within a wider context of teaching Navajos English through poetry.

From Ponies to Arrows

In 1933 a short eight-line poem was published in *Indians at Work*, a U.S. government publication (Hirschfelder and Singer 1992). The poem was composed by a collection of Navajo students at Tohatchi School in New Mexico (on the Navajo Nation, a boarding school at the time). This poem, "If I Were a Pony," is one of the first published poems by Navajos. Here is the poem:

> If I were a pony,
> A spotted pinto pony,
> A racing, running pony,
> I would run away from school.
> And I'd gallop on the mesa,
> And I'd eat on the mesa,
> And I'd sleep on the mesa,
> And I'd never think of school.
> (Brandt 1937: 44)

Let me start with something personal here. I cannot read this poem without sensing the desire that these young Navajos had to leave the school, to be like the "running pony." Indeed, when I have shared this poem with Navajos, they have often remarked on the courage of the young Navajos who wrote this poem. They too have heard this poem as a critique of Western schooling. The poem was written in English. Other poetry in English would follow, and like this early poem, it too would use English as a way to critique outside educational practices. Note the irony of the publication venue for this poem, a U.S. government publication. The content of the poem must have been utterly beside the point, which was to highlight Navajo literacy in English.

This pattern repeats. The first poetry that I have found published in the *Navajo Times* occurs May 16, 1962. The poet is Eugene Claw. I have not been able to locate any more poetry published by Claw. The four poems appear in a short-lived feature of the *Navajo Times* called "Poets Corner." The introduction to these poems articulates a view of Navajo poetry—written poetry—as an exemplar of English-language command. The poems are iconic, then, of English language mastery. Here is the brief introduction to Eugene Claw's poems (orthography and spelling as in original):

EDITORS NOTE: The following short poems were written by Eugene Claw, a Navajo Junior at Manuelito Hall and display a fine grasp of the English language as well as imagination and good poetic syntax.

What are we to make of this short but fascinating introduction? Why is it important to assert that the poems "display" command of English? Or that they exhibit "imagination?" And what precisely is "poetic syntax"? Indeed, one poem by Claw is titled "Illiterate Navaho" and sets up a contrast between Western educational knowledge and Navajo knowledge, here reckoned as "illiterate." Western knowledge is associated with literacy and Navajo knowledge is associated with primary epistemic knowledge (things one can see, touch, and hear). The value these poems have seems to cluster however around the "fine grasp" of English, which is then supplemented by "imagination and good poetic syntax." It is the display of English that is primary.

Claw's poems, especially "Illiterate Navaho," seem to resist a simple reading as merely a display of English. Here is that poem. I have attempted to retain the spacing of the poem as reproduced in the *Navajo Times*. I do not know if this matches the format Claw had in mind when he wrote it.

Illiterate Navaho

I believe only what I see, feel,
    and hear, as they exist,
I know I feel the sun comes from
    the east to the west

I tend not to believe what I can't
    see, feel, and hear,
fool would I be to say I know the
    intangibles
Only will I be intelligent to accept
    just the tangibles,
Educated in my own way, yet I
    live happily, and satisfied,
This is my knowledge, which I
    believeth and live.

Again, this poem appears to be a critique of Western educational practices. Written by a student in a Western educational setting at roughly the same time that Blackhorse Mitchell was writing "The Drifting Lonely Seed" (circa 1963), it challenges the knowledge being dispensed at such schools. As Claw writes, the speaker is "educated in my own way, yet I / live happily, and satisfied." It is not necessarily Western education that will lead to happiness and satisfaction, to the exclusion of the knowledge of "illiterate" Navajos. Rather than merely displaying a "fine grasp of the English language," Claw seems to be challenging Western educational practices. The irony is that Claw's "fine grasp of the English language" is used in the service of that critique.

During the late 1960s and early 1970s the Bureau of Indian Affairs sponsored the Creative Writing Project under the leadership of T. D. Allen. Allen taught at the Institute of American Indian Arts in Santa Fe. As a part of that project, Allen edited six volumes of the anachronistically titled anthology *Arrow*. These were collections of prose and poetry written by Native American students. Many young Navajos were published in these collections. Prizes were awarded for the outstanding submissions and the works were often judged by major figures in the then-burgeoning Native American literary scene. For example, in volume 4, N. Scott Momaday and William Stafford were the judges. However, by the end of 1973 government funding for the project ended. Volume 6 would be the last volume. The primary forms published were poetry, partly because they were shorter and thus more could be published, and partly because students tended to write more poetry than prose. Even the title of the journal evokes ideological images of Native Americans. It places Native Americans, like the use of arrows, in the past or as anachronism. It is reminiscent of Brenda Farnell's (2004: 33) discussion of the ways Native Americans have been imagined in particularly stereotypical ways, all in the name of "honoring" Native Americans.

In volume 1 of *Arrow*, T. D. Allen outlines the goals behind the Creative Writing Project. In the autumn of 1968, the Bureau of Indian Affairs allotted special-education funds for the project, which was aimed at Native American high-school students. As Allen (1969: vi) writes:

> The project's purpose was to provide American Indian high school students some training in the craft of writing along with the opportunity and encouragement to write. The immediate goal was to help students to discover themselves as persons with something to say, to help them acquire skill in making their statement and, incidentally, skill in using English.

There are a number of issues to unpack in this brief statement concerning the purpose and goal of the Creative Writing Project. That Allen felt that it was important for Native Americans to "discover themselves as persons with something to say" seems a bit presumptuous. It is certainly related to the stereotype of the "silent Indian." Allen says as much. "The ultimate goal was to help cure the silent-stolid-Indian syndrome." However, as Susan U. Philips (1993) has shown in regard to Warm Springs Native American students, "silence" may have more to do with discourse strategies and learning strategies than with not having "something to say" or with any "syndrome" (see also K. Basso 1991; Scollon and Scollon 1981; Webster 2012a; see also Hymes 1996a). Indeed, the suggestion that it is the American Indian student who must be "cured" places the onus of the "problem" on American Indians. Teaching methods are not the problem, according to this view; they are neutral. We will see in the transcript below that Mitchell explicitly states that Allen's classroom was not a place where he felt he could ask questions or speak freely (lines 16–17, 47–48, 52–57). In fact, Mitchell will explain that he had much to say, but that he could not speak in class and that is why he wrote his poetry. The problem that he had expressing himself was the constraints that the classroom placed upon him. There is no reflection by Allen on the notion that learning styles and speaking styles may differ cross-culturally. In place of the "silent" Indian, Allen posits the "confused" and grammarless Indian.

More important, however, was the goal of teaching Native American students the ways to express themselves, that is, the rules of Western "rhetoric." A crucial, although "incidental," factor for learning to express themselves was the use of English. The poems in *Arrow* are predominantly in English. There is very little code-switching in the poems collected. The poems are examples of English proficiency. It cannot have been only an "incidental" goal of the initiative for the students to "acquire . . . skill in using English," for the first two goals Allen mentions, "discover[ing] themselves" and expressing themselves, can be achieved, are being achieved today, without the use of English. There are many Indigenous poets, not just the Navajo poets I discuss here, who write in their indigenous language. The primary goal of the Creative Writing Project must have been to find a method to teach English. Creative writing was that method. Later, in the same introduction, after describing all the "plus by-products accruing," Allen once again turns "incidentally" to English. Allen has this to say: "They are, incidentally, acquiring skills and a bit of the art of English usage" (1969: vii). Again poetry and creative writing are methods of teaching English, which I argue *was* the primary goal. Allen's repeated use of *incidentally* strikes too much the note of happy coincidence to be taken seriously. Poetry, then, was used as a method for teaching literacy, and a clearly defined literacy at that: English literacy.

Miracle Hill and "Reading Loose"

In 1967, Blackhorse Mitchell, with the help of T. D. Allen, published *Miracle Hill: The Story of a Navaho Boy*, a semiautobiographical work that includes two poems, through the University of Oklahoma Press. The book created a bit of a sensation and was reviewed by N. Scott Momaday in the *New York Times* and by Dan Thrapp in the *Los Angeles Times*. Through a number of book signings along with the reviews in major newspapers, *Miracle Hill* was a very public book in 1967. The *Navajo Times* also reviewed Mitchell's book that year. From my conversations with some of Mitchell's Navajo contemporaries, it does appear that the book was more public off the Navajo Reservation (as the Navajo Nation was still called at the time) than on it. I still recall talking with a classmate of Mitchell's from Shiprock, New Mexico—who had a number of wonderful stories about him—and asking her about his book; her reply was that the first time she heard about Mitchell's book was when I mentioned it to her a few days earlier. Mitchell, for his part, has noted that he was reluctant to call attention to the publication of the book and preferred to let other people do that. Other Navajos I spoke with did not remember the original book coming out in 1967, but they did recall the reissue of the book in 2004.

I first met Mitchell in the fall of 2000 while I was doing dissertation fieldwork on and around the Navajo Nation concerning the emergence of written Navajo poetry. Besides his book, in 1968 Mitchell had been awarded a special prize in the Navajo Tribal Centennial literary contest for his poem "The New Direction" (a call to modernism that Mitchell now "would write differently") and his poem had been published in the *Navajo Times*. Having been one of the first published Navajo poets and one of the more well-known

Navajo authors, Mitchell was an important consultant for my work. He later became an important language instructor for me. He is a fluent speaker of Navajo and is literate in Navajo. He has written poetry in Navajo, which is unpublished. Since my initial fieldwork in 2000 and 2001, I have spent much time with Mitchell. During the summers of 2007 to 2012, I stayed with him at his house while I did further research on Navajo poetry and poets.

Written in 1963, when Mitchell was close to eighteen years old, *Miracle Hill* has since been reissued in 2004 by the University of Arizona Press, without the introduction by Allen, as *Miracle Hill: The Story of a Navajo Boy*. Allen's name is no longer on the cover and there is a new foreword by Paul Zolbrod. There is also the subtle shift from *Navaho* to *Navajo*, aligning more with current practices on the Navajo Nation. Terry Diener Allen, it should be noted, was also an author. She and her husband, Don Allen, wrote a number of novels and nonfiction works under the name T. D. Allen (which are also Terry Allen's initials) about the West and Native Americans. Perhaps the most famous of those works is *Navahos Have Five Fingers* (1963). That Allen already had a relationship with the University of Oklahoma Press is important for understanding how Mitchell's book wound up being published there. As one Navajo consultant pointed out when discussing the book and Mitchell, Allen did encourage Mitchell to write, and she did get the book published. As that consultant further noted, whatever the reasons for the book being published, once it was published it was no longer under Allen's control, and Navajos could and did make of it what they would. Allen, as this Navajo consultant noted, was both paternalistic (or maternalistic) and sympathetic toward Mitchell.

Miracle Hill is the story of Broneco, a young Navajo boy, and the events that led him to go to boarding school and later to the Institute of American Indian Arts in Santa Fe. It grew out of Mitchell's experience in the Bureau of Indian Affairs's Creative Writing Project. On the cover of *Miracle Hill* we find a hand-drawn picture of Tsé Bit'a'í (Winged Rock or Shiprock)—not the Miracle Hill of the title—and the following words: "By . . . Blackhorse Mitchell and T. D. Allen." In a review of *Miracle Hill* in *American Anthropologist*, Dorothea Leighton (1968) took this to mean that Terry Allen was the coauthor of this book. Although the language of the book is certainly Mitchell's (by degrees), as are the stories, Allen massively mediated what is in the book, according to Mitchell. Mitchell claims that Allen wanted a positive image of the boarding school and worked to make that so.

In the introduction to *Miracle Hill*, Allen (1967: vii) makes a plea for readers to "please read loose." Allen claims Mitchell lacks "grammar." Many Native American languages were devalued and dismissed because

Euro-Americans believed that traditionally understood Native American languages lacked grammar (see Hymes 1996a: 208). Allen has applied this paradigm, merely replacing the Native American language with Navajo English. In a later work (1972: 91), she will claim that Mitchell's grammar is "tangled" and that "writing in English presented almost insurmountable difficulties" for him. She is at pains to excuse his English-language skills, claiming his work is "more documentary than aesthetic or literary"—more, and this is her word, "primitive" (1967: viii). Allen likens Mitchell's work to primitive art. In essence, she apologizes for his literary voice. She goes on to claim that, "in spite of confused tenses and genders and sound-alike words, [Mitchell] was writing in sensory terms" (xi). Rather than understanding the structure of Navajo English, Mitchell is "confused." According to Allen (and, as we will see, many reviewers), Mitchell's regularized use of plural -*s* marking on the irregular noun *sheep* is a mistake. Mitchell has explained to me on numerous occasions that he prefers the form *sheeps* for the plural of *sheep*. This is a decision that he has made. *Sheeps* makes more sense to him. It is not a mistake. Mitchell is aware of negative evaluations regarding *sheeps* and other Navajo English forms (from phonology to lexical choices to syntax). I have seen him apologize for his Navajo English to audiences composed largely of non-Navajos. I have not seen him apologize for his Navajo English to audiences composed largely of Navajos. The plural marking on *sheeps* is an intimate grammar, an emotionally saturated use of language that runs the risk of negative evaluation by outsiders but that can create a common bond of sociality, an intimate sociality, among Navajos.

Here is the danger of using Navajo English, which is what the book is written in: it is subject to outside inspection and evaluation, outside scrutiny, based on criteria and expectations that are not local. Navajo English is a local way of speaking and writing that differs from mainstream English on phonological, morphological, syntactic, semantic, and discourse-related grounds. Guillermo Bartelt (1981, 1983, 2001) provides a useful overview of some of the features of Navajo English (see also Webster 2004; Leap 1993a, b). Some of the features of Navajo English are carryovers from Navajo, some are regularizations of irregular mainstream English forms, and some are based on the distinctive historical trajectory of Navajo English as a local way of speaking and writing, which does not completely coincide with the historical trajectory of mainstream English. Navajo English is spoken at the supermarket, at the tire shop, at the trading post, in homes, and at the local mutton stand. It is written on signs on and around the Navajo Nation and in e-mails. Note that Navajo English is also—like English more generally—not a homogeneous phenomenon. Rather it is—like all languages—a set of heterogeneous practices based on local registers and the unique histories of linguistic individuals.

However, because Navajo English is spoken and written by marginalized peoples, it can always be dismissed or devalued using outside assumptions about "standard" English and outside aesthetic principles (see Woodbury 1998). Leighton Peterson (2011) provides a telling example: the Navajo English–language skills of Elsie Mae Cly Begay were dismissed by "media professionals" who saw early versions of the documentary *The Return of Navajo Boy*, which is about her and her family. A pervasive belief in mainstream American culture is that linguistic differences equal linguistic deficiencies (see Hymes 1987a, 1996a; Lippi-Green 1997; J. Hill 2008). Here there are echoes of Deloria (2004). The expectations about Navajo English are that it is a "primitive" and "incompetent" English. English must be a foreign language for Navajos (see Meek 2006 on this point). What is not taken seriously is that Navajos may have a deep and perduring felt attachment toward their Englishes, that Navajo English can be an intimate and deeply felt grammar, and that Mitchell might be doing something with his use of Navajo English besides mere documentation.

Allen, however, does praise Mitchell's penmanship. She reproduces a page of his "beautiful handwriting" (1967: ix). Penmanship was a topic focused on at boarding school (as elsewhere), and Allen's printing of the page seems to act as a display of Mitchell's technological competence, which is to be marveled at (even Navajos that I know have, in fact, marveled at the aesthetics of Mitchell's handwriting). Although Mitchell may have mastered the graphic art of handwriting, Allen repeatedly makes clear that this mastery is only ornamentation, superficial, for the reality is that "the thing you, the reader, and . . . Blackhorse . . . Mitchell don't have in common is grammar. He has made the effort to meet you halfway. He has learned your vocabulary (with some fascinating use variations) and he has learned some bits and pieces of your linguistic patterns" (vii). Allen assumes that the language that Mitchell uses is incomplete ("bits and pieces"). Not understanding the structure of Navajo English, not knowing that there is no gender on pronouns and that plurality is regularized on irregular and mass nouns, Allen presents Mitchell's work as an incomplete (incompetent) attempt to write some putative "standard" English (note here that she assumes a homogeneous readership of a homogeneous English). Mitchell's book is a failure to reach that standard. Allen does not take seriously the possibility that Mitchell was expressing himself in the language he was competent in, that rather than being an incomplete attempt, it was a successful use of Navajo English for creative purposes. Instead of reading Mitchell's work "loose," perhaps we might read it seriously.

Even Mitchell's creativity can be explained away. Allen writes, "Imagery and sensory detail come through partly because of the author's not-quite-at-homeness with the English language. He does not translate literally from his thoughts in Navaho, but he does translate, and in the process a certain color and point of view are retained. Much of this happens out of something ingrained in a Navaho which is inherent in him and his language" (viii). Here Allen articulates an essentialist position, positing something "inherent" in Navajos and their language that leads to the "imagery and sensory detail" found in Mitchell's work. That Mitchell might have been actively selecting his images and sensory details and then writing them down seems to be lost on Allen. Mitchell has explained to me how he handwrote each page of what would become *Miracle Hill*, and then would rewrite, and rewrite, and rewrite the pages making corrections as he went. He also modeled the introduction of characters and changes of scene in his book on the writings of Sir Walter Scott's *Ivanhoe* and other writers he had been introduced to at school.

Later Allen conflates language with writing (common, as we will see, in the reviews as well). In discussing what she calls Mitchell's "aborted English," Allen explains some of his language uses as being based on "trying to learn our words by ear." She sees the written form as the "correct" form that speakers do or do not fail to "enunciate" (xi). She assumes that the written form is the language and that the actual speaking of language is, more or less, a deficient form of the written form. This is a pervasive language ideology that conflates written discourse with spoken discourse (see J. Milroy 2001). It assumes that people are trying to speak as if they were writing and not that writing and speaking are two sometimes overlapping and sometimes distinct endeavors.

The Reviews Are In

Having laid out something of the ways that T. D. Allen framed Mitchell's work, let us pause and look at the kinds of reviews that Mitchell's *Miracle Hill* received when it was first published. Many of the following reviews are quoted from a notebook collection of reviews that Blackhorse Mitchell kept. The reviews were cut out of newspapers, but there is incomplete information concerning the original places of publication of many of the reviews. Hereinafter, I will cite the author of the review and note that the review can be found in Blackhorse Mitchell's collection of reviews. I will give the publication date when known and any other pertinent information. I also have a copy of that collection of reviews. I thank Mr. Mitchell for sharing those reviews with me and for letting me make copies.

Many reviewers followed Allen's lead and apologized in one form or another for the language used in the book. Many took Allen's introduction at face value. Robert Ford (1967, Blackhorse Mitchell Collection) states that Mitchell's "command of English is still not absolute, for he constructs some writing as would a Navaho." Note that Ford assumes that Navajos are incapable of writing in "standard" English. Note that this implies a single "absolute" English. Ford praises the book for its "simplicity." He then goes on to praise, and echo, Allen. "The editor-mentor declined to make any changes of a major nature. It was a wise decision for the lapses from grammar only add to the personality of the book." Mitchell's work is again a "lapse from grammar" that "only add[s] to the [childlike] personality of the book." Or as Peggy Durham (1967, Blackhorse Mitchell Collection) writes in the *Oklahoma Journal*, "Mitchell writes as a child would write— and while this may sound obvious in view of his inexpert command of English, this 'childishness' has nothing to do with his vocabulary. It has to do with his way of seeing and presenting." This childlike point of view is, Durham adds, not marred by "Indian philosophy" or "rationalized bitterness toward the white man." Vincent Starrett, in the *Chicago Tribune* (August 28, 1967), writes this about Mitchell's language: "if your reaction to a colorful high-stepping verb is merely an urge to conjugate it, if a pungent sentence merely stirs you to grammatical analysis, and if the word *sheeps*—to be more specific—irritates you even mildly, go back to your epics by writers who take the rules of grammar seriously." According to Starrett, Mitchell's work should not be confused with an "epic" and Mitchell does not take "the rules of grammar seriously." But if Starrett suggests that Mitchell is not a serious writer, Maggy King in the *Monterey Peninsula Herald* (August 19, 1967) argues that "the writer is the real McCoy—a real Navaho of today, telling the story of his life; and his struggle with English shows only how earnest is his desire to learn and improve." For these reviewers, Mitchell's book satisfies the expectation that Navajos will lack a competent command of English and that such incompetence in English will also be linked with a childlike or primitive essence (common, by implication, to all Navajos).

Other reviewers of *Miracle Hill* were less kind or less condescending. One review suggested that Allen should have done more editing (Stensland 1971: 1198). Brian Garfield writes in the *Saturday Review* (September 9, 1967: 37) that Mitchell's "tale is not for the general reader. The language is too strange; there is little incident and less characterization; he does not even give enough information about his family and his people. [Mitchell] is completely silent, for example, about the dances and songs and sand-paintings of the Navaho." For Garfield, not only is Mitchell's language "garbled," the story is also not titillating or exotic enough. Joan Seager, in the *Denver Quarterly* (1968), takes Allen to task for not editing the book more thoroughly. She states that Mitchell's "grammatical errors simply detract" from the quality of the book. She goes on to state, concerning Mitchell, that the fact "that he is also a Navajo could have been given finer and more valid expression by a narrative uncluttered with the errors of a foreign language imperfectly learned." Note that for Seager, English is clearly not Mitchell's language; it is a foreign language for him. For these reviewers, Mitchell's book fails because of his language (or lack of language) and because he does not adequately meet the expectations of Navajo exoticness.

What is striking in these reviews is how preoccupied they are with Mitchell's supposed lack of English-language abilities. Most take Allen's characterization of the writing process at face value. They do not ask more fundamental questions about Allen's role in the shaping of the form and content of the book. Mildred Hart Shaw, in the *Daily Sentinel* (October 15, 1967), does note that "Mrs. Allen has written a patronizing, school-teacherish, unperceptive introduction to Mitchell and his book. It does no credit to either." But as Deloria (2011) notes in discussing an earlier version of this chapter, any "pleasure that ensues" from Shaw's review should be taken as "fleeting," because "the weight pressing relentlessly down on the system is that of non-Indian language ideology and expectation." Shaw's voice is the "anomaly" (180). Some reviewers, including Dorothea Leighton (1968), do attempt to place Mitchell's language use within the context of Navajo English. But, as I have argued elsewhere, whereas many critics claim that the Navajo language is quite complex, they see Navajo English as relatively transparent (Webster 2010c). It lacks complexity. Many reviewers, in one way or another, approached this book as an incompetent English that highlighted the primitive or childlike quality of its author (that is, Mitchell's English was "charming" and reflective of his "childlike" view of the world) or a failed English that lacked enough documentation of Navajo exoticness (that is, Mitchell had failed at writing English and he did not even provide enough exotica to make the book worth reading). Few took the trouble to see this book as something else entirely.

"The Drifting Lonely Seed"

In the introduction, Allen includes a poem that Mitchell wrote titled "The Drifting Lonely Seed" (Mitchell 1967). Mitchell wrote the poem circa 1963. According to Mitchell, it is the first poem that he ever wrote. The following is an extended excerpt from Allen's introduction to *Miracle Hill* that purports to describe the creation of "The Drifting Lonely Seed." I quote it at length because I will contrast it with a discussion that I had with Mitchell during the summer of 2008 about the creation of this poem. I have replaced a nickname that Mitchell was known by at the time with his current name, Blackhorse, throughout the excerpt (italics are in the original).

One day I [Allen] said, "I think readers would like to know how you first decided you'd like to write. It was during orientation, wasn't it?"

"Yes," [Blackhorse] answered.

"Well, try to remember all about it," I suggested. "Your readers will want to know how you got started, and you have skipped over that part."

He sat at the long table in our writing studio with a pad of paper before him and his chin in his palm. Finally he asked, "What was that you gave us that day? A kind of seed or something, I think."

"I don't know for sure, but I believe it was a milkweed," I said. "Don't worry about its name, though. Don't you remember, I've told you not to label things? Remember your five senses. Give your reader your sense impressions and let him have the fun of imagining it as it was to you."

In a few minutes, instead of giving me the paragraph or two I was waiting for to insert into Chapter XV, [Blackhorse] laid a short poem on my desk.

"[Blackhorse]," I scolded, "I thought you were going to help me fill in—"

"I just wrote this to get wound up," he said.

The poem he wrote to get wound up was:

The Drifting Lonely Seed

From the casein dark-blue sky,
Through the emptiness of space,
A sailing wisp of cotton.
Never have I been so thrilled!
The drifting lonely seed,
Came past my barred window,
Whirling orbit, it landed before me,
As though it were a woolly lamb—
Untouched, untamed, and alone—
Walked atop my desk, stepping daintily,
Reaching forth my hands, I found you,
Gentle, weightless, tantalizing.

I blew you out through barricaded window;
You pranced, circled round me,
*Sharing with me your airy freedom.**

Thus wound up, [Blackhorse] went on to write what I had asked—how he decided that he wanted to write: "To put the past history in writing so it will always be remembered someday!" (T. D. Allen 1967: xiv–xv)

Allen presents Mitchell as failing to follow her instruction to write about how he began writing. Instead of doing as she had instructed, he writes a poem to get "wound up." Allen clearly presents herself as the mentor here. She explains to Mitchell not to worry about the labels and that she will insert pages into chapter 15. Mitchell has explained to me that Allen was concerned to make sure that overtly negative statements about the boarding school were excluded from the manuscript (see also Zolbrod 2004: xix). Allen "corrected" some of the language that Mitchell used in the text and limited the content of the manuscript. She was attempting to fit the manuscript into an image, a set of expectations, of what Mitchell, as a Navajo, should be. As Deloria (2004: 11) notes, such expectations of Native Americans are "dense economies of meaning, representation, and act . . . the ways in which popular culture works to produce—and sometimes compromise—racism and misogyny." Mitchell, as he once explained to me, was and is trying through his work to express to a dominant society that he is a "human being." Mitchell was trying to engage in a dialogue about such expectations. My understanding of Mitchell's work has come about through conversations with him. This is why it is important for me not to summarize our conversations but rather present actual transcripts of those conversations.

Not all of Mitchell's critiques of the boarding school were overt. The poem that Allen claims he wrote to get wound up can be read as a critique of the boarding school and as a meditation on being at home—away from the boarding school—with one's sheep. Mitchell offered that reading to me. During the summer of 2008, the two of us were sitting in his living room. We were talking about poetry and, specifically, his poetry. It was not the first time we had talked about his poetry, and it would not be the last time that summer. It was July 9, 2008.

---

* "The Drifting Lonely Seed," from *Miracle Hill: The Story of a Navajo Boy* by Blackhorse Mitchell. © 2004 The Arizona Board of Regents. Reprinted by permission of the University of Arizona Press.

Thematically, Mitchell's poem resonates with the poem "If I Were a Pony." Both are ostensibly displays of English command but are more pointedly critiques of school. In both cases, however, the theme of the poem seems to have been beside the point for its editor, respectively Allen and the editors of *Indians at Work*.

What follows is a fragment of our conversation from that July day. The transcript begins 26:28 into the discussion and concludes at 31:14, and has been organized into lines based on breath-pause structure.*

AW:	When you first started writing poetry	1
	that was because	2
	you were in school	3
BM:	Mhm	4
AW:	And you were I assume learning to write English	5
BM:	RIGHT	6
AW:	And so poetry was a way to learn to write English?	7
BM:	I think it was mostly describing	8
	or my thinking was I was trying to say something	9
	because a lot of times	10
	when you're in a boarding school	11
	your teacher does not allow you	12
AW:	Mmm, I see	13
BM:	They kind of don't allow you	14
	and there you're trying to say	15
	you want to speak a:nd	16
	you don't, you don't have MUCH	17
	you're, you're to sit there and learn	18
AW:	Mhm	19
BM:	That was the kind of thing	20
	SO:	21
	the best way was I'm gonna write about	22
	like the dormitory	23

---

* As always, I organize the transcript into lines not to argue that Mitchell is speaking poetry but rather to highlight something of the cadence, rhythm, and discourse structuring of Mitchell's talk. A space between lines indicates a longer pause; small capitals signal loudness and emphasis; the use of a colon indicates lengthening (either of vowels or consonants); brackets provide information not on the digital recording; the use of parenthesis indicates an aside made by Mitchell; for ease of reference I number the lines beginning with 1; and BM stands for Blackhorse Mitchell and AW stands for Anthony Webster.

NOBODY sees what	24
what what what horrible things	25
or what the impact is to stay in the dorm at the time	26
The bell rings and then they say, "stay in you can't get out"	27
you go to your room	28
and you're sittin' there	29
you're restless	30
only thing you can do is look out the window	31
BUT HERE	32
look I can go in and out	33
and you can too	34
so: it's the whole freedom	35
but in the boarding school	36
you have to	37
you have TIME limit	38
So those were just some of things that I:'m	39
talking about	40
and then when I'm WRITING	41
it always has to do with	42
freedom	43
And a:h I think the first first ah	44
[BM gets up, walks across room and gets *Miracle Hill*]	
first ah poem that I was working on	45
there was no chances	46
[BM comes back and sits]	
there was no chance of like	47
to ASK question	48
even though the instructor say, "you need to ask question"	49
AW: A:h	50

Let us pause midway through the transcript and walk through a bit of it; I want to focus on the issues of language, poetry, and the boarding-school experience. Lines 1 through 3 are my attempt to summarize the previous discussion that Mitchell and I had directly engaged in. Mitchell's "mhm" confirms my general summary. In line 5, I am checking to make sure that the language instruction was in English. Mitchell's emphatic "RIGHT" confirms that the language was English and probably signals that this is an obvious point, for him and for me. In line 7, I ask Mitchell if he thinks that poetry was a way to learn English. Mitchell takes this as a question of why he was writing in English. My question in line 7 posits a reason for why Allen was having Mitchell write poetry. Mitchell instead begins to describe why he was writing poetry. Instead of taking Allen's position—that poetry would aid in teaching him English—Mitchell counters by asserting that he was writing poetry for his own reasons. Reasons, I might add, outside of the control of Allen. As Mitchell clearly states in lines 9 through 12,

> I was trying to say something
> because a lot of times
> when you're in a boarding school
> your teacher does not allow you

In class, one was "to sit there and learn" (line 18). Or again, "there was no chance of like / to ASK question" (lines 47–48). Note here that Mitchell emphasizes the word *ask* as well. Class, as discussed in chapter 2, was a place to be silent.

Mitchell creates a contrast between the boarding-school environment and the immediate environment in which we are situated during our conversation. In line 32, Mitchell emphatically contrasts the *there* from line 29 with the *here* of Mitchell's home. He states in lines 32 through 35,

> BUT HERE
> look I can go in and out
> and you can too
> so: it's the whole freedom

He immediately contrasts that "freedom" with "the boarding school" (line 36). In lines 41 through 43, Mitchell summarizes why he was writing in boarding school:

> When I'm WRITING
> it always has to do with
> freedom

He is emphatic about writing, and his use of *freedom* echoes with its earlier use in line 35. Mitchell was not writing to learn English, he was writing in English to express his desire for freedom. It is at this point (lines 44–47) that Mitchell stood up from his couch and walked over to a table and picked up his 1967 edition of *Miracle Hill*. He reiterates that "there was no chance to like / to ASK question" (lines 47–48). Let us take up the second half of the transcript here.

BM:	And so hunh	51
	if you're	52
	if we're FREE to ask questions	53
	in my	54
	it may be different	55
	but in this case	56
	there was none	57
	And after writing this	58
	the first poem	59
	that I ever came up with	60
	she thought this was great	61
	She didn't see what I'm trying to s:	62
	STILL she didn't see what I was trying to say	63
	as a student	64
	so I wrote	65
	because I saw this	66
	cotton	67
	somehow it came past the window into the classroom	68
	and it was just	69
	I was watching it	70
	and then I thought, "wo:w"	71
	so this is what I did	72
	I put	73
	the DRIFTING lonely seed	74
	FROM the casein dark-blue sky	75
	through the emptiness of space	76
	a sailing wisp of cotton	77
	NEVER have I been so: thrill	78
	the drifti:ng lo:nely: see:d	79
	came past my barred window	80
	whirling orbit	81
	it land before me	82
	as though it were a woolly la:mb	83
	(see where I'm thinking)	84

UNtouch, UNtame, and alone	85
walk atop my desk	86
stepping daintily	87
REACHING out my hands I found you	88
gentle, weightless, tantalizing	89
I blew you out through barricaded window	90
you prance	91
circle around me	92
sharing with me your airy freedom	93
Now if she was intelligent	94
she would have found what I'm saying	95
and she thought that was a gre:at pi:ece of writing	96
AW: What did she think it was about	97
BM: She thought I was learning my tense	98
AW: Ah	99
BM: Grammar skills	100
AW: She thought you were learning your tense grammar, I see	101
BM: She didn't see:	102
my thinking is:	103
listen to me	104
again	105
as an instructor	106
she did not see what I'm saying	107

In lines 58 through 71, Mitchell recounts his understanding of how and why the poem was written. He notes, not without irony, that Allen—who remains nameless throughout this discussion (a rhetorical device found in much Navajo discourse both in Navajo English and in Navajo)—"thought this was great" (line 61). In lines 62 through 64, Mitchell makes it clear that Allen was not approaching his poetry as the informed thoughts of an individual. Allen simply does not understand what Mitchell is trying to do. As he movingly says,

She didn't see what I'm trying to s:
STILL she didn't see what I was trying to say
as a student

The emphatic use of "STILL" was jarring when Mitchell and I were talking. "STILL" seems to evoke the frustration that he felt and feels toward

Allen. "STILL" is the linchpin of his discussion of this poem and of T. D. Allen; it carries the rhetorical weight of his frustration.

Mitchell then explains that a piece of cotton had floated into the class-room, and he felt a connection with that floating cotton. Note that Mitchell was quite sure what the object was when it came floating into the classroom. Also, he does not state that his writing the poem was inspired by Allen telling him to work on how he "got started." Rather it was the connection he felt toward the cotton, the fact that the cotton was free, that had inspired him.

Mitchell then "reads" the poem from the book. *Reads* seems like the wrong word here, and I would rather replace it with *performs*; this perfor-mance is certainly not a mere verbatim reproduction of the language of the written poem. Note the contrast that Mitchell creates between the "airy free-dom" of the cotton and the "barred windows" and a "barricaded window" of the classroom. The cotton is described as "UNtouch" and "UNtame" with the stress on the "un" in both cases (line 85). It is also described as "gentle, weightless, tantalizing" (line 89). The cotton is free, and "barred windows" and a "barricaded window" confine Mitchell.

In line 83, Mitchell likens the cotton to a "woolly lamb," and in line 84 he makes a telling aside to me, "see where I'm thinking." Mitchell and I have talked a great deal about the fondness that he had for sheepherding when he was a boy and that he has had for much of his life. During the time that Mitchell was out herding sheep he would often compose songs. The image of a "woolly lamb" is an expression of Mitchell's desire to be outside with his sheep and of his desire not to be at the boarding school, not to be surrounded by "barred windows," not to be at a place where he could not speak. It is an expression of a desire for freedom.

Mitchell's most pointed critique follows directly after he has finished performing the poem. He states in lines 94 through 95 that "if she was intelligent / she would have found what I'm saying." Instead, Allen thought it was a "gre:at pi:ece of writing." Mitchell is ironic here and bitingly so. Allen had no idea what the poem is about, yet she was convinced that it was a great piece of writing. As with Mitchell's handwriting, the content was beside the point for Allen. Rather, it was the mere ability to write that seems to have been important. If Allen was concerned about overt critiques of the boarding-school experience, this poem by Mitchell is a covert critique. As Mitchell notes in lines 41 throughout 43,

When I'm WRITING
it always has to do with
freedom

This poem is a longing for freedom, freedom from the boarding school and the constraints of his teachers, including Allen. Mitchell has embedded this poem within the politics of the boarding-school matrix. With apologies to Peggy Durham (1967, Blackhorse Mitchell Collection), perhaps here after all is some "rationalized bitterness" toward white educational practices.

In line 97, I ask Mitchell what Allen believed the poem was about. Mitchell's answer is telling. Instead of having anything to do with content, Mitchell believes that Allen was concerned that the poem showed that Mitchell was learning to use English tense and "grammar skills" (line 100). He reiterates his fundamental point in line 102: "she didn't see." He then adds, "my thinking is: / listen to me." According to Mitchell, Allen did not listen. He states this again in lines 105 through 107:

Again
as an instructor
she did not see what I'm saying

Note that in line 107, rather than contracting *did not* into *didn't* as he had done in line 102, he gives both words independently. This adds emphasis to his statement about Allen's inability to understand what he was writing.

Performing Navajo English Poetry

Earlier I suggested that to say that Mitchell "read" his poem to me on that day in July would be to mischaracterize what he was doing. Although he got up, retrieved a copy of *Miracle Hill*, sat down, and opened the book to the page of the poem (that is, he displayed all the trappings of "reading"), he was performing this poem in his Navajo English. While he may have started with the assumption of reading the poem to me, Mitchell clearly had what Hymes (1981: 79) called a "breakthrough into performance" (see also Bauman 1984). What mattered here was the emotional evocativeness of the performance—the shared social intimacy between performer and audience—and not any fidelity to what was written. According to Mitchell, T. D. Allen saw this poem as a display of the ability to use English tense. Note that, in lines 78, 82, 85, 86, 91, and 92, Mitchell does not use the past-tense marker *-ed*, found in the published poem (the past-tense form does occur in lines 80 and 90). Following Bartelt (1981, 1983, 2001), I would argue that Mitchell's use of what looks like an English present tense is a Navajo English imperfective mode and aspect marker. As Bartelt (1981: 382) notes, "much of the idiosyncratic tense usage found in Navajo English is a result of the use of English tenses as a vehicle for the expression of Navajo aspects and modes. Specifically, the English present tense seems to be used for the transfer of the Navajo usitative mode, imperfective mode, and continuative aspect." In a longer discussion of Mitchell's *Miracle Hill*, Bartelt (2001: 97–98) posits that Mitchell is discursively alternating putative English tense markers for mode and aspectual reasons.

In line 78, the use of *thrill* indicates a momentaneous aspect in the imperfective mode. Its use brings immediacy to the moment of excitement. This immediacy is replicated again in line 82 with the use of *land* (again, I would argue, in the momentaneous aspect in the imperfective mode). In line 85, the use of *untame* and *untouch* evoke the usitative mode, suggesting that, unlike Mitchell, the floating cotton is always untamed and untouched. *Walk* (line 86) appears to be in the continuative aspect in the imperfective mode, as do *prance* (line 91) and *circle* (line 92). The use of a Navajo English imperfective adds immediacy to these events. It is interesting that the oral performance of this poem contrasts in its use of tense marking with the written version, the very grammatical feature that Allen was concerned about Mitchell learning. Mitchell also changes *forth* in the published version to the more informal *out* (line 88).

There are, however, echoes of other voices in this poem, and in *Miracle Hill*. Over the course of the summer of 2011, Mitchell and I discussed lexical choices found in this poem and in the book as a whole. The repeated references to God in *Miracle Hill*, Mitchell tells me, are Allen's insertions, predicated on her Christian and "missionary" zeal. For example, lines like the protagonist Broneco's exclamation "For heaven sake! God of All Mighty, help me!" (2004: 221) were, according to Mitchell, an Allen insertion. Mitchell's view of Allen was that she both wanted to teach Navajos to write and to "save" their souls. This insertion by Allen is particularly interesting because it is in the quoted speech of the protagonist—a young Navajo boy trying to find his way in the world—Broneco. Broneco becomes the ventriloquial figure for Allen's Christian exhortation. The voice one hears is Allen's through Broneco and under the authorship of Mitchell. The name Broneco is also an Allen insertion. Mitchell has explained to me that the name of the character—roughly based on him—was meant to be *Bronco*, but he misspelled the word; he asked her to change it later, but she decided to keep it. Allen displays her baptismal power here. She has the authority to name. Mitchell, however, would challenge the Western baptismal power to name him when he had his Bureau of Indian Affairs–school-enforced name legally removed. The 2004 reissue is by Blackhorse Mitchell, not, as was the 1967 edition, Emerson Blackhorse Mitchell.

As for Allen's editorial choices in the poem, Mitchell tells me that *forth* was one. It was not a word he would have used, and, indeed, in the performance of this poem that day in July 2008, he did not use it. On the other hand, before a non-Navajo audience at Southern Illinois University in Carbondale in November of 2009, Mitchell did use *forth*. These are his words to change as the context changes. In such ways, Mitchell asserts his authorship over this poem. These are his lines and his words to manipulate. Then there is *daintily*. Mitchell was very clear that this word was an insertion by Allen at the time. Yet at multiple readings of this poem, the *daintily* is always there. When Mitchell and I have talked about this, he has told me that while it was an Allen insertion, he has a certain fondness for *daintily* and enjoys the word. For Mitchell, this word works in the poem and he has decided to leave it there (for now, anyway). While *forth* still sounds, to Mitchell, like Allen's voice, *daintily* is now a part of Mitchell's voice. *Daintily* is satisfying in form for Mitchell now. If there is an echo from Allen there, then it is an echo that is also a part of Mitchell's voice. He has made an intimate communion with *daintily*.

Today, Mitchell is a noted performer on the Navajo Nation and internationally. Many people know where he stands. He has performed at the inauguration of a Navajo Nation president as well as in the Czech Republic. He has performed at major universities and at off-reservation venues in border towns. In such performances he often reads some of his poetry and performs his songs. At the Cortez Culture Center in Cortez, Colorado, he would do demonstrations of sand paintings for tourists in the summers while I was staying with him (see image 6). At such performances not only would he demonstrate sand painting, he would also try to educate tourists about the humanity of Navajos. Sometimes this took the form of indirectly critiquing audience members for their expectations about Navajos. He describes himself on his website as a "Diné teacher, artist, writer, musician" and offers for sale copies of the revised version of *Miracle Hill*, CDs of his sheepherding songs, and a copy of *Mud*, the documentary about Navajo pottery in which he stars. In all of these works, Mitchell continues to engage with the wider world, to remind them that Navajos are "human beings"—that is, to remind Anglo readers that Navajos and Anglos are coeval, of the same time and place and sharing an overlapping history (Fabian 1983).

Conclusions

One way to read *Miracle Hill* is as a love story. It is a love story between Blackhorse Mitchell and his intimate grammar, his English. One way to read "The Drifting Lonely Seed," perhaps Mitchell's preferred reading of it, is as a critique of boarding school and a plea for freedom. These readings do not match the expectations of Mitchell, expressed by Allen and the reviewers of *Miracle Hill*, to be primitive and childlike. They do not match the expectations that saw his English as "foreign" to him, "garbled," "lacking in grammar," and "confused." The "primitiveness" of Mitchell's work was read as iconic of his primitiveness, and the childlike language became iconic of his childlike nature. Ideas about language are read as iconic of speakers (Irvine and Gal 2000). The "confused" grammar is a sign of "confused" thinking. Claims that Native American languages (English or otherwise) lack grammar or are confused are not new, and not new either are the ways that such putative confusion has then been read as iconic of the confused thinking of Native Americans. The racist logic here is essentially that so-called modern languages have grammar (often codified in writing) and so-called primitive languages lack it, and that this lack of grammar reflects the limited cognitive abilities of "primitives." Mitchell is certainly not confused about why he wrote "The Drifting Lonely Seed," nor is he confused about his language choices. The poem, according to Mitchell, is an argument for freedom and against the stultifying regimes of knowledge that the boarding school meant to inculcate in him. While it is certainly true that not all features of Mitchell's Navajo English are equally salient to him and within the limits of his linguistic awareness (limits we all have; see Silverstein 1981; Kroskrity 2010), certain features clearly are salient and Mitchell has built up certain felt attachments to them over time. They have become feelingfully salient, in part, due to the pressure exerted by Allen and others through their critiques of his English.

Here I think it is useful to invoke Ellen Basso's (2009) concern with the ordeals of language, a counterpoint to intimate grammars (see also Rodríguez and Webster 2012; Webster 2012a). An intimate grammar is one spoken even in the face of outside scrutiny. For Basso, ordeals of language are those moments when language is withheld, when, as she says, "we permit our own voices to be powerfully affected by the language of the dominant" (122); when, for example, some Navajos that I know avoid speaking Navajo in Farmington, New Mexico, in order to avoid racist comments, or feign monolingualism in Navajo in order to avoid the scrutiny of their (Navajo) English or to disengage from outsiders. Mitchell's work asserts his love for English, his English (some of his work not examined here asserts his love for Navajo too), even in the face of outside scrutiny, of which T. D. Allen's (1967) introduction to his book is an example. Recognizing Mitchell's literary uses of Navajo English means recognizing Mitchell's linguistic competence, his "voice," defined as the moments when individuals can tell their stories in their way using all their preferred expressive options. Indeed, Mitchell has found "voice" even in words that were originally Allen's insertions. He has grown intimate with them through repeated performances.

Here is a conundrum. Other than Bartelt's work—and Bartelt is a sociolinguist (to be sure)—Mitchell's work has not received much attention from outside literary scholars. Not a word about Mitchell's *Miracle Hill* is in Susan Brill de Ramírez's (1999) *Contemporary American Indian Literatures and the Oral Tradition* (though see Brill de Ramírez 2007), nor is there a mention in Amelia Katanski's (2005) *Learning to Write "Indian": The Boarding-School Experience and American Indian Literature*, and there is nothing in Robert Dale Parker's (2003) *The Invention of Native American Literature* (to pick three works that do discuss other Navajos). These are all fine books, but a silence exists here, a silence predicated on an inability—I would suggest—to understand what Mitchell was doing. Mitchell's book does not fit the expectations of literary critics. Or perhaps worse, Allen's introduction has been taken at face value because it confirms certain expectations.

At a poetry performance in Window Rock, Arizona, in 2001, Luci Tapahonso was quite clear that *Miracle Hill* was one of the foundational books for her. Although Tapahonso may be the most famous Navajo poet on the Navajo Nation, Mitchell's book is now widely known and widely enjoyed by Navajos with whom I have spoken. A number of other Navajo poets have also commented on the importance of Mitchell's book in their coming to believe that they could become writers and poets. When Navajo filmmaker Bennie Klain was looking at possible movie ideas, Mitchell's book was an obvious topic. Some Navajos get Mitchell's book in a way that outside literary critics do not, which is partly due to the language and partly due to the fact that many Navajos can imagine themselves in the situations that Mitchell describes. This is so even if there are echoes of T. D. Allen in the words of *Miracle Hill*. These Navajo readers recognize themselves and their languages—their voices—in Mitchell's work. As one Navajo consultant noted, Mitchell "writes the way I speak," and in writing that way, he has provided a degree of "comfort." Another Navajo consultant said that Mitchell's language "validated our language." And another consultant stated that they were "fiercely proud of the language" Mitchell used in his book. For some Navajos, Mitchell's use of Navajo English in *Miracle Hill* is not unexpected at all. Rather it is deeply and intimately satisfying. The language of the book fosters a common sociality, a common social intimacy. This is the expressive work of intimate grammars.

This is not to claim that all Navajos appreciated the use of Navajo English in Mitchell's book. One Navajo consultant was rather dismissive of Navajo English and agreed with Allen's introduction that these were errors of grammar. It is also not to claim that most Navajos have read the book. Another Navajo consultant of mine had not read the book, but liked the idea of a book "written by a Navajo for Navajos." Still another Navajo consultant had never heard of the book. Mitchell and one of his relatives have both told me about how Mitchell gave the book—when it first came out in 1967—to one of his aunts. He later found the book, with pages removed, in the outhouse. As he noted, his aunt could not read and the book was useless except as toilet paper. The fault was his in giving the book to his aunt and expecting her not to use it. However, the vast majority of Navajo poets and writers whom I have worked with know the work and wish to promote it. Esther Belin, for example, was working to get the book used for incoming freshman at Fort Lewis College in Durango, Colorado. According to Mitchell, Luci Tapahonso and Laura Tohe were instrumental in getting the book reissued by the University of Arizona Press.

Such appreciation and respect for Mitchell's language is not confined to Navajos. Recently, at the Native American Literature Symposium in March 2010, during a panel discussion on the work of Dogrib (Northern Athabaskan) author Richard Van Camp, Acoma poet and scholar Simon Ortiz called attention to the "beauty" of Mitchell's English in *Miracle Hill*. Ortiz noted that Van Camp was following in the tradition of authors like Mitchell. Ortiz encouraged literary critics to engage with Mitchell's work and his "beautiful English." Ortiz, I believe, was calling attention to the silence that surrounds Mitchell's book among literary critics.

As Deloria (2004: 4) notes, "The world we inhabit is the shared creation of all peoples, though the costs and benefits have been parceled out with astonishing inequality, as have the notions about who has been active in that creation and who has been acted on." Understanding the dominant outside expectations about American Indian languages (including Englishes) and what forms those languages can take may suggest something of the ways astonishing inequalities have been naturalized. The recognition of American Indian Englishes as languages worth taking seriously, as "beautiful Englishes" and intimate grammars, would be one useful starting point in destabilizing such inequalities. To recall Belin's comments from the beginning of this chapter, it is time to understand Navajo English as a Navajo (Diné) language. It is long past the time when we were "perplexed that they even had tongues at all."

CHAPTER FOUR

Beauty of Navajoland

It is important that awake people be awake
—WILLIAM STAFFORD, "A RITUAL TO READ TO EACH OTHER"

The scene is November 17, 2004, Swarthmore College, Swarthmore, Pennsylvania. Blackhorse Mitchell stands before a packed audience of students and faculty. Ted Fernald, a linguistics professor who has been active with the Navajo Language Academy (see Fernald and Platero 2000), has invited Mitchell to perform at Swarthmore. It is nighttime. Mitchell is dressed in black pants, a black vest, and a white and black shirt. He has performed a number of songs for the audience. At the beginning of the performance that night, Mitchell has been introduced by a young Navajo woman who is a student at Swarthmore College. Throughout the night Mitchell addresses the young lady about the Navajo language and about the reservation.

Mitchell has traveled to Swarthmore from his home on the Navajo Nation near the community of Shiprock, New Mexico. He has performed on and around the Navajo Nation a number of times. I videotaped him numerous times while I was doing fieldwork on the Navajo Nation in 2000 and 2001. Mitchell and Fernald have both invited me down from Wesleyan University in Middletown, Connecticut, where I am a postdoctoral fellow.

Mitchell, whom we met in the last chapter, is perhaps most famous to outsiders for his book *Miracle Hill*, originally published in 1967 and reissued by the University of Arizona Press in 2004 (see Zolbrod 2004). On the cover of both the 1967 edition and the reissued edition is an image (not the same image) of Tsé Bit'a'í (Winged Rock or Shiprock), a rock formation that can be seen from miles away. Tsé Bit'a'í is not "Miracle Hill." Mitchell's book is well known among Navajo artists and writers, though in 2000 and 2001 the book was virtually impossible to locate on the Navajo Nation outside of the libraries at Window Rock, Arizona, and Tsaile, Arizona (where the main campus of Diné College is located). After the reissuing, the book was available during the summers of 2007 and 2008 at 'Ahwééh/Gohwééh, a coffee shop in Shiprock run by Gloria Emerson that sold a number of books of poetry by Navajo authors and also sponsored poetry readings. It has since closed. During the summers of 2007 to 2011, the reissued copy was also available for purchase at Cool Runnings, a music store in Window Rock that has also produced two CDs of Mitchell's music (they are available for purchase there as well). To many Navajos, Mitchell is best known for his "sheepherding songs" (songs that he has composed while watching his sheep). When I did my initial fieldwork on the Navajo Nation on the emergence of contemporary Navajo poetry, he had also begun to read his poetry again (he had published a number of poems in the late 1960s and early 1970s).

Mitchell has just finished singing his song "American Bar," about a young Navajo man who is in love with a Navajo woman who runs off to the big city. When she comes back to the Southwest she tells the young man to meet her at the Greyhound station in Gallup, New Mexico. The young man finds her instead coming out of a local bar (the American Bar of the title) with two "cowboys" on her arms. The young man then drives back to the Navajo Nation alone. Mitchell has put down his drum and picked up a large black binder from the podium that contains much of his writings. This is not the first poem that Mitchell has read from the binder.

My transcript of what happens next, a reading of the poem "Beauty of Navajoland,"* attempts to capture some of Mitchell's performance features. The transcript has been organized into lines based on breath-pause structure (Tedlock 1983). Quoted material, including the poem, has been indented. Small capitals indicate an increase in loudness. Other information concerning the performance is included in brackets.

I'll read to you	1
when people come to the Navajoland	2
they always say,	3
"My goodness [said in higher pitch]	4
your country is beautiful	5

---

* The term *Navajoland* (a rough translation of *Dinétah*) is used by Navajos for the Navajo Nation, but it is also associated with the promotion of the Navajo Nation as a tourist destination. For example, the hotel in St. Michaels, Arizona, on the Navajo Nation is named Navajoland Inn & Suites. Mitchell's use of the term carries both associations.

The rocks   6
the mountains   7
man, you have a country."   8
When I hear that   9
I always look on my own road   10
and what I see   11
I'm the opposite   12
so I wrote   13
  "Beauty of Navajoland"   14
  Plastic bags blowing in the wind   15
  aluminum   16
  beer cans shining in the country [nervous laughter from audience]   17
  flies enjoying waste on Huggies disposal   18
  AND   19
  an empty bottle of Zima ornaments the roadside   20

  The beauty of Navajoland   21
  little big trashes drifting in the gale of wind   22
  run-over dogs and coyotes   23
  vultures feasting on deteriorating smell of meat   24
  and the crows flying away with the eyes of the kill   25

  "The beauty of Navajoland,"   26
  you say   27
  those polluted dark clouds are not the real clouds   28
  the rivers and streams contaminated   29
  by redneck piss and dungs   30
  and uranium in the flowing innocent river   31

  The beauty of Navajoland   32
  bra strap   33
  hanging on the roadside guidepost   34
  crucifix with plastic bouquet of flowers   35
  standing and reminding in humiliations   36
  and   37
  coal stripping of Mother Earth   38
  and flood of acid rain   39

  Is not the beauty of Navajoland   40
  [applause]

That's how I view Navajo Nation   41
there is no beauty   42

UNLESS they clean up [5-second pause]   43

Power plants and all the ugly filth   44
then I'll be proud   45
but I'm not proud   46

I see all of this   47
I see my Navajo Nation people lecturing   48
they wear all these jewelry   49
turquoise   50
saying "Mother Earth"   51
And I would be laughing   52
I kinda look at myself   53
I'm not gonna come out here   54
Wearing all these   55
Except this watch [shows silver watch from under sleeve]   56
but I'm not gonna come over here   57
play a wild medicine man [makes motion up and down his chest
    of regalia]   58
with a lot of [leans forward as if weighed down by regalia]   59
walking around [hunched over] [audience laughter]   60
no, that's not my style   61
I'd rather come over here   62
and be myself   63
that's what I like to do [stands back up]   64
so that's what I've been working on   65
writing [closes binder and takes it to podium]   66
the book title [moves back toward audience]   67
doesn't talk about beauty   68
just talks about the country   69
the land as it was   70
back in the   71
I would say   72
kinda like the late '40s   73
that's what I grew out of   74
and that's the what the book is about   75
[This is followed by Mitchell's song "Brand New Vehicle."]

The title and recurrent refrain of Mitchell's poem is clearly ironic. It is a form of "echoic mention"—here echoing and reversing the words of a tourist (Sperber and Wilson 1981; Hymes 1987b). When Mitchell wrote this poem, he tells me, he intentionally centered it on the page so as to break from a practice he was taught at boarding school. Blackhorse Mitchell began writing poetry while he was in boarding school in the 1960s. He has written poetry in both Navajo and Navajo English. Most Navajo poets write in English or Navajo English. Many Navajo poets code-switch from English into Navajo in their poetry (Webster 2009). Some Navajo poets—Rex Lee Jim, Nia Francisco, Laura Tohe, and Blackhorse Mitchell—write poetry that is entirely in Navajo. However, literacy in Navajo is still relatively uncommon among Navajos (see McLaughlin 1992). Poetry in English and Navajo English reaches not only a wider audience of non-Navajos but also a wider audience of Navajos. Few Navajo poets are full-time poets. Most have other jobs. Mitchell, for example, teaches college courses at Navajo Technical University.

The plural marking on *dungs* is an example of Navajo English, a local way of speaking and writing. As we saw in the last chapter, some reviewers of Mitchell's work have understood the use of a plural marking on *dungs* or *sheeps* or *popcorns* or an alternation in tense markings as a "confused" use of some putative "standard" English; Mitchell has explicitly stated, for example, that he prefers *popcorns* over *popcorn*. Local languages like Navajo English are often stigmatized and devalued, then read as iconic of the "confused" nature of their speakers (see Webster 2010c; Blommaert 2005). Mitchell is quite aware of outside evaluations of his English as deficient, but for him *popcorns* simply makes more sense. In the transcripts we find that Mitchell consistently uses *dungs*, both in the performance in 2004 and in the conversations I had with him in 2008. It is also how he has written it in the versions he has given me, first in 2004 and again in 2008 and 2009.

In lines 2 through 14, Mitchell sets up the motivation for writing this poem. He explains, through the use of quoted speech, that "when people come to the Navajoland" they often marvel at the "beauty" of the country. Mitchell's poem is a challenge to the touristic view of the Navajoland. Instead, Mitchell describes the realities of the Navajo Nation as he "sees" them looking at the land around him. After line 17, there is a smattering of nervous laughter from the audience. Mitchell has told jokes that night and invited a faculty member (Ted Fernald), a visiting linguistic anthropologist, and two ladies from the audience to dance, much to the amusement of the audience. The audience seems unsure of how to take this poem. Mitchell continues. After the applause at the end of the poem, he goes on to say in lines 41 and 42, "that's how I view Navajo Nation / there is no beauty."

Mitchell then loudly announces, with "UNLESS" in line 43, that this could change. The change would come about if—and here Mitchell pauses mid-clause for five seconds between "UNLESS they clean up" and what it is he wants cleaned up. It is an uncomfortable pause because what he closes the clause with is "power plants and all the ugly filth." He must make his point explicitly. In line 45, he notes that if such things are done, then he'll be "proud." In line 47, Mitchell switches to a discussion of certain "Navajo people lecturing" about "Mother Earth" (line 51). These Navajo people are what some Navajos see as stereotypical Navajos, Navajos covered in turquoise jewelry. Mitchell contrasts himself with those Navajos by point-ing out that he is not covered in jewelry (save for his watch). Indeed, he adds a nice comic element in lines 58 to 60, where he gestures to his chest covered with imaginary jewelry, so much jewelry that he stoops over as he speaks in lines 59 and 60. The audience laughs. Instead of that, Mitchell says as he stands back up, he will be himself (line 64). Certainly Mitchell's use of "Mother Earth" can be seen as tapping into a set of expectations which he believes the audience may hold (Gill 1987), but it is simulta-neously a critique of the invocation of Mother Earth by certain Navajos. Like Mitchell's challenge of a touristic view of Navajoland, this too is a challenge to the expectations that the audience may have about Navajos and Navajoland.

In line 65 Mitchell puts an emphasis on "SO," usually a good indicator, in my experiences of watching Mitchell perform, that he is summarizing his previous comments and is about to change topics. *So* is used here in a manner similar to the use of the Navajo discourse marker *'áko* 'so' (Webster 2004). Indeed, Mitchell proceeds to say that he has been writing (line 66). However, throughout the night Mitchell has also been discussing his 1967 book *Miracle Hill* (reissued that year by the University of Arizona Press). It is that book he refers to in line 67. During line 66 he has taken the black binder with his poetry in it back to the podium and put it down. During line 67, he then moves back toward the audience. In lines 68 to 75, Mitchell wants to clarify that *Miracle Hill* is not a book about "beauty." His book is not like the people who visit the Navajo Nation who are always talking about the "beauty of Navajoland." Rather, his book "talks about the coun-try / the land as it was" (lines 69–70). It does not create an idealized view of Navajoland. After line 75, Mitchell walks back to the podium to retrieve his drum. He will conclude the performance with his song "Brand New Vehicle." That song talks about how, after you buy a new vehicle, you will have people wanting to be around you (a recording of this song is included on Mitchell 2006).

Why Write About Ugliness?

Why do some Navajo poets write poetry that describes "ugliness" on the Navajo Nation and what do they believe they are doing by writing that poetry? This chapter examines those questions by focusing on Blackhorse Mitchell's poem "Beauty of Navajoland." Here I build on themes developed in the previous chapter concerning the poetry of Mitchell, Navajo English, misrecognition, and astonishing inequalities. Having presented Mitchell's performance at Swarthmore College, I now want to think through the implications of such a performance. In particular, I want to work through a local theory of what poetry can accomplish as a form of social action. But in doing this, I need also to place this poem within a larger context of concerns about proper ways of speaking. Contrary to an injunction on the Navajo Nation, *doo ajinída* 'don't talk about it', Mitchell and other Navajo poets argue that it is only by talking about "ugliness" that it can be restored to "beauty." We need to understand these terms as bivalent terms, terms that reside in two linguistic systems. We are dealing with the iconicity of linguistic forms across languages.

Much of this chapter—like some of the previous chapter—will revolve around transcripts of conversations that Mitchell and I have had about his poetry. Here I will intersperse with my own analysis three excerpts from the summer of 2008 that deal with "Beauty of Navajoland." In doing this I am following David Delgado Shorter's (2009) recent book on performing Yaqui history. Like Shorter, I hope to "write social science that emphasizes the intersubjective and social dynamic between me and community members" (4; see also Tedlock and Mannheim 1995; Molina and Evers 1998; Denetdale 2007). Such a perspective takes seriously Julie Cruikshank's (2005: 3) call for research that attends to the "stubborn particulars of voice." In these excerpts, Mitchell explains, among other things, what his poem is about and what the motivation was for writing it. He also teases me about eating too much salad and paying for translations. These are not the only conversations I have had with Mitchell about this poem, but they reveal some of the tensions in our conversations and the ways that Mitchell repeatedly embeds the poem or parts of the poem in our discussions.

Navajo Poetry as *Hane'*

One local theory of poetry, as expressed by Navajo poets like Rex Lee Jim and Blackhorse Mitchell, is that poetry functions to make one think, to reflect, and that such reflection should then motivate one to proper behavior (see Webster

2009). Related to this is the view of some Navajos that proper language use can change the world (see Reichard 1944; Witherspoon 1977; McAllester 1980; Field and Blackhorse 2002). This belief in the creative power of language use (Reichard 1944; Witherspoon 1977) is one of many language ideologies found on the Navajo Nation today (see Field 2009; Webster 2009).

Many Navajo poets have described contemporary poetry as a form of *hane'* (story, narrative). Indeed, many Navajo poets link their poetry with traditional Navajo narratives through formal poetic devices (see Webster 2004, 2009). Part of the meaning of *hane'* is that it is something to be publicly shared (see also Peterson 2006), and many Navajo poets mentioned that contemporary Navajo poetry centrally is meant to be shared (see Webster 2009). Among Navajos, narratives—from "Mą'ii Jooldloshí Hane'" ("Stories of the Trotting Coyote") to contemporary poetry—can be used as "indirect" forms of critique (see Toelken and Scott 1981).* Indeed, there is also a subgenre of contemporary Navajo poetry that is based on Navajo Coyote stories (Webster 2004). One purpose of telling Coyote stories is to get people to think. W. W. Hill and Dorothy Hill (1945: 317) quote a Navajo consultant explaining why Coyote stories were told. "The old men used to tell these stories when we were young so that we would think. They told us these stories to make us think." As Barre Toelken (1987) has ably demonstrated, for many Navajos, Coyote stories are not merely for entertainment, they are about changing the world. In fact, Toelken and Scott (1981) and Toelken (1987) challenge the received view that Navajo Coyote stories were directed primarily toward children and served merely as entertainment. Toelken points out that this view misses the importance that aesthetic practices have in bringing about change in the world (see also Reichard 1944; McAllester 1954, 1980; Field and Blackhorse 2002). Likewise, the use of stories to get people to "think" also resonates with a general Navajo notion that I have heard, *t'áá bí bee bóholníih* 'it's up to her/him to decide' (see also Lamphere 1977). People should be allowed to make their own decisions and their own interpretations.

Excerpt 1

July 9, 2008. This fragment occurs about midway through the recorded conversation. It is midafternoon and we have been talking about what poetry does. As is typical in our discussions about poetry, Mitchell has focused in

---

* On "indirectness" among Navajos see Field 1998, 2001.

on a specific poem. In this case, that poem is "Beauty of Navajoland." As in previous transcripts, small capitals indicate loudness, colons mark lengthening, and brackets supply relevant contextual features of the conversation.

AW: You once said to give an imagination to someone
    an that's
    so that's
BM: I WANT people to really see it
    like the beauty of Navajoland
AW: Mmhmm
BM: You can go on the road
    an saw saw those things then
    I I want
    I want somebody
    to laugh an say
    "god damn it this guy's r:ight"
AW: Mmhmm
BM: Not
    just to say o:h:
    the WAY it's written is awesome
AW: Right
BM: That's not
    that's
    that's not
    THAT'S no good
    I want uh people actually
    o:h look out there an say
    "look at that dirty sky
    oh Jesus I read that somewhere I think Blackhorse wrote it about it"
    OR AT LEAST somebody was standin out there an says
    "I'm glad it's raining"
    an then they start scratchin
AW: Hh
BM: And then they say "what's wrong" and they might
    maybe the doctor says
    "you you should stay outta the rain because it had a lot a acid"
AW: Hh hh
BM: I DON'T WANT my
    my poem to
    to be

```
        jus:
        said
        I want it proven sayin
        it is true
        I want somebody to go down tuh
        San Juan River take their shoes off an
        just swarm their feet around an then all of a sudden uh shit
            crosses the feet [2-second pause]
        an say, "what is this
        there's a lot a salad in it
        I think it's a white man's"
AW:    [laughter]
        A lot of salad in it
BM:    Y:eah
AW.    [laughter]
BM:    SO
        THAT'S
        that's what I'm
        lookin at [2-second pause]
AW:    Hh hh [5-second pause]
BM:    THAT'S what my poem:
        I want my poem
        to say
        I don't want it just read
AW:    Hm
BM.    I don't wanna stand there tuh in the poetry sla:m an jus
        just
        giving action:
        body movement an hands
        that's
        poetry slam
AW:    Mm hmm
BM:    Kinda make people
        see
        the gesture an all this
        I don't wanna do it that way
        so when I'm reading my poem I rather have that
        ugly facial expression [2-second pause]
AW:    But you don't wanna be me:an:
BM:    Hm mm
```

AW: Or co:ld
BM: No
> just medium
> I don't wanna be like [name of non-Navajo poet]
> uh
> not [name of mutual Navajo acquaintance with similar name] yeah
> [name of non-Navajo poet]
> he: doesn't like
> Americans
> "THAT'S COLONALISM
> U:H:
> WHITE SO-CALLED WHITE THEY CAME ALONG TAKE AWAY ALL
> THE INDIAN LAND"
> that's the way he talks
AW: Hh hh hh [2-second pause]
BM. But
> I don't wanna say that
> I can say that but
AW: Mm hmm
BM: But it's just
> the way of putting it
> an
> so eh in this case
> it's jus:
> it's just something that I wanna say
> an
> something that
> people
> should begin to think about
> that's all
> that's what I'm sayin

Excerpt 1 begins with my repetition of a turn of phrase that Mitchell and other Navajo poets have used, about "giving an imagination" through *hane'*. Mitchell stresses that in his poetry he wants people to "really see it." Likewise, his poems are "true" and can be "proven" by observation. The conditions he describes in "Beauty of Navajoland" are a reality and if people can see these things—that is, imagine them—then they may "begin to think about" them. In the terms of Scott Rushforth's (1992, 1994) analysis of Northern Athabaskan ways of knowing, Mitchell wants secondary epistemic knowledge—his poem—to be validated by primary epistemic knowledge, that is, personal experience. Instead of people treating the writing as merely "awesome," Mitchell wants them to be motivated by it to "see" and to "think." That is, to recognize what is really going on around them. In fact, as we saw in the last chapter, in another discussion about another poem, Mitchell chastises his former teacher for being overly impressed with grammatical structures and not interested in what he was trying to say.

Mitchell contrasts himself both with slam poets and with another Native poet who is not a Navajo. This poet, according to Mitchell, has a confrontational style. Mitchell raises his voice when speaking like this poet. Note that Mitchell does not disagree with what that poet is saying about colonialism but rather is concerned with what he perceives as that poet's confrontational style. More than one Navajo poet has suggested that an overtly confrontational style is not the "Navajo way" (see also Lamphere 1977; Field 1998, 2001). Some Navajos that I have spoken with have evaluated certain poets negatively for what they see as an overtly confrontational style. Mitchell's view on slam poetry is complicated because he often speaks with great appreciation for the slam-poetry style of Navajo poet Zoey Benally (on Benally's poetry, see Wheeler 2008). Mitchell, for his part, prefers a less showy style.

Thinking, Seeing, and Listening

Navajos, like other Athabaskans (see Cruikshank 1998; Nevins 2004; Meek 2010), put a premium on proper "listening." As Cruikshank (1998: 144) notes, "Indigenous storytelling assumes a relationship between speaker and listener. A listener becomes knowledgeable by hearing successive tellings of stories and may mull over, reinterpret, and absorb different meanings with each hearing." When I asked Blackhorse Mitchell who was the audience for this poem, his response was, "anyone who could pick it up and listen."

In an insightful discussion about Western Apache language ideologies, that is, Western Apaches' views on the uses of language, Keith Basso (1996: 84) notes that "Western Apache conceptions of language and thought are cast in pervasively visual terms. Every occasion of 'speaking' (*yałti'*) provides tangible evidence of 'thinking' (*natsíkęęs*), and thinking occurs in the form of 'pictures' (*be'elzaahí*) that persons 'see' (*yo'įį*). Prompted by a desire to 'display thinking' (*nil'įį́ natsíkęęs*), speaking involves the use of language to 'depict' (*'e'ele'*) and 'convey' (*yo'ááł*) these images to members of an audience, such that they, on 'hearing' (*yidits'ag*) and 'holding' (*yotą́'*) the speaker's words, can 'view' (*yínel'į́'*) the images in their own mind." Basso's description, based on his work with Western Apaches, who are linguistically and culturally related to Navajos, echoes the descriptions that Mitchell gives of what he is trying to do through in his poetry. Many of my discussions with Mitchell are in "visual terms" (*look* and *see* recur throughout the transcripts).

Mitchell's comments also resonate with the work of Gary Witherspoon (1977). As Witherspoon points out in a chapter on "Creating the World Through Language," for some Navajos, "knowledge [*ééhózin*] is the inner form of thought [*ntsáhákees*], language [*saad*] is the inner form of speech [*yáti'*], . . . thought is the inner form of speech, [and] . . . knowledge is also the inner form of language" (32–33; see also House 2002). For some Navajo poets, proper or beautiful language use, that is, poetry, can "stimulate thought," as Rex Lee Jim described it to me (Webster 2006b: 44). Or as Blackhorse Mitchell explained in an interview I did with him on February 17, 2001, "poetry should have a rhythm, it should tell a story, it should make your reader really think, see clearly what's happening." Jim, for example, suggested that his poem "Tó Háálį́" ("Spring," Jim 1998: 12–13), which concerns vulgar English graffiti and littering at an important place for Navajos, was an attempt to get Navajos to "think" about what they were doing (see also Webster 2009). When Mitchell critiques a former Anglo teacher of his, he describes her inability to understand one of his early poems as her failure "to see what I was trying to say." When Mitchell explains what he wants his poetry to do, he frames it as getting people to "think" about what he is saying, so that they can "really see" it.

By "seeing" things clearly, one can be motivated to act. As John Farella (1984: 35) points out, in discussing Navajo philosophy, "if the mind can be changed, the world changes." Or as David McAllester (1954: 72) long ago noted with reference to Navajo aesthetics, "beauty is that which *does* something"; that is, that which heals, protects, and sustains (see also Field and Blackhorse 2002).

Excerpt 2

July 9, 2008. It is evening, and Blackhorse Mitchell and I are again sitting in his home outside Shiprock. We are again talking about his poetry. We have spoken on and off all day about his poetry. I am asking him what he is trying to accomplish with his poetry. He begins to respond, I turn my digital recorder on. Here is a fragment of that conversation.

BM: So it's just like
    the way I would write
    the this is just one good example
    an:
    the only way I would write my poem is in the middle uh
    a chaos

AW: Mm hmm

BM: Meaning
    I would find
    uh people
    WHOLE LOT A people, not just one

AW: Mm hmm

BM. That's
    the only way
    if I get bored
    if I get distract
    maybe at a conference

AW: Ah ha

BM: Maybe at a gathering an:
    it's what people say
    it just so happened that [clears throat]
    this [clears throat]
    lady was
    called in:
    to attend a writer's conference

AW: Mm hmm

BM: [community name]

AW: Okay

BM: An:
    she comes in
    an she stands there
    an she reads
    a couple of paper I forgot the name a the lady
    she said [2-second pause]
    "MY GOD
    YOU NAVAJOS
    when I was coming in from
    Tuba City
    OH MAN
    HO:W beautiful your Navajo land is

you got all that nice open country"
and what was I thinkin
I'm just sittin there I say
"oh: my God
what is she saying
haven't she looked around
hasn't she seen
what's
alongside of the highways
oh Jesus
what was she looking at
WHERE WAS SHE LOOKIN"
and SO
my poem
I went an put
"BEAUTY
of NAVAJOland"
plastic bags
blowing in the wind
aluminum
beer cans
shining in the country
fli:es enjoying WASTE on
Huggies disposals
AND
an empty bottle of Zima ornaments
the road side
the BEAUTY a Navajoland
little a big trashes drifting in the gale of wind
run-over dogs and coyotes
v:ultures
feasting on deteriorating smell a meat
AND
the crows
flying away with the eyes of the kill [2-second pause]
"the beauty of NAVAJOland,"
you: say:
THOSE polluted dark clouds are not the real clouds
the rivers
an streams contaminated

by redneck piss and dungs
AND
uranium in the flowing innocent r:iver
the BEAUTY of Navajoland
bra: strap
hanging
on the roadside guidepost
crucifix with plastic bouquet of FLOWERS
STANDING an remi:nding in humiliations
AN
coal stripping of M:other Earth
an
flood of acid rain
is not the beauty of
Navajoland
AW: Ah
BM: That's
what I wrote
AW: Can I have a copy of that?
BM: It'll cost you
AW: That's fine
BM: [laughter]
AW: [laughter]
BM: ANYWAY
THAT'S
what I WROTE
an that's what I mean
if you
look at this
it's something I see
that
people don't see
so:
whoever said
the word *beauty*
I go, "by golly if
there's beauty on Navajoland
how come you
you have this
we HAVE this"

is what I'm saying
AW: Mm hmm
BM: An I was just hoping that
whoever: read this
an it's true
I I:
I got real
real:
I got to the grip
Like
bra strap hangin on the roadside guidepost would be:
I see that
eh ya you know guidepost and somebody thinks that's
that's something great to hang
somebody:
maybe they throw the poor
they use the old lady or:
screw for half of the night an then throw her bra strap up there
Navajo
uh either the new Navajo is thinking ah that's
that's cool
to me that's not cool
an then
[clears throat]
crucifix with plastic bouquet of flowers
whenever somebody died along the roadside they put all a this
this decoration of plastic bouquets
and I don't like that
AW: Right
BM: I don't like lookin at it
that's not nice
they should put it
in a cemetery where it belongs
AW: Mm hmm
BM: But
people don't
why
why do we get in
into this bandwagon
so:

ALL ALL a this
and then
[laughter]
we
you find
councilmen
you find great people
they always stand there says
"MOTHER EARTH"
what did they know a Mo:ther Earth
you know
so:
a lot a things that happen
a no nobody pays attention to
what Mother Earth wants
THAT'S
that's why I wrote it like that I was
mad
at that point

In Excerpt 2, Blackhorse Mitchell performs his poem "Beauty of Nava-joland" for me during our interview. In many discussions I have had with many Navajo poets, they have performed their poetry for me (see Webster 2009, 2010c). Indeed, here Mitchell echoes some of his discussion of the poem at Swarthmore College. Mitchell elaborates on the Anglo woman coming onto the reservation and commenting on how "beautiful your Navajo land is." His poem is a response to this woman's inability to "see" the realities of the Navajo Nation. As he explains, the realities are things he sees, but that other "people don't see."

But if Mitchell is critiquing the Anglo woman for not really seeing Nava-joland and rednecks for pissing in the San Juan River, he is also critiquing Navajos for doing "ugly" things. He singles out Navajos for putting bra straps on guideposts, for leaving empty cans and bottles of beer after they have partied, and for putting up crucifixes with plastic flowers to commem-orate an individual's death. In another conversation, Mitchell describes all of these things as "ugly." Mitchell also echoes his discussion at Swarthmore when he singles out various "great" people who talk about Mother Earth without really understanding what "Mother Earth wants." He is aware of the strategic use of various bivalent terms like *Mother Earth* that will resonate with Anglo American outsiders and tourists.

From Mother Earth to Shitrock

Let me now add that some Navajos I know, certainly not all, sometimes do talk of Mother Earth. As we see in the above transcript, Mitchell uses the term outside of the performance setting. Some Navajos that I have worked with have glossed the Navajo term *Nahasdzáán* as 'Mother Earth'. They note that embedded within this term is *asdzáán* 'woman'. Some Navajos refer to the earth as *nihimá* 'our mother' or *shimá* 'my mother'. Gary Witherspoon (1977: 91–94) documented such usage in the 1970s. Gladys Reichard ([1950] 1963: 19) noted that "essential parts, as well as the earth itself, are called 'our mother.'" As Witherspoon explains, "a mother is one who gives and sustains life . . . and by both definitions the earth is a mother to the earth surface people [human beings]" (92). Witherspoon challenges a view of the use of *-má* 'mother' as a metaphorical extension when applied to the earth, sheep, cornfields, and mountains. Rather he argues that those things and human female parents all share the quality of "sustenance" that defines the term. This aspect of Navajo can carry over to Navajo English. As a result, *mother* is bivalent in mainstream English and Navajo English, and indeed, the use of *mother* by Navajos can sometimes be confusing to those who expect it to map onto mainstream English uses of *mother*.

Some Navajo poets, when I interview them about this subject, will mock Navajo politicians' uses of Mother Earth as a cynical ploy to tap into Euro-American stereotypes, or they will say that politicians use the phrase without an adequate understanding of what it actually entails. They will then point out that, of course, "Navajos do believe in Mother Earth, we call the earth *shimá* or *nihimá*, you know. *Nahasdzáán* means Mother Earth." For some Navajos, Mother Earth is a salient concept in Navajo English and linked to the Navajo language. In Rex Lee Jim's (1998: 12–13) poem "Tó Háálį," he translates the line *Nahasdzáán shimá ha'níigo* as "Earth, my mother." I have heard Jim read this poem in Navajo to audiences primarily composed of Navajos (see Webster 2009).

Driving north from Window Rock (the capital of the Navajo Nation) to Tsaile, Arizona, (site of the main campus of Diné College) one finds a number of homemade signs along the road imploring people to "keep the Navajo Nation beautiful." These signs become less common the closer one gets to Shiprock (also the location of a satellite campus of Diné College). Mary Lawlor (2006: 58) notes the sign outside Window Rock that says, "Welcome to the Navajo Nation: Explore Scenic Parks." The Navajo Nation does market itself as a tourist destination. On the website for the Navajo Tourism Department (http://www.discovernavajo.com, last accessed January 15,

2010) a film, *Welcome to the Navajo Nation*, describes the importance of "Mother Nature" to Navajos and highlights the scenic beauty of the Navajo Nation. Such an image is certainly crafted to entice non-Navajos to visit the Navajo Nation, but it is not alone. Regional Southwest magazines like *Arizona Highways* and *New Mexico Magazine* certainly play up the Navajo Nation as an enticing tourist attraction as well. Leah Dilworth (1996) has explored some of the history of the ways that the Southwest and Navajos have been imagined. She notes the role of the Fred Harvey Company in constructing an aesthetic view of Navajos (see also Bsumek 2008; Mithlo 2008).

When I speak with tourists on the Navajo Nation, they tend to highlight a view of the Navajo Nation as "scenery." Some lament the poverty. Letters to the editor in the *Navajo Times* occasionally include letters from tourists chastising Navajos for not keeping their reservation clean or not taking care of their dogs. Sarah Krakoff (2008: 30) observes that "many non-Indian visitors to this stark, high desert region are overwhelmed by the signs of third world poverty, including roving stray dogs, roadside trash, alcoholic (and recently, methamphetamine addled) hitchhikers, and a landscape pock-marked by mining and other forms of resource extraction." Following the work of Harkin (2000, 2004) and Nadasdy (2005) on the kinds of outside expectations one encounters concerning Native peoples and their relationship to the environment, one can sense in Krakoff's discussion and in the letters that crop up in the *Navajo Times* a disappointment with Navajos for not living up to a romantic ideal. Lawlor (2006: 60) describes herself as an "educated tourist" on a visit to the Navajo Nation for research on its public face. She views Shiprock—the "town," not the "dramatic rock formation"—as "easily mistaken for any border town, or, perhaps more accurately, for any middle-American strip zone" (88, 89). One wonders what she was expecting. Again, Navajos—not the landscape—fail to live up to romantic ideals.

Lawlor also notes that "Navajo people use both names [*Tsé Bit'a'í* and *Shiprock*] today, at least in public discourse" (89). Tsé Bit'a'í (Winged Rock) is the name for the rock formation. I have not normally heard the community of Shiprock referred to as Tsé Bit'a'í. In my experiences over the course of the last decade, some Navajos have referred to the Shiprock community in Navajo as Naat'áanii Nééz (Tall Leader) or Toohdi (At the Water/River). In English, Navajos from both Shiprock and elsewhere on the reservation sometimes call it "Shitrock." Navajos also recognize the poverty and desolation in Shiprock, but seldom have I heard them misrecognize Shiprock as a "middle-American strip zone." Some Navajos do lament the fast-food restaurants in Shiprock. Some Navajos, though, are quick to point out that the KFC serves mutton stew. One Navajo poet I interviewed in 2000 insisted that I interview her at the KFC. She was quick to call my attention to the mutton stew on the menu. Chat-&-Chew, a local eatery, remains popular. Other Navajos I know generally avoid the chain restaurants in Shiprock and prefer to eat in Cortez, Colorado (about forty-five minutes north of Shiprock) or Farmington, New Mexico (about a half-hour east of Shiprock) when they can eat out. But Farmington is a problematic place in its own right.

Just outside Shiprock, at the exit to one of the major power plants in the Four Corners region, is a sign that reads "Wake Up You Bunch of Nuts, We All Live Downstream" (see image 1). Below that sign is another sign with an image of four public figures urinating into the San Juan River and a question in large red print: "Showing Our Concern for the Environment?" In the bottom corner of that sign, in smaller print, is the question "The truth hurts doesn't it?" If you are driving to Farmington the sign is on your right. When you drive back to Shiprock the sign is on your left. At the intersection with the exit, there are traffic lights. The signs are conspicuous. R. G. Hunt II, a local Anglo businessman, put the signs up in frustration with what he saw as the environmental problems caused by the power plants that litter the Four Corners region. He told me in June 2012 that he felt the sign had, at minimum, cost the power plant some employee morale. One Navajo poet I talked with in the summer of 2008 said she was surprised that the sign was still up. According to her, it had been up for a couple of years. She had assumed the power plant would have had it removed already. Hunt told me that the sign had been up for twelve years and that the power plants had requested that he take the sign down. He had refused. As my poet consultant noted, every time Navajo employees of that power plant leave work, they are confronted by that sign and have to "think" about what they are doing.

One afternoon, Gloria Emerson asks me to go down to the San Juan River with her and take pictures of the river and the garbage that lines the river. Emerson is careful to direct me to take photos of all the garbage along the river. She is working on a project about the importance of water and about the condition of the river that she later presents to an audience in Shiprock. Unfortunately, the event is poorly attended.

Doo Ajinída (Don't Talk About It)

Sitting in Tsaile in a dorm on the campus of Diné College on a cold March evening in 2001, a young Navajo college student, who also writes poetry, laments to me that contemporary Navajo poets are not talking about the important issues on the Navajo Nation. He tells me that Navajo poets are good at criticizing "white people," but that they are less inclined to criticize the myriad issues that are confronting Navajos on the reservation: issues, he says, like poverty and pollution. I respond by noting the poetry of Nia Francisco (1994), with its gimlet eye on the myriad of social issues confronting Navajos. He has not heard of Francisco's book. I might have also mentioned the early work of Gloria Emerson (1971), which critiqued the social and political ills on and around the Navajo Nation. When Rutherford Ashley's book of poetry is published in 2001, one Navajo praises the book and tells me that Ashley is one of the only Navajo poets talking about social and economic issues on the reservation. On the other hand, in 2000 I also heard one aspiring Navajo poet state that the poetry of Esther Belin was too political.

Years later, in July 2008, with Navajo-Hopi poet Venaya Yazzie, I bring up the conversation I had with the young Navajo college student. Yazzie, along with Gloria Emerson, Esther Belin, and Tina Deschenie, has been active in Dooda Desert Rock (*dooda* means 'no'), an attempt to block the construction of the Desert Rock power plant on the Navajo Nation in the Four Corners region. Dooda Desert Rock is spearheaded by Elouise Brown, a Navajo who lives in the area where the power plant would be located (Horoshko 2008: 16). Yazzie's activities have included a 2008 exhibit at the Center for Southwest Studies at Fort Lewis College in Durango, Colorado, titled *Connections: Earth + Artist = A Tribute Art Show to Resistance to Desert Rock*, and a poetry and art session in March 2009 titled *Connections: Earth + Artist II* at the Navajo Studies Conference in Shiprock. During that event, which was lightly attended, Yazzie described some of the opposition she encountered from Navajos over the art exhibit in Durango. In my interview with Yazzie in July of 2008, she points out that one of the issues that Navajo poets face is a concern with *doo ajinída* 'don't talk about it'. She has had people tell her that some of her politically engaged poetry says things that are best left unsaid. *Doo ajinída*, as another Navajo consultant explains to me, is often associated with *'aseezí* 'gossip'. As Yazzie explains to me, the phrase *doo ajinída* encapsulates the idea that "you don't talk about these things, cuz that's what happens when no one's around and you don't want other people to know that's what happens." The phrase makes explicit an "ordeal of civility," that is, the "acquiescence to a tradition of politeness [that] . . . results in a consciousness of participating in one's own subjugation" (E. Basso 2009: 127). Using *doo ajinída* in this context suggests, in a way akin to the cultural intimacy described by Herzfeld (1997), that you should not write about social, political, and environmental issues on the Navajo Nation because outsiders, primarily Anglos, might overhear and have their various negative stereotypes about Navajos confirmed.

Navajo poets that I know are quite aware of these outside negative stereotypes, for example, the notion that all Navajos are alcoholics (on some of the stereotypes about Native Americans see Meek 2006; J. Hill 2008; see here also Deyhle 2009). Indeed, a number of Navajo poets have pointed out the tension involved in simply ordering a beer at a border-town bar or restaurant. The moment you order that beer, they tell me, you can be seen as confirming a stereotype. This is especially true in a border town like Farmington. Many Navajos have told me that Farmington was once known as the Selma (Alabama) of New Mexico. One Navajo woman told me it was unfair to compare Selma and Farmington because, she said with a smile, she had heard that Selma had changed. Farmington is often described by some Navajos as a "racist" or "redneck" town. I have heard astonishingly racist comments about Navajos in Farmington. Some Navajos refuse to do business in Farmington because of the racism they see. Some Navajos that I know, who speak Navajo freely on the Navajo Nation, are sometimes reluctant to do so in Farmington. Navajo poet Zoey Benally has told me about how she did not want her slam-poetry team associated with coming from Farmington. While Farmington was the largest city in the area, members of the team did not all come from Farmington and they disliked the association. They preferred to be "from the Four Corners region" (it was both more accurate and less offensive). However, in the face of Farmington's bad reputation, some Navajo poets are quick to add various caveats. For example, many Navajo poets speak highly of the recently closed bookstore and cafe Andrea Kristina's, which had hosted art exhibits and poetry readings by Navajos. But, in general, many Navajos consider Farmington a "dangerous" place. And by a dangerous place, Navajos sometimes mean a potentially violent place.

Navajo poets are also aware of outside expectations that trivialize and exoticize them. They encounter such expectations at poetry readings and conferences (see Belin 2009). At poetry readings off the reservation that I have attended, Navajo poets are often confronted with questions from audience members that constitute ordeals of language, demands to maintain the imagined civility of an unequal society. I have seen Navajo poets asked about their thoughts on the ancient Navajo writing system shown on the television show *The X-Files* and I have seen them asked whether or not they were "shamans." In the former case, the poet directed the questioner to talk with me because I was an "expert on Navajo writing." In the latter case, the poet responded that he was not "a medicine man" and thus subtly corrected the questioner. In both cases, the imagined civility was maintained by Navajos suppressing responses that would have highlighted the condescending assumptions behind the questions.

Adding to all of this is Desert Rock. The Desert Rock power-plant project is supported by the government of the Navajo Nation and by many Navajos. Some have explained to me that Desert Rock will create jobs and spur "economic development" on the Navajo Nation. Other Navajos—including poets—counter these arguments by suggesting that there will be few jobs actually created and that these jobs will be menial-labor jobs (janitors and security guards). They note that most Navajos lack either the education or the educational opportunities to get high-paying employment at a "high-tech" power plant. Finally, these Navajos note that the power from this power plant will not go to Navajos but rather to Texas or California. Indeed, in the letters page of the *Navajo Times*, there has been a spirited debate about Desert Rock. This, I might add, includes a letter written by Venaya Yazzie and published in February 2008. Navajo critics sometimes label those involved with Dooda Desert Rock as "troublemakers."

In the chorus of a poem for *Connections: Earth + Artist = A Tribute Art Show to Resistance to Desert Rock*, Tina Deschenie addresses some of these issues. She writes, "Those people protesting, they're just trouble makers, / Protesters, trying to be like AIM." AIM is the American Indian Movement, which was a politically active American Indian group in the 1970s whose activities included a number of high-profile protests and occupations (Fixico 2004: 388). As Yazzie noted in an interview I did with her, "a lot of Navajo people are very apathetic to anything that goes on that's political, they just don't wanna get involved." This apathy is a concern expressed by other Navajo poets as well.

When I spoke with Blackhorse Mitchell about *doo ajinída* he too equated it with a prohibition against gossip, but he also noted that "you have got to talk about" issues like the environment. He said that the injunction *doo ajinída* should be used, for example, when someone tells someone "to go to hell." As he said, "you don't say wrong things like that, don't tell your neighbors to go to hell." Mitchell's description of the right use of *doo ajinída* is reminiscent of a familiar point in much of the literature about Navajos. Toelken (2003: 111) describes it this way: "For Navajos, actually uttering words creates the reality of their world . . . hence people avoid speaking of things they don't want to see appear in the world around them." The injunction *doo ajinída* is about not saying things that are not already in existence. Yazzie and Mitchell, on the other hand, both say that there are some issues that must be discussed, most likely because they already exist.

The state of the Navajo Nation is one such issue. They seem to agree, then, that the injunction *doo ajinída* is being misapplied, or as Mitchell said, "distorted," when it is used against poets discussing issues like power plants on the reservation or treating Mother Earth cavalierly.

Some Navajo poets have suggested that being an overtly politically active Navajo poet would decrease one's chances of getting published. As Deschenie noted in an interview I did with her in July 2008 about venues for Navajo poets, "there's just so few publishers." Many Navajo poets have expressed to me a feeling that there are stereotypes among publishers of what a Navajo poet should write about. More than one Navajo poet has told me about a poetry manuscript that was rejected for "not being Navajo enough." Navajo poets, like other Navajo artists, know that tourists and non-Navajos often have expectations about what they should write about or paint (see Dilworth 1996; Denetdale 2007; Bsumek 2008; on the political economy of such expectations see M'Closkey 2002; for a more general survey of stereotypes of Native peoples see Graham 2002 and Deloria 2004). One Navajo poet/artist explained that she does both artwork that will satisfy tourists' expectations and artwork that she feels is important but is unlikely to sell. This is the double bind of the Indigenous art market (see Marcus and Myers 1995; Myers 2001, 2002; Povinelli 2002; Bunten 2008; Mithlo 2008). One Navajo poet described the Navajo Nation as a "zoo," a place where tourists can come and gawk at Navajos (see image 2). Such comments show the deep ambivalence that some Navajos have toward marketing the Navajo Nation and themselves as a tourist destination or attraction. That ambivalence can be heard in Mitchell's poem as well.

Navajo poets are aware of these multiple tensions emanating both from outside, non-Navajo expectations and from other Navajos. To write poetry that is critical of tourists or that calls attention to the economic, environmental, and social issues on the reservation is still a risky undertaking. Based on my experience, there are now certainly more Navajo poets actively engaged in environmental and other social and political causes than there were in 2001. Gloria Emerson has recently described the Shiprock region to me as the "hub of Navajo poetry." In the summer of 2008, Navajo poets like Zoey Benally, Clifford Jack, Venaya Yazzie, Gloria Emerson, Esther Belin, Tina Deschenie, and Blackhorse Mitchell all lived in the Shiprock region. All of these poets write politically engaged poetry. Whether it is Clifford Jack's poetry challenging stereotypes about Navajos or Tina Deschenie's, Esther Belin's, and Venaya Yazzie's poetry in support of Dooda Desert Rock, Shiprock is not just a hub for Navajo poetry, it is also a center of Navajo activist poetry.

Excerpt 3

July 20, 2008. This interview begins after Blackhorse Mitchell has shown me how he has centered some of his new poetry to challenge the way he was taught to write poetry at the boarding school. Mitchell and I are sitting in his living room.

AW: So I just want to start with
something you just said
that the "Beauty of Navajoland"
the reason you centered it
BM: Mmhmm
AW: Because you a:
wanted to make it different
BM: Mmhmm
AW: Than the way they taught you at boarding school
BM: Yes
AW: Could you say something about that [light laughter]
BM: Well the [light laughter]
my thinking
have TOTALLY changed
from the boarding-school life
looking at the "Beauty of Navajoland"
is like
looking at all the things that have changed
SO
way down at the end
when I said like
[4-second pause]
the beauty of Navajoland
would be like um
"bra strap hanging on the roadside
guidepost
crucifix with plastic bouquet of flowers
standing and reminding in humiliation
AND
coal stripping of Mother Earth
and flood of acid rain
is not"
ACTUALLY I don't call it the beauty of Navajoland

    maybe it is thought of as Christmas
    if you pick up all these materials
    like bra strap, Huggies
    AND
    [laughter]
AW: [laughter] I see
BM: And you put all of these
    throw away beer cans
    and if you put it on a Christmas tree
    maybe it would make a good decorations
    but
    it wasn't meant to be
    it seems like [clears throat]
    the first line
    where it says
    "the plastic bag blowing in the wind"
    that's what you would find in the street
    even in Farmington
    the clean town
    you would find that
    like, "aluminum beer cans shining in the country"
    that means in the open country
    people party and they just throw stuff
    and then it says, "fly enjoying waste on the Huggies disposal"
    it seems like that's another thing
    people just throw Huggies
AW: Mmhmm
BM: Away
    either alongside of the road
    and you find flies
    and it's jus, jus all these things
    how should they be dealt with
AW: Mm
BM: And that's just a question
    like um
    ALL the things that I'm looking at
    like
    "little big trashes drifting in the gale
    that's run-over dogs an coyotes"
    and you find vultures

as well as the crow
"feasting on
deteriorating smell of meat"
that's what you find here on the highway
you find all of these ugly smells
and you wonder
so I put it
ah in a POEM form
that people never really look at these things
and then hunh
I put like, "'the beauty of Navajoland'
YOU SAY"
this is anybody
tourists are coming into Navajoland
and saying, "oh how beauty [high pitch on quoted portion]
your land is
and the country"
they might look at Shiprock
without looking down
and they look down
or
look across the sky
they might find, "the polluted dark clouds
which are not the real clouds"
and not knowing the rivers and streams
are contaminated by redneck piss
and dungs
SO it's not only Farmington
but wherever the river flows
and there's
Aztec
and Durango
and Silverton
and up the way
I'm sure these people
they just
SOMEWHERE they take care of it
but along the river
they do wild things
AW: Hmm

BM: And who knows
    people go to the river and piss in it
    and
    and it just flows
    that's what I'm talking about
    we NEVER know
    what goes on up the river
AW: Mmhmm
BM: As well as
    from here
    from Shiprock
    down the river
    and as I was saying that
    people dumping trash in the gullies
    and when flood rain
    washes them away
    washes them into the San Juan River
    we're just as bad
    and it goes down to Page
    and I'm sure
    there's a lot of things
    under
    the big lake Page
    I'm just thinking about
    how many
    junk
    is under there
    and
    on the surface
    people are boating
    and enjoying
    just boat riding and fishing [done in a singsong voice]
    but what's
    way down there
    at the bottom
AW: Right
BM: Is what I'm saying
    we're not rea:lly
    looking at the environment
    like or

taking care of the environment
like we're supposed to
so
all all of this
that's
what I was talking about
AW: Mhm
BM: And I feel
it does cover
like the coal stripping
and then the power plants
because
like all the things that go on
around Navajo country
and people are not really:
looking at it
or what they saying
and I thought
I'd write it
to that point
that this is the new era
this is today
AW: Mhm
BM: That I'm talking of
2000

In Excerpt 3, Mitchell again walks me through the poem. I have been, by this time, on the Navajo Nation for a little over two weeks. I have talked with many of the poets involved with Dooda Desert Rock and I have talked with Mitchell about the issues involved most nights. When I ask him to talk about his centering of the lines of "Beauty of Navajoland" as a challenge to the regimes of the boarding school, Mitchell takes it as an opportunity to discuss the ways his views have changed over time. Mitchell no longer writes like he did in *Miracle Hill*. His writing has changed not just in the alignment of lines on the page but in that his "thinking has totally changed" since boarding school. Mitchell has an interesting comic touch with his notion of using the trash on the Navajo Nation as Christmas-tree decorations, suggesting that one can find "beauty" in the trash if it is used correctly. Ironically, as Mitchell pointed out to me on a subsequent visit in 2014, a roadside memorial has been placed at the turnoff to his home (see image 7). Such roadside memorials, as it was explained to me, both call attention to death and potentially attract ghosts. In this way, they are ugly. He has plans to "beautify" the memorial. The negative consequences of uranium mining, explicitly mentioned in Mitchell's poem (though not in this excerpt, as it happens), are a topic many Navajos—poets and nonpoets alike—have been concerned with (see Brugge, Benally, and Yazzie-Lewis 2007). Mitchell clearly taps into a pervasive concern here. Indeed, Venaya Yazzie's (2008) letter to the *Navajo Times* about Desert Rock also invokes the ramifications of uranium mining and embeds them within Navajo narrative traditions involving the slaying of monsters (see Zolbrod 1984).

We also hear echoes of the performance from Swarthmore here. Once again Mitchell notes that it is "tourists" who make these claims about the "beauty of Navajoland." Tourists may look at the "dramatic rock formation" of Shiprock, but they might not "look down" at the people living there. They might not "see" what is going on. Again, Mitchell wants people to "see" through his poetry.

In this conversation, Mitchell talks about the San Juan River. He points out that upriver, even in the deeply ironically "clean town" of Farmington, rednecks—Mitchell's term for racists who live there—defile the river with dung and piss. Mitchell's comment about the plastic bags in Farmington is particularly interesting because Farmington, unlike Shiprock or most communities on the Navajo Nation, has regular garbage-collection services. Mitchell goes on to follow the course of the river, pointing out that "it's not only Farmington but wherever the river flows and there's Aztec [New Mexico] and Durango [Colorado] and Silverton [Colorado]." As Mitchell states, "we *never* know what goes on up the river." Mitchell again does not give Navajos a pass here. Rather than only blame "rednecks," Mitchell also notes that Navajos dump "trash in the gullies." This is a conversation Mitchell and I have had many times. In one such conversation, Mitchell noted that this is an "ugly thing" to do. According to Mitchell, Navajos "are just as bad" when it comes to "contaminating" the river. Mitchell continues to follow the river, moving from the gullies around Shiprock back to the San Juan River and then finally to Page, Arizona. Mitchell imagines all the "junk" in Lake Powell (a major tourist destination in the Southwest) as people go about enjoying "just boat riding and fishing." Mitchell says this in a singsong voice that draws out the contrast between their ignorance of what is going on above water and what is "way down there at the bottom."

On Beauty and Ugliness

When Blackhorse Mitchell uses the term *beauty*, it should not be confused with the mainstream English term *beauty*. Instead, it should be understood as a lexical item in Navajo English (a local language), much like the plural marking that Mitchell uses on *dungs*. It resonates not so much with Western notions of beauty as with Navajo views on *hózhǫ́* 'beauty, harmony'. The same is true of Mitchell's use of *ugly*. We confuse the matter by assuming that mainstream English and Navajo English are isomorphic (an assumption wholly licensed by the inequality between these linguistic systems and between their speakers [Hymes 1996a; Blommaert 2005; Webster 2010c]). They are not. We need to understand Navajo English terms like *beauty*, *ugly*, and *Mother Earth* as bivalent with the corresponding mainstream English terms. Here I follow Kathryn Woolard (1998: 6) and understand bivalency as "a simultaneous membership of an element in more than one linguistic system." Such forms are based on a phonological iconicity across linguistic systems. In this case, the two linguistic systems are Navajo English and mainstream English.* *Beauty* and *ugly*, to adapt a term from linguistics, are "false friends." Phonologically iconic forms—bivalent forms (if not polyvalent)—are often misrecognized as having identical or near-identical semantics or meaning. They appear to have the same meaning because of superficial similarity of form, but in fact they have distinct historical trajectories and semantics. I am not claiming, however, that *beauty*, for example, is equivalent with *hózhǫ́*. *Hózhǫ́* is formed from the very productive and interwoven verb stem *-zhǫ́* 'beauty, harmony, peaceful, orderly'; the Navajo English term *beauty* is neither as productive nor as interwoven in a host of expressive forms as the Navajo term is (see Woodbury 1998 on "interwoven"; see Witherspoon 1977 on the productivity of *-zhǫ́*).

What I am arguing is that for some Navajos, including Mitchell, *beauty* is a Navajo English expression for something akin to the Navajo term *hózhǫ́* (see Witherspoon 1977; Lamphere 1969). It is not an approximation of some normative "English," but rather a distinctive local way of speaking and writing. Likewise, for Mitchell, *ugly* is a Navajo English expression for something

---

* I assume, following Paul Hopper (1987), that grammar is a by-product of use, a certain sedimenting of recurrent patterns through repeated use. Rather than see language use as informed by some putative "universal grammar," we should instead see languages as "emergent grammars." These emergent grammars are locatable, as Bakhtin (1986) would remind us, in the concrete utterances of socially located speakers (see also Johnstone 1996). Languages are, then, relatively and never completely shared patterned ways of speaking and sometimes writing.

akin to *hóchxǫ'* 'ugly, disorderly' (see Lamphere 1969; Witherspoon 1977; Farella 1984). Over the years, Mitchell has made a number of comments about the "ugliness" of various things on and around the Navajo Nation. At first, I took this to be a strange aesthetic judgment. However, over time, I have come to realize such comments are about the disorderly and out-of-control qualities of these things. As Witherspoon (1977: 186) notes, *hóchxǫ'* is used to describe "things and beings out of control." Lamphere (1969: 281) glosses *hózhǫ́* as 'pleasant conditions' and *hóchxǫ'* as 'ugly conditions' (see also Haile 1947). Various things are ugly, like bra straps on guideposts and redneck piss in rivers, in the sense that they are out of control and disorderly. As has been repeatedly noted about Navajo ritual, one of the primary goals of much ritual is to restore order or beauty, *hózhǫ́* (see Witherspoon 1977; Farella 1984; Toelken 2003). Mitchell's poem, through its attempt to get listeners to think and see, is also an attempt to restore order, to restore "beauty."

I would argue that one can also understand why Rex Lee Jim reads his poem "Tó Háálį́," with its use of English vulgarity, to Navajo audiences composed of both adults and children (see Webster 2009). Jim is trying to get Navajos of all ages to see the ugliness and to "think" about that ugliness. This is at least partially why Jim has described his poetry as "thought poems" (Webster 2006b). Indeed, in an interview I did with Tina Deschenie in 2008, she recalled a poetry performance by Jim in 2001 where he read a number of his critical poems in Navajo—including "Tó *Háálį́*"—to a Navajo audience. She noted that many Navajos in attendance "gasped." Deschenie, who was involved in the first *Connections: Earth + Artist* exhibit, saw Jim's performance as important. Jim, I would argue, was trying to get Navajos to "see" and "think" about the current state of the Navajo Nation. Like Mitchell, he was attempting to restore order and "beauty." Yet some Navajos use the injunction of *doo ajinída* to critique and silence such calling of attention to the ugly realities on the Navajo Nation. David Kamper (2010: 161–62) has made a similar point about Navajo union organizers speaking out about controversial issues. He argues that one way of understanding Navajos who voice concern about important political issues is to see this action as an attempt to restore *hózhǫ́*. Yet, as he notes, there is also the risk that such voicing of views will be seen as disruptive. This, then, is an ordeal of language (E. Basso 2009).

Conclusions

Why do some Navajo poets write about contemporary environmental and social issues? Based on the discussions with Mitchell, I think we can now sketch out something of what he is attempting to accomplish with his poem "Beauty of Navajoland," and answer the question in the process. When Mitchell describes various "ugly things" in this poem, he is inviting his audience to listen to what he is saying. He wants his audience, in listening, to see, that is, to visually imagine, what he is describing and to recognize the truth in his descriptions; this is a felt iconicity between the world as it is and the world as he describes it in his poetry. He is inviting people, based on these visual images, to think then about what is going on on the Navajo Nation. If his listeners engage in such thinking, Mitchell hopes things on the reservation can change. He is not telling Navajos (or non-Navajos) what to do; that would be presumptuous (see Lamphere 1977; Field 2001). He is, instead, helping Navajos to make their own decisions. In the performance at Swarthmore, Mitchell must make some of this explicit for the non-Navajos in the audience. Mitchell also, repeatedly, has made some of his argument explicit in the conversations he and I have had about this poem. But, as with his verbal trip down the San Juan River, he has also invited me to imagine these issues. Like the Coyote stories described by Toelken and Scott (1981: 104), Mitchell's poem "suggest[s] a set of ethics for humans." Like Coyote stories, the poem does not explicitly explain these ethics. They are not normally explicitly explained. Rather, the expectation is that the listener/reader will—through reflection, that is, thinking—infer them (Toelken and Scott 1981: 110). And as Cruikshank (1998) and Keith Basso (1996) have argued, such reflection comes from repeated engagement with the stories.

Mitchell's poem, then, has at least two audiences, both nicely encapsulated at the Swarthmore College performance in November 2004. This is a dialogue both with outsiders and with Navajos. On the one hand, the poem is directed at non-Navajos or potential tourists to the Navajo Nation. Mitchell is urging potential tourists to really "see" Navajo country. "Seeing" means not engaging in a superficial appraisal of the reservation as mere "scenery," as banally "beautiful." Moreover, Mitchell wants potential tourists to listen to what he is actually saying and to see beyond stereotypes, both positive and negative, of Navajos. And as Mitchell reminded me after reading an earlier version of this chapter, he also wants to "reach out" and remind outsiders—who he sees as having inordinate power compared to Navajos—that he is a "human being" with "feelings." Mitchell's poem is iconic of his humanness. On the other hand, the poem is also aimed at Navajos. And here it is important to remember that throughout the performance at Swarthmore, Mitchell repeatedly addressed the young Navajo woman who had introduced him. What Mitchell was doing through the performance of this poem was, I believe, trying to get both potential tourists and Navajos to listen, to think, to see, and then to act in a proper manner to rectify the "ugliness" he was describing. His poetry performance, an aesthetically pleasing use of language, was, to paraphrase McAllester (1954), *doing* something. For Mitchell, and for some other poets, describing what is happening on the Navajo Nation is the first step in getting people to see and think about that truth. It is not gossip, nor is it troublemaking. It is an accurate description of the current situation. Mitchell's poem is an attempt to restore order and harmony—or as he says in his local language, Navajo English, beauty—to Navajoland. Mitchell is trying to change people's minds, and in so doing, to change the world (Farella 1984).* The challenge, as some Navajo poets understand it, is to get more Navajos to "listen" and "see clearly what's happening."

Today there are a growing number of Navajo poets writing about environmental and social-justice issues. Such poetry is not just focused on external forms of colonialism or racism—criticizing "white people," as the young Navajo college student said back in 2001—but rather takes a critical stance toward events on the Navajo Nation like the attempt to build the Desert Rock power plant. Many Navajos, not just poets, who live around the Shiprock region are quite aware of the economic, social, and environmental issues that confront them on a daily basis. Actions like the art exhibit in support of Dooda Desert Rock suggest that some Navajos are attempting to change those realities. This resistance can also be seen in some Navajos' refusal to eat at the fast-food restaurants that populate the Shiprock community. One also can see teams of Navajo high-school students picking up litter on the sides of the road. Signs throughout the Navajo Nation encourage people to not litter (see image 4). Navajos engage in such activities not to fulfill some ecological-Indian stereotype but to fundamentally improve the conditions of their lives. That is also why poets write poetry about environmental and social-justice issues. Taking the "stubborn particulars of voice" (Cruikshank 2005: 3) seriously can allow us to understand something of what it means when some Navajo poets say their poetry is *hane'*. It also means recognizing local languages like Navajo English and attending to the bivalency of words across linguistic systems, not assuming phonological iconicity means semantic isomorphism. It can also allow us to begin to appreciate what some Navajo poets consider to be the purpose, the work, of poetry that calls attention to the ugliness—the disorder—on the reservation. And to appreciate why it is important to accurately describe that ugliness.

----

* I am not claiming that all Navajo poets understand their poetry in this way, but I hope to have suggested that some do. It is probably not a coincidence that both Mitchell and Jim are also "medicine men," or "practitioners" as they are also known on the Navajo Nation.

Epilogue

In the summer of 2012, I was out doing research on the Navajo Nation and attended the opening reception of the "TIME Project on Diné Bi Kéyah" at the Navajo Nation Museum in Window Rock. *TIME* is an acronym for *Temporary Installations Made for the Environment*. The TIME Project is put on by New Mexico Arts in conjunction with various local communities. In 2012, New Mexico Arts had teamed with the Navajo Nation. A series of art installations had been constructed on and around the Navajo Nation. Some of the artists involved were Navajo, most were not. Among the artists involved were Esther Belin and Venaya Yazzie. Yazzie and I were at the opening reception together. Yazzie, Belin, and a non-Navajo artist, Andrea Polli—an associate professor of art and ecology with appointments in the College of Fine Arts and the School of Engineering at the University of New Mexico—had teamed together for an installation titled *Binding Sky*. The installation was described in the *Gallup Journey*, a local monthly, in the following manner:

> Binding Sky is a 3-fold experience that involves public art, oral history
> and education in and around the Navajo Nation. This project aims to bring
> the complexities of the inter-relationships between air, people and tech-
> nology on the Navajo Nation to greater public attention. Artists worked
> with a social media group on this project, which uses the medium of air to
> convey its stories, through audio, and new media (cell phone apps, web-
> sites, video, etc.) to bring audiences on a journey through Navajo country.

The blurb is deceptive in the ways that it hides the social and environmental critique embedded within the installation.

At the urging of Belin and Yazzie, I drove up to the Shiprock area of the Navajo Nation to take a look at and experience the installations. There were two of them. One was at the library at Diné College's Shiprock campus and the other was at The Original Sweetmeat Inc. in Waterflow, New Mexico (see image 3). The installation at Sweetmeat was a bench with various images represented on it. One could also pick up a CD (labeled *binding sky*, with the website URL *www.bindingsky.org* also written on it) and a transcription of the conversations on the CD. Among the conversations recorded is one between Damien Jones (a Navajo educator and medicine man) and Blackhorse Mitchell. Here is a bit of what Mitchell says on the CD. I have transcribed the conversation and made changes to the version that accompanies the CD. Most notably, I use pause and intonation units as a guide to representing the organization of Mitchell's words. The transcription that accompanies the CD is in prose, but given the strong intertextual links with Mitchell's poem "Beauty of Navajoland," I represent his words as a breakthrough into a poetry performance.

> Aluminum beer cans rolling across the highway,
> you call that beauty?
> Na:h,
> you find trash along the highway you call that beauty na:h,
> even bra strap
> dangling on the guidepost.
> Is that beauty? NO: uh-uh.
> And
> plastic flowers
> you know those where accident took place is like a graveyard that they
>   put there
> and it's it's not beauty.
> It just makes you wonder
> and run-over dogs
> and crows eating up and pulling intestine
> across the highway.
> You find all that called beauty. No: uh-uh.
> And then the smog and all the other stuff,
> SEE going back to how I see Navajoland.

Here, in condensed form, is Mitchell's "Beauty of Navajoland," with references to bra straps dangling on guideposts, plastic flowers used in roadside commemorations to the dead, aluminum beer cans strewn about, and the carcasses of dogs as food for carrion birds. There is the refrain of *Is that beauty?* that is answered negatively both in the performance here and in the poem as discussed above. Mitchell's poem, which looks honestly at Navajoland, can now circulate more widely: people can stop at Sweetmeat and sit on the bench, stare out at the power plant (the bench orients the gaze toward it; see image 5), and take the CD with them (or perhaps merely skim the transcription provided). The installation, like Mitchell's poem, compels the viewer and listener to see and hear and think about the role of power plants on the Navajo Nation, to reflect on the ugliness that can be found there, and in so reflecting, to begin the process of restoring beauty.

When I stopped at the installation and sat on the bench staring at the power plant on June 16, 2012, the owner of Sweetmeat—an older man in a baseball cap and clothes that had seen work—came out to chat with me. R. G. Hunt II was the man responsible for the sign discussed earlier in this chapter that called attention to the ramifications of the power plant. Both the power plant and the sign are visible from Sweetmeat. Hunt is not Navajo, but has been the long-time owner of the meat store. To simplify his views a great deal, over the years he has grown increasingly concerned about the environmental destruction he has seen around him.* His sign was one in a series of actions that he has taken to call attention to his concerns. As we stood talking that June day about environmental concerns and other things, I asked Hunt what he thought of the bench and the work of Yazzie and Belin. Hunt replied that he was glad they had done it. Then he told me, "The bench makes me happy, because it says to me that I'm not alone."

---

* For those interested, Hunt's prepared statement to Congress about the environmental issues in northern New Mexico where he lives is available online: http://democrats.energycommerce .house.gov/Press_111/20091210/hunt_testimony.pdf.

Image 1. Sign outside Shiprock, New Mexico, July 2008. Photo by author.

Image 2. Esther Belin and Venaya Yazzie calling attention to the "zoo-like" quality of the Navajo Nation, Canyon de Chelly, Arizona, November 2007. Photo by author.

Image 3. Binding Sky bench exhibit at Sweetmeat, Waterflow, New Mexico, June 2012. Photo by author.

Image 4. Sign discouraging litter on the Navajo Nation (with Tsé Bit'a'í in the distance), July 2014. Photo by author.

Image 5. The view from the bench at Sweetmeat, with power plant in the distance, June 2012. Photo by author.

Image 6. Blackhorse Mitchell and author at the Cortez Culture Center, Cortez, Colorado, July 2010. Photo courtesy of Damien Jones.

Image 7. Roadside memorial near Blackhorse Mitchell's home, Shiprock, New Mexico, July 2014. Photo by author.

CHAPTER FIVE

"We Don't Know What We Become"

If we are to understand a fair part of linguistic change, comprehend the use of language in speech and verbal art, take account of all the varied speech play in which a competent speaker may indulge, and to which he can respond, we must study his real and lively sense of appropriate connection between sound and meaning.

—DELL HYMES (1960: 112)

One summer afternoon in 2010, at a coffee shop in Farmington, New Mexico, I was working with a Navajo consultant on translating some of contemporary Navajo poet Rex Lee Jim's poetry from Navajo into English. My consultant and I were talking about Jim's (1995: 35) use of *hózhóónshchíín* for 'plastic' in a poem. My consultant was particularly amused and satisfied by Jim's use of this word. Here *hózhóón* 'beauty' has been combined with the adjectival enclitic *-shchíín* 'facsimile'. This is not the only term for 'plastic' in Navajo. Both Young and Morgan (1987: 423) and Neundorf (1983: 623) give *tó doo bidééłníní*, literally 'that which is impervious to water', as a form for 'plastic' (see also Peterson and Webster 2013). The turn of phrase was thus particularly salient because a different word could have been used. Some of what my consultant found so amusing about Jim's use of *hózhóónshchíín* was that it evoked a whole host of other terms in *-shchíín* (e.g., *'awééshchíín* 'doll, facsimile of a baby') and that it appeared to be a bit of social commentary about Anglo-Americans, who create "facsimiles of beauty." My consultant had also just heard a report about the manufacture of plasma televisions releasing a little known but potentially dangerous chemical into the environment. Plastic, like the plasma televisions, was an example of, as he said, "fake beauty." He felt the reported problem with plasma televisions was an example of the ways that Anglo-Americans attempt to create "beauty" without really thinking about the ramifications of what they are doing. Plastic was like that as well. Created as a form of "beauty," it has ended up becoming—as Blackhorse Mitchell's poem in the last chapter described—a source of ugliness.

In the previous chapter, I suggested that some Navajo poets used their poetry to call attention to the ugliness (*hóchxǫ'*) in the world and in so doing to attempt to restore *hózhǫ́* (order, beauty, control). In this chapter, I want to look a bit more into that question and turn to poetry written in Navajo. A number of years ago, Hymes (1965) chastised anthropologists and others for relying on overly romantic translations of Native American song-poems. Hymes argued that vocables or so-called nonsense forms that lacked semantic meaning had structural import in the organization of the songs and that rather than be excluded from translations, they needed to be included (see also, on Navajo vocables, Frisbie 1980; McAllester 1980). He went on to state emphatically that in the study of Native American poetry and poetics, "the study of languages is too important to be left solely to linguistics (in any narrow sense of the term), the texts too valuable to be interpreted by any who ignore linguistics" (337). This book has been an extended defense of Hymes's point.

This chapter takes as its point of departure a poem written in Navajo by Rex Lee Jim, which uses the velar fricative [x] as an expressive feature that indicates an affective stance toward the actions and actors in the poem. This affective stance is about "lacking control." The distinction between control and lacking control is important in Navajo (linguistically and culturally). Working backward from this poem, I point to two sets of language-documentation practices in the mid twentieth century, showing how Gladys Reichard recognized the use of the expressive or presentational feature and hence documented it, while Edward Sapir and Harry Hoijer systematically erased the feature from their linguistic description of Navajo. This is reminiscent of missionaries who erased Navajo punning practices, seeing confusion instead of speech play there. In this chapter I look at the use of phonological iconicity and punning as an important component of Navajo verbal art. My goal is not just to translate Jim's poem (though there will be some of that) but rather to discuss the way that Jim uses the expressive device of the velar fricative—along with consonantal rhyme, predicated on punning—to indicate an affective stance toward the actors and actions in the poem. I also want to place this poem within a broader Navajo aesthetic (an aesthetic Jim creatively taps into). I am not, however, offering an interpretation of what Jim meant by this poem. Many Navajos that I have worked with have been reluctant to speculate on the "whys" or "whats" of a given poet's meaning, instead offering an interpretation based on the images evoked by a poem (Webster 2009). In general, Navajo poets should not force an interpretation onto the reader or listener, nor should the listener or reader force an interpretation onto a poet: this is an important principle of what one might term Navajo ethnoliterary criticism and resonates, as I noted earlier, with a wider Navajo ethos of *t'áá bí bee bóholníih* 'it's up to her/him to decide' (see Rushforth and Chisholm 1991). Stated most simply, people should be allowed to make their own decisions, including their own interpretations.

Na'ashchxiidí

The poem that is the focus of this chapter comes from Rex Lee Jim's all-Navajo collection of poetry *saad* (the title means 'word, language'; I follow Jim's practice of not capitalizing the title). The book was published in 1995 by the Princeton Collections of Western Americana. It is important to emphasize that the entire book is in Navajo, including the page numbers and the title page. The poem we are concerned with here—it does not have a title—can be found on page *tádiin dóó bi'ąą tseebíí* 'thirty-eight'. Both Blackhorse Mitchell and I have seen Jim perform this poem on the Navajo Nation (I recorded it on three different occasions). The book is for sale by Jim at his performances, but I have not found it available at other places that sell Navajo books of poetry on the Navajo Nation and in the surrounding area (see Webster 2009). I will also discuss Jim's performance of this poem in Window Rock, Arizona, on July 18, 2001.

I first present the poem and a translation I made in collaboration with Mitchell. I also had the poem translated by other Navajos and will inter-sperse some of their commentary in with the discussion of the translation in the next section.

na'ashchxiidí
bíchxį́į́h
ní'deeshchxidgo
ni'iihchxįįh
chxąą' bee
nániichxaad
(Jim 1995: 38)

the badger's
nose
stretched round*
shitting
with shit
is full

In its brevity and its dense use of sound, this poem is very much like the other poems in *saad* (see Webster 2006b). Indeed, when I interviewed Jim about some of the poems in the book, he told me that "sounds were very important." He also noted that his poetry was "sorta sneaky." Elsewhere, Jim has pointed out the role of what I call sound affinities and phonological iconicity (sounds echoing sounds) in his poetics.[†] The notion of sound affinities owes a debt to Dwight Bolinger's (1940) "word affinities" (actually, I suggest that *sound affinities* is merely a more apt name for the same phenomenon) and phonological iconicity owes a debt to David Samuels's (2001) discussion of Western Apache punning (see also Webster 2009, 2010a).

Translating the Poem or Seeing the Morphemes but Not the Feeling

Of all the chapters in this book, it is in this chapter that I must ask the reader's indulgence concerning linguistics. In what follows, I will be describing in some detail features of the Navajo language. I understand that for many readers this may be quite burdensome, but I believe that understanding the linguistic and ethnopoetic structure of Jim's poem is important for recognizing what is going on in it. That the Navajo language differs from English in rather radical structural ways will, I believe, also be informative for the reader who may not appreciate the kinds of differences that can occur across languages. Navajo and English facilitate different poetic and expressive possibilities.

Here I offer a run-through of the basic morphological components of Jim's poem. The first thing to note about the poem is that each line includes the sound sequence *-chx-*, which can be described as a voiceless palatal affricate (written with <ch> in Navajo orthography) followed by a velar

---

* That is, dilated, stretched into roundness.

† In a video for *Princeton Alumni Weekly*, Jim (2010) describes the role of sound in one of his poems. I will discuss the poems in this video later in the chapter. Jim is not the only Navajo poet to exploit phonological iconicity for poetic purposes.

fricative (written with <x>). The repetition of this sound sequence, or *conso-nant cluster*, from line to line is a form of consonantal rhyme. The consonant cluster is always at the beginning of a verb or noun stem. I should also note that this stem-initial consonant cluster *chx-* is due to the insertion of the velar fricative according to an expressive phonological process that I describe below. All of the forms in this poem that have this consonant cluster can also appear (both in spoken and written discourse) without the *-x-*.* The velar fricative is, in fact, not commonly produced in any of these words.

The first line in the poem, *na'ashchxiidí*, is the nominalized verb form that means something akin to 'badger'.† In a poem that appears earlier in *saad* Jim writes it as *na'ashchiidi*, without the *-x-*. Elsewhere the form is also written *nahashch'idí*. It can be glossed as 'the one who scratches, gropes, paws around' (the word-final *-í* is the nominalizing enclitic that turns the verb phrase into a noun). Like many Navajo names for animals, this form is sometimes recognizable to Navajos as a morphologically complex word (that is, some Navajos can and do segment the form into its constituent mor-phology), while others understand the form as just the conventional word for something akin to 'badger' (that is, the morphology of the word is not readily apparent to them). Indeed, there is some question as to which verb stem is involved in the form used by Jim. There are two likely candidates. First is *-ch'id* 'to paw, scratch', which is the stem conventionally given for the form *nahashch'idí* (see Young and Morgan 1992: 106). However, note that this form has the glottalized (ejective) affricate *-ch'-*, not the plain affri-cate *-ch-*. Another verb stem, which does not have the glottalized affricate, is *-chid*, which Robert Young and William Morgan (1992: 83) describe as relating "to the abrupt movement of the hands in 'grabbing, reaching, touching, placing the hand, sticking the finger, gesturing, releasing.'" It has a related, homophonous verb stem, *-chid*, which describes action that is "'jittery, fidgety' — presumably describing the aimless movements of the subject's hands" (85). Note that this homophonous verb stem seems to indicate a movement of the hands and arms in a "noncontrolled" manner (see Cook and Rice 1989: 28). Note also that Reichard ([1950] 1963: 382)

---

* This is a voiceless velar fricative [x]. There is also a voiced velar fricative, written in Navajo orthography as <gh>, which can also be used as an expressive feature. This *-gh-* alternates with *-x-*. When the expressive feature follows an aspirated alveolar or palatal affricate or a voiceless fricative in the stem-initial position, it is *-x-*; when it follows a nonaspirated alveolar or palatal affricate or voiced fricative, it is *-gh-* (see Young and Morgan 1943: 142; Reichard 1948). Both forms of the feature have the same expressive function. See also Mitchell and Webster 2011.

† For a discussion of this animal's role in Navajo myth see Reichard (1950) 1963.

presents the 'badger' form as <na'actcidi:>, which in the current Navajo orthography would be *na'ashchidii*. Reichard was aware of the glottalized consonants in Navajo and did indicate them (xxxi). That she did not indicate glottalization in this word is, therefore, evidence that it did not occur. Since I have not found examples of the use of the velar fricative after a glottalized affricate, I am operating under the assumption that the form used in Jim's poem, at least, is the one with the plain affricate. I've also wanted to suggest the range of homophones (or potential puns) for this verb stem. In any case, the verb stem is marked with the *si-* perfective prefix and has either the prefix *nahi-* 'one after another' or *na'a-* 'around'. Despite its complex morphology, all the Navajos that I have asked about this form translated it simply as *badger* or *rodent*.

The second line presents fewer uncertainties: *bi-* 'his, her, its' and *-chxíįh* 'nose'. This form is most commonly found without the velar fricative as *bichíįh* 'his, her, its nose'. This is an inalienable noun with a possessive prefix. For the translation, Mitchell achieved the indication of possessive, marked on the noun in the Navajo original, by using the English possessive suffix on *badger* in the first line.

The third line consists of *ní'deeshchxid*, glossed as 'fleshy, thick in a circle' (Young and Morgan 1992: 83), plus what we will call the relative enclitic *-go* (see, however, Mithun 2008). Young and Morgan present the form as *ń'deeshchid*; it is common for the /i/ and the alveolar nasal /n/ to fall together and produce a syllabic /ń/ (see McDonough 2003: 95). The form is based on yet another verb stem with the shape *-chid*. While Young and Morgan (1992: 83) have suggested that this verb stem "relates to the mouth," both Mitchell and the Navajo consultant I mentioned earlier were clear that it related to the mouth and nose. It might be best to think of the stem as relating to both the oral and nasal cavity (perhaps the "snout"). Note that in the form given by Young and Morgan there is no *-x-* indicated. Mitchell translated the form as *stretched round*, describing the nostrils of *na'ashchxiidí*.

The fourth line, *ni'iihchxįįh*, is based on the verb stem *-chąą'* 'to defecate', which can also occur as an independent noun *chąą'* 'defecation'. The form is most likely built with the *si-* perfective preceded by *na'ahi-* 'around'. Mitchell translates it as *shitting*, but in conversations we have had he has also noted that the form has a sense of "shitting around." Another Navajo translated the line as "shits all over." Again, the *-x-* is optional in this form. Young and Morgan do not represent the form with the velar fricative (76).

The fifth line has the noun *chxąą'*—the independent noun mentioned above, with expressive *-x-* inserted—plus *bee* 'with'. Here *bee* is used in an instrumental sense. As in all of the previous lines, the velar fricative is optional. Young and Morgan give the noun stem without *-x-* and gloss it with 'excrement, manure, offal' (75). This is the only line in the poem that has multiple words in it. Both Mitchell and the other Navajo I consulted on the poem translated the form as *shit*.

The sixth and final line has the form *nániichxaad* and this is glossable as 'to be full of food (a person)' (Wall and Morgan [1958] 1994: 119). This form is based on the verb stem *-chaad* 'swell, bulge' (Young and Morgan 1992: 73). Here one finds the prefix *ná-* 'to return to a state, condition, place' plus thematic prefix *ni(i)-*, which is used for 'roundness'. As Young and Morgan explain, this form can be glossed morphologically as 'to swell back up, recover a bulging appearance' or 'to get full eating'. Again, the *-x-* is wholly optional here and is not indicated by Young and Morgan. Mitchell translates this line as merely *is full*. The velar fricative is not commonly produced in any of the words in this poem.

Having worked through the morphology of the poem, I am reminded of a conversation I once had with Rex Lee Jim in early 2001, where I showed him a translation of one of his poems based on the morphology of phrases in it. Jim replied, "You got all the words correct." I understood this to mean that while I could segment Navajo morphology, I had no understanding of what the words actually meant. As Sapir (1929a: 209), discussing what came to be known as linguistic relativity, suggested, "the understanding of a simple poem, for instance, involves not merely understanding of the single words in their average significance, but a full comprehension of the whole life of a community as it is mirrored in the words, or as it is suggested by their overtones." This chapter takes Sapir's insight about the loci of linguistic relativity in poetry seriously. It is, then, to the "overtones" that I now turn.

Expressive Features in Native American Languages

Languages do not merely refer to things in the world (Jakobson 1960). They also, among other things, create felt attachments and attitudinal stances toward their referent by way of expressive features. A discussion of the semantico-referential meaning of a poem, then, is only a partial discussion of it. Sapir ([1915] 1985) presented a fine-grained analysis of the expressive features found in Nootka mythic narratives and also in ordinary stereotyping of the speech patterns of various marked members of Nootka society. Sapir's seminal article noted the creation of affective associations between linguistic forms and people through "consonantal play," both humorous and disparaging, in literary uses of reported speech (181).

In an influential article, Hymes (1979) argued for the expressive role of the voiceless lateral [ɬ] and voiceless alveolar fricative [s] in Takelma mythic discourse. Correcting a position taken by Sapir, Hymes argued that alternation between expressive prefixes in the reported speech of bears expressed varying degrees of social distance from those actors. A prefixed [ɬ], a speech sound linked with Athabaskans, expressed a greater social distance than did the use of a prefixed [s], which was linked with the neighboring (and perhaps distantly linguistically related) Siuslaws. As Hymes (1981) says, such uses of expressive forms were a "choice in use" (69), they were optional forms. The alternation of these expressive forms aided in constructing an affective stance toward the characters. "The *s*- prefix seems somewhat closer in emotional distance, somewhere in the range of diminutive meanings that have to do with condescension, sympathy, even affection on the part of an audience. . . . The [ɬ] prefix seems somewhat greater in emotional distance, somewhere in the range of diminutive meanings that have to do with condescension, perhaps, but also deprecation, disdain, for coarseness and stupidity" (74). Hymes goes on to make a similar claim about the alternation between *wa-*, *a-*, and zero prefixes for bears in Clackamas. In each case, Hymes (2003: 207) showed how careful attention to "presentational" or "expressive" meaning provided insight into the attitudes toward the characters who spoke in such a manner or were named in such a manner. It did not change the semantico-referential meaning of the words, but it changed the affective attitude toward the speaker of those words or the characters that took such forms (see also Hymes 1998: 19–22).

Woodbury (1987: 685) has challenged a received view of the "'double articulation' of language," whereby "syntactic (not phonological) representations receive semantic interpretation, and . . . phonology is a purely formal, interpretive component of grammar." According to this view, phonological units build meaning-bearing morphological, lexical, and syntactic units, but phonology, in and of itself, does not bear meaning. Dani Bird and Toben Mintz (2010: 10) explain this view as follows: "In any particular language, words, new or old, must draw from a stable, small set of nonmeaningful units called phonological units. So in human language the meaningful messages (both sentences and words) are infinite in variety by virtue of the fact that words are produced from a system of combining a finite set of meaningless units." In contrast to this view, the examples from Central Alaskan Yup'ik—from foot cloning to vowel doubling—that Woodbury (1987) is concerned with show the ways that Yup'ik speakers display an affective stance (specifically, "benign, slightly pedantic patience") that bears meaning; that is, "speakers use it to organize and contextualize information and to enhance the expressive value of a line, rather than alter its truth-functionality" (708). Woodbury argues for "meaningful phonological processes" and against any strict division between phonology and meaning-bearing units of language (see also Bolinger 1940 and Jakobson 1960 for other critiques of the received view).

As can be seen, then, expressive features in Native American languages have been a topic of some interest on the part of linguists and linguistic anthropologists, especially in the ethnopoetic tradition (for useful discussions see Sapir [1915] 1985; Reichard 1948; Hymes 1979, 1981, 1996b, 1998, 2003; Toelken and Scott 1981; Tedlock 1983; Berman 1992; Silverstein 1994; J. Hill and Zepeda 1998; Sherzer 2002; Woodbury 1987, 1998; Bunte 2002; Friedrich 2006; Webster 2009; widening the horizon, see also Rumsey 2001, 2007; on issues of expressivity and phonation, J. Hill and Zepeda 1999; Sicoli 2010). To be sure, though, expressive features have not been at the forefront of recent concern with endangered languages (but see Woodbury 1998; Samuels 2004b; Nuckolls 2010; Webster 2010b). There, the concern has been with Indigenous "words for things" and "lost words, lost worlds," that is, loss of the kinds of ecological knowledge that are encoded in the semantic domains (see, for a sampling, Harrison 2007 and Nettle and Romaine 2000; for critiques of this literature see J. Hill 2002; Nevins 2004; Moore 2006; and Moore, Pietikäinen, and Blommaert 2010). Such discussions have been relatively unconcerned with felt attachments to linguistic forms and the expressive features that can evoke such connections.

While it is beyond the scope of this chapter to explain why the uses of expressive features have been largely "neglected" (Nuckolls 2006) in the linguistic literature, I would like to note two relevant points. First, as Samuels (2004b) has noted, many of our modernist visions of languages are based on a "referentialist" view of language, according to which language is understood as being about referring to things in the world. This is, as Richard Bauman and Charles Briggs (2003) have argued, a profoundly modernist language ideology. Expressive features of languages, for example, especially those features based on iconicity (a resemblance of something to someone), have been largely ignored or trivialized because they were deemed "prelinguistic" or "primitive" (see Farnell 1995; Nuckolls 1999; Samuels 2004b; Webster 2009). When a linguistic feature does not contribute to semantico-referential meaning, it violates a basic assumption of Western language ideologies: language = reference. As Bauman and Briggs note, this conflation of language with reference has sometimes amounted to a totalizing language ideology, a *monotelic* view that sees reference as all that languages do or should do (see also Hymes 2000: 334). Punning, expressive features, and poetic language are, in this view, to invoke John Locke's famous phrase, a "cheat and abuse" of language (see Bauman and Briggs 2003: 36).

A second point, related to the first, is that the shift from a relatively phonetic-centered concern with documenting languages to a phonemic view of languages has led to many expressive features simply not being recorded (Hymes 2003; for a critique of "formal" phonology see Port and Leary 2005). As Hymes (2003: 207) explains, this shift from phonetics to phonemics is intimately tied up with concerns about "reference."

> Descriptive linguistics developed on the basis of the kind of contrast that underlies the phonemic principle. Only differences in referential or propositional meaning were addressed. The general term "language" was reduced to that one, basic dimension of language. . . . The phonemic principle led many linguists to omit features of the second sort [expressive meaning] from their recordings of texts from the 1930s onward. Recordings that included nonphonemic features were even thought of as "old fashioned" and of no scientific use.

Hymes goes on to say, "we want to be sure that features that were part of the teller's performance, conveying emphasis and attitude, are represented. . . . In Wishram and Chinookan languages, these features especially include vowel length, shift of stress, and vowel color" (207). The phonemic view had the potential to obscure locally evocative ways of using language. Sapir, to his credit, in his work with Nootka and Takelma, tended to record expressive features because he had not yet decided on the phonemic inventory of a language when he was recording it. Later linguists and linguistic anthropologists would ignore nonphonemic or expressive features because they did not fit a narrow view of "grammar" (see below).

Control in Navajo

Before returning to the velar fricative, I want to first discuss an important distinction in Navajo, both linguistically and culturally, between control and lacking control. I mentioned this distinction above, and also touched on it in the previous chapter in relation to "ugliness." Here I want to suggest some ways that the distinction between controlled and uncontrolled interanimates and resonates through Navajo linguacultural practices. Reichard ([1950] 1963: 5) once noted, "Good then in Navaho dogma is control. Evil is that which is ritually not under control." While I would not go so far as to speak of "dogma," there is an important distinction among some Navajos between things that are "controlled" and things that are "out of control." The anthropological literature on this topic is immense (see Reichard 1944, [1950] 1963; Kluckhohn 1949; Wyman 1970; Witherspoon 1977). Control and lack of control are important components of the meanings of the verb stems *-zhǫ́* 'control, order, beauty, harmony' and *-chxǫ'* 'lack of control, disorder, ugly'. Witherspoon (1977: 44) describes them this way: "*hózhǫ́* may be conceived of as the imposition of form, order, harmony, beauty, and, therefore, good upon the world. When *hóchxǫ'* occurs in one's world, it is as though things have returned to original chaos." Or as he describes them earlier, "*hózhǫ́* is everything that is good, harmonious, orderly, happy, and beautiful. The opposite of *hózhǫ́* is *hóchxǫ'* which, of course, is the evil, the disorderly, and the ugly" (34). As we saw in the last chapter, *hóchxǫ'* is often expressed in Navajo English (a local way of speaking and writing) as *ugly*.

The importance of control is not just relevant to some Navajos culturally. It is a sometimes noted feature of Northern Athabaskan languages that some verb stems fall into pairs distinguished by whether they indicate an agent engaging in an activity in a "controlled" manner or in a "noncontrolled" manner (Scott Rushforth, personal communication, 1996). Eung-Do Cook and Keren Rice (1989: 28) describe the distinction as between doing things in a "careful, humble controlled manner" and things "done less carefully, more quickly." In discussing this distinction in Slave (Northern Athabaskan), Rice (2001: 238) says, "it turns out that the stems, while conveying largely the same information, have a very different sense about them. In one case, the verb embodies a way of carrying out the event that is highly valued culturally—it is humble, polite, and so on. . . . The other verb stem does not embody this; it is not negative in force, but rather ordinary." Cook and Rice (1989: 27) point out that Navajo, too, appears to have a distinction between "controlled" and "noncontrolled" verb stems. They give three examples, which I reproduce here (for the third example, I have added references to the verb stems in Young and Morgan 1992). The first member of each pair is the "controlled" verb stem and the second "noncontrolled."

'ééś	-taał	'move or act with foot'
-k'ą́ą́h	-tlááد	'burn'
-nííh	-chííd	'act with hand, arm'

The stems *-níí̦h* and *-chíí̦d* are listed by Young and Morgan (1992), respectively, as *nii'* (451) and *chid* (83). The latter is found in the first line of the
poem by Rex Lee Jim. Note that it denotes a movement that is not controlled.

The Expressive Work of *-x-* in Navajo

Navajo has an expressive phonological process whereby *-x-* is inserted after
the initial consonant of the stem. In an early paper, Gladys Reichard (1948)
called attention to this expressive device in Navajo. She described it this
way: "a more forceful action, a state exaggerated in size or quantity, or
a pejorative may be expressed by aspirating the voiceless stem initial so
strongly as to form a consonant cluster." She termed the resulting formation an "augmentative" (15). In Reichard's (1951) mammoth and important
grammar of Navajo she listed a number of contrasting pairs of stems where
the addition of "aspiration," as she called it, changed not the semantico-
referential meaning of the words but their expressive implication (for
example, from neutral to pejorative). I present a number of such pairs from
Reichard (1951: 141–42; I have amended the forms to present them as they
are currently written in Navajo orthography and I have added Mitchell's
remarks about some of these forms in parenthesis (see Table 1).

Looking at the table presented, we can readily see that two of the forms
that Jim uses in his poem are also included in Reichard's list: *-chíí̦h* vs.
-chxíí̦h and *chąą'* vs. *chxąą'*.

I would like to make one caveat on Reichard's work before continuing.
While Reichard's work is the first to indicate the importance of this expressive feature in Navajo, she makes a claim that I would like to qualify. As I
noted above, Reichard (1948, 1951) consistently terms this process "aspiration" or "strong aspiration." Reichard's use of this term is misleading.
Aspiration does occur in Navajo, but the insertion of the velar fricative is
not an example of it. I agree with Joyce McDonough (2003: 86, personal
communication, 2010) that the *-x-* is not in fact aspiration but a velar fricative (see also McDonough and Wood 2008).

Reichard was not the only linguist to call attention to the use of this
expressive feature in Navajo, though she was by far the only one to fully
engage the topic. Young and Morgan (1943) in *The Navaho Language* state
that "a depreciative sense is injected by inserting *gh* after an unaspirated,
or *x* after an aspirated consonant. Thus, *są'* 'star'; *sxą'* 'that such and such
star'; *dził* 'mountain'; *dzghił* 'that such and such mountain'; *dząądi* 'here';
dzghąądi 'here' (with an intonation of disgust or displeasure)" (142; in this

Table 1. Expressive Function of Velar Fricative

-tih	'cover, wrap'*	-txih	'protect, conceal'

(*Mitchell does not use the velar fricative in this verb stem.*)

-sał	'move like a feather'	-sxał	'heavy obj[ect] (as person) moves like a feather, gracefully'

(*Mitchell describes the insertion of the velar fricative here as like the description for the "light fall of the first snow on the ground." From conversations with Navajo consultants it appears that the distinction is between something "floating" and [with the -x-] something [heavier] "floating" and "falling."*)

-si	'make numb'	-sxi	'paralyze, deaden'
sǫ'	'star'	sxǫ'	'a fearful star'
-sǫs	'glitter like copper'	-sxǫs	'glitter like a red star'

(*Mitchell describes this as a glittering "deep pink."*)

-tsaaz	'grow big'	-tsxaaz	'grow very large'
-chah (-cha)	'cry'	-chxah (-chxa)	'scream'
chą́ą́'	'manure, excrement, faeces'	chxą́ą́'	'excrement' (vulgar)

(*Mitchell suggested this was not so much "vulgar" as had the sense of 'smelly' and 'nasty'.*)

-chin	'have, exude odor'	-chxin	'have strong odor'
-chį́į́h	'nose'	-chxį́į́h	'muzzle'
-chǫ'	'bad'	-chxǫ'	'wicked, essentially bad'
-łaał	'hate'	-łxaał	'be exasperated'

* These are Reichard's glossings and should not be understood as "literal" translations. Reichard is attempting to capture the sense implied in the "augmentative." Elsewhere, Reichard (1944) was critical of those who would attempt literal translations from Navajo into English. Having worked with Navajo now for over a decade, I share her caution.

quotation and those that follow I have regularized the punctuation and formatting of Navajo forms and English glosses). Later, in their own mammoth
dictionary, they write, "*h* used as a depreciative-augmentive in certain stems
is written *x*, as in *łitsxo* 'orange' (*łitso* 'yellow'), *t'áá 'ałtsxo* 'absolutely all'
(*t'áá 'ałtso* 'all'), *hółchxon* 'the place stinks' (*hółchon* 'the place stinks' —
less emphatic)" (1987: xiv). Mitchell has glossed *łitsxo* as 'dirty yellow' (see
also Landar, Ervin, and Horowitz 1960: 381–82). Young and Morgan (1992)
also note that a number of stems seem to "occur more frequently" with the
-x- form. For example, the verb stem *-chǫ'* 'bad, ugly, sulk, dirty, filthy'
"occur[s] most frequently in intensive form, with *-x-* (*chxǫ'* in lieu of *chǫ'*)"
(96). Likewise, the verb stem *-tsxas* 'whip, lash' seems to always occur with
the *-x-* (592; Reichard 1948: 16). The verb stem *-chosh* 'rumpled, disheveled, bushy' also "often appears in intensive form as *chxosh*" (Young and
Morgan 1992: 95). I have given these verb stems (*-chxǫ'*, *-tsxas*, *-chxosh*)
because they occur in other poems in Jim's *saad* always with the *-x-*.

From the above research and from my own investigation we can see
that the expressive velar fricative (both the voiceless and voiced forms) is
inserted after the initial consonant (either a coronal fricative or a coronal
affricate) of a stem (noun or verb); *-x-* after an aspirated or voiceless coronal
fricative and *-gh-* after an unaspirated or voiced coronal fricative. The insertion of the expressive feature does not work in all Navajo words. Mitchell,
for example, suggested that *-tih* 'cover, wrap', *tó* 'water', and *'awéé* 'baby'
could not take the velar fricative. In each case, the form violated the pho-
notactics described above.*

It seems clear that the use of the velar fricative indicates an affective
stance. The discussions by Reichard and by Young and Morgan describe
that stance as variously functioning to indicate an "augmentative," a "pejorative," an "intensive," or a "depreciative." Here I wish to suggest a slightly
different interpretation and this will lead us back to the poem by Jim. First,
Mitchell, in describing what the *-x-* does, has said that it is "very descriptive" (that is, it is evocative of certain characteristics). Second, when distinguishing the sense of the expressive form in minimal pairs, Mitchell often

---

* In Reichard's (1951: 19) grammar she notes that there is a regular allophonic process that
velarizes and rounds the aspiration of [t] before /o/. There is no pejorative or augmentative
sense to this process. McDonough and Wood (2008), based on spectrograph analysis, describe
/t/ (along with /k/) as a complex stop and not a simplex stop. They argue specifically that
"the *t* and *k* phonemes are phonemic as well as phonetic heterorganic affricates /tx/ and /kx/"
(441; see also Young and Morgan 1987: xv). The velar fricative, then, is already present in
the phoneme /t/ and is not used for expressive purposes.

came back to the terms "too much," "dirty," "ugly," "awful," and "an extra description" relative to the unmarked form. Let us look at some examples here. In one case, Mitchell noted that "the word *nizeedi* [your opposite-sex cousin] is a clean-cut description of a cousin and if the *x* falls in there like *nizgheedi* would indicate the two [cousins] had been sleeping together or sharing blankets." Here the moral force of the use of the velar fricative seems clear. The difference between *chin* and *chxin* is the difference between "dirt" and "dirt with grease, really dirty." The difference between *bichąą'* and *bichxąą'* was the difference between "just a blend of shit" and "very dirty and nasty" shit that "smells awful."

I would now suggest that the distinction discussed above between controlled and noncontrolled, which is both culturally salient and linguistically salient for some Navajos, is relevant to an interpretation of the expressive function of -*x*-. First, the affective stance of augmentative or pejorative toward such-and-such may be coupled with the view that such-and-such is lacking in control (that is, *hóchxǫ'*). Things that are "too much," "nasty," "ugly," or "disorderly" are things that may well lack control and therefore need to be returned (through ritual) to order or control (Toelken and Scott 1981: 86). The very kinds of things, then, that would be depreciated, pejorated, or augmented can also sometimes be understood as things that would lack control. For example, *nizgheedi* does not so much suggest that the cousin is "dirty" as indicate that the cousin is behaving in a manner that lacks control. The use of the velar fricative may, then, imply an affective stance, in addition to augmentative or pejorative, that something also lacks control.

Second, note that the verb stems -*ch(x)ǫ'* 'ugly, disorderly, bad, pout', -*ts(x)as* 'whip', and -*ch(x)osh* 'rumpled, disheveled' are almost always produced with the velar fricative rather than without. This seems likely because they are all things that are "disorderly" or "out of control." Mitchell explained, for the form *nichxǫ́'í* 'it is ugly', that "we most always use *x* when we say that" (this is the same verb stem -*chxǫ'*). Indeed, -*chxǫ'* is the prototypical verb stem for describing things that are "ugly" or "disorderly," things, that is, that need to be brought back into control or order or balance or *hózhǫ́*. Likewise, both a whiplike action and disheveled hair, for example, are things that are also "disorderly" and "out of control" or, again, in Navajo English, things that are ugly. In fact, Young and Morgan (1992: 592) describe the verb stem -*tsxas* in the following manner: "act in a violent whipping-lashing manner, whip, strike with a slender flexible object, slam (as in slamming a door, or slamming down an object)."

There is, then, a potentially dual association with the use of the velar fricative: (1) using the velar fricative for things that are augmented or pejorated may imply that they are also out of control, and (2) the use of the velar fricative in the consonant cluster -*chx*-, as in Jim's poem, can evoke the verb stem -*chxǫ'* 'ugly, out of control, disorderly'. I turn to this second point next. Before I return to the poem, I would like to observe, recalling a point made by Hymes (2003) above, that the use of -*x*- as an expressive feature, which does not change semantico-referential meaning, meant that the form could also be ignored by linguists. Reichard (1948: 17) makes this point as well, in reviewing previous collections of Navajo textual materials. "The Sapir-Hoijer [1942] texts do not differentiate the regular forms from the augmentatives because they treat both types of initial as a single phoneme." In Harry Hoijer's (1974) *A Navajo Lexicon*, for example, he never includes the -*x*- on any of the verb stems noted above. Thus, the verb stems are -*chǫ'* 'bad, ugly, ill-natured, evil' (220), -*chosh* 'unevenly cut, ragged' (219), and -*tsas* 'whip' (182) (I have updated Hoijer's orthography to match the current Navajo orthography). Indeed, Hoijer also misses the distinction between *łitso* 'yellow' (186) and *łitsxo*, conventionally glossed as 'orange' but also with a sense of 'nasty yellow' or 'dirty yellow'. Thinking the expressive -*x*- unimportant because it did not contribute to the semantico-referential meaning of a lexical item, he did not include it in his lexicon. Hoijer (Sapir and Hoijer 1967) goes so far as to dismiss Reichard's view concerning the use of -*x*- to indicate "augmentative" or a "pejorative" sense. He claims that it is a "nondistinctive feature" and can therefore be excluded from the serious work of describing Navajo morphology and phonology (7).* Leonard Faltz (1998), in an insightful discussion of the Navajo verb, spends a good deal of time discussing the verb stem -*cha* 'cry' without noting that there is an optional expressive form -*chxa* 'scream, cry without control, wail' (see Reichard 1951: 142). Credit, then, must be given to Reichard, Morgan, and Young for recognizing the expressive work that the velar fricative did and for including it in their grammars and dictionaries. Not every linguist did.

---

* The book (Sapir and Hoijer 1967) is based on Sapir's data, but Hoijer is the author of much of the narrative discussion in the book (1). I am struck by the fact that Hoijer is responding only to the claims of Reichard and not to the similar claims made by Robert Young and William Morgan (1943, a book Hoijer was aware of: 124). Hoijer goes so far as to state, "it is probable that the contrasts Reichard notes are not regular grammatical processes but are instead the result of an emphasis in speaking by reason of emotional context" (7). This statement utterly misses the pejorative and depreciative sense the expressive feature can have and ignores that the velar fricative is quite common and regular in certain verb stems like -*chxǫ'*. Hoijer's discussion of Reichard's work echoes the dismissal of such work described by Hymes (2003; see above). For a discussion of some of the dynamics between Hoijer and Reichard see Falk 1999.

-x- Marks the Spot

As a first approximation of a Navajo ethnopoetics concerned with ethnoliterary criticism, I would like to suggest that the expressive use of *-x-* in Jim's poem resonates or echoes with the *-x-* that is normally found in expressions like *nichxǫ́'í* 'it is ugly' or *hóchxǫ'* 'ugliness'. I find this most likely because Jim not only repeats the sound *-x-* throughout the poem but in fact creates a consonantal rhyme by way of the repetition of the consonant cluster *-chx-*. This is, of course, the very consonant cluster found in the verb stem *-chxǫ'*. The velar fricative, as noted above, resonates across a number of lexical items, especially those more prototypically found with the velar fricative, like *hóchxǫ'*. Jim highlights this sound affinity or phonological iconicity even more by repeating the consonant cluster *-chx-* throughout the poem. Here phonological iconicity is a resemblance between words or consonant clusters, where sounds echo off of each other. As I discuss later in this chapter, such expressive and poetic features based on phonological iconicity—from puns to poetry—are much appreciated by some Navajo (see Webster 2009, 2010a). Jim's use of the velar fricative is a richly layered and textured poetic accomplishment. To make this point, let us go through the poem adding in comments that Mitchell made about the various forms. This will be supplemented by comments that I have elicited from other Navajos about this poem. I rely on Mitchell's discussion for a number of reasons. First, like Jim, Mitchell is a poet. Second, like Jim, Mitchell is also a medicine man (though they do not do the same chantway). Third, like Jim, Mitchell has spent a fair amount of time thinking about the Navajo language. Fourth, Jim and Mitchell have known each other for many years. To summarize my argument here, in each line of the poem, the expressive consonant cluster is *-chx-*, a cluster that iconically evokes the stem *-chxǫ'* through phonological similarity and thus suggests that that stem's lexical meaning of lack of control applies. To make this point, let us go back through the poem, this time adding in comments that Mitchell made about the various forms.

  The introduction of *na'ashchxiidí* 'badger' with the velar fricative indicates a pejorative affective stance toward this character. As Mitchell noted, without the *-x-* this might be a 'badger' from a storybook or Disney DVD, "these animal characters in those movies, there is no ugliness, it's nice and clean movies." But with the *-x-* there is a pejorative sense and, also, a sense of 'badger' being out of place, ugly, and uncontrolled. First, it is possible, as I argued above, that the verb stem here is *-chid* 'to move hands and arms in a noncontrolled manner'. Second, the addition of the *-x-* in conjunction with *-ch-* suggests, because it evokes the *-chx-* sound in *hóchxǫ'*, that not only are the hands, arms, or paws moving in a noncontrolled manner, but they are moving in an "uncontrolled" manner. 'Badger' lacks control. Behaving (including speaking) in a controlled manner, as has been widely noted in the literature, is a basic tenet of Navajo philosophy (Witherspoon 1977; see also Rushforth and Chisholm 1991: 146–48). Reichard (1951: 370) makes the association between what she sees as *h* (aspiration) and *x* (a velar fricative) being out of control in the following passage: "Since x-speaking is related to the augmentation and exaggerated emphasis . . . , it may be that the Navaho consider those persons who exaggerate the articulation of *h* or *x* as 'affected' or 'raving.'" When a speaker overuses the velar fricative, it may suggest that the speaker is "raving" and out of control. This is another potential resonance for the use of the velar fricative in this poem.

Let us turn to the second line, *bichxį́į́h* 'its nose'. Note that Reichard (1951: 142) translated *-chxį́į́h* as 'muzzle'. In my conversations with Mitchell, he has variously tried to explain the expressive work done by *-x-* by lexicalizing it into English. Mitchell has used terms like "big nose," "fat nose," "dried and cracked," and "ugly nose" to describe the expressive quality of the line *bichxį́į́h*. Another Navajo that I have worked with on this poem suggested "protrusion." The velar fricative expresses a pejorative stance toward 'badger's' nose, while the consonant cluster *-chx-* evokes— through phonological iconicity with the verb stem *-chxǫ'*—an out-of-controlness or ugliness. The character *na'ashchxiidí* is uncontrolled both in behavior and appearance.

The third line, *ní'deeshchxidgo*, which Mitchell translated as *stretched round*, was described by Mitchell as follows: "its nose is widened out," "its nostrils, horrible looking," "the rim of its nose is open wide," and "it's expanding its nose, getting big." It seems that *na'ashchxiidí*'s nostrils are flaring in a "horrible," uncontrolled manner. The behavior of 'badger' here is uncontrolled and "ugly" (that is, *hochxǫ'*).

The next line—*ni'iihchxįįh*—suggests that 'badger' is taking a "nasty shit." It is a "shit" that "smells awful." It might be the case that 'badger' has lost control of his bowel movement and has become incontinent. This seems suggested, anyway, by Mitchell's comment that the form has a sense of "shitting around" and another Navajo's suggestion, "shits all over." In any case, it is a vile shit that 'badger' is taking. This is, of course, affirmed in the fifth line. Here we find *chxąą' bee* and as noted above the use of the *-x-* here indicates that 'badger's' defecation is "too much," "like you filled up the toilet bowl," "dirty," "nasty," and "smells awful."

This brings us to the final line: *nániichxaad* 'becomes full (bulges or swells) with food' or as Mitchell translates it, *is full*. Mitchell has described the use of the -*x*- here as indicating that 'badger' "overate," "ate till it was too full," "its belly became too round," "ate till they became ugly with a round belly hanging out," and "it ate more than it needs." As Mitchell further noted, "we shouldn't overeat, we shouldn't have a round stomach." The velar fricative here indicates an affective stance that is both augmentative and pejorative. Thus, the use of the -*x*- in conjunction with -*ch*- seems to indicate that 'badger' ate in an uncontrolled manner; that it ate too much, much more than it needed. Note also that the vowels that follow the consonant cluster in the six lines of this poem transition from high front /i/ (*na'ashchxiidí* and the subsequent three lines) to low central /a/ (the final two lines). In producing these vowels, the mouth physically gets more open, larger and rounder, as one reads down the poem. The mouth thus replicates—iconically—the very fullness of *nániichxaad*. Indeed, comparing *nániichxaad* to *náníchid* 'swelling goes down', for example, we sense the synesthetic sound symbolism according to which high front vowels like /i/ are associated with smallness and more open (low central or back) vowels are associated with largeness (see Webster 2009: 56). The use of the consonantal rhyme of -*chx*- in each line foregrounds that sound and suggests—through phonological iconicity—a felt connection with the verb stem -*chǫ'*.

While Mitchell stressed that each listener of this poem would get "a different image, a different picture" and that Jim was "creating a descriptive picture" and "playing around with words" in this poem, he did note that, for him, the poem suggested that "we don't think about what we are doing, we don't know what we become." *Na'ashchxiidí* is not behaving in a proper manner and according to Mitchell the -*x*- seems to add the view that 'badger' does not "think about what it is doing." 'Badger' is not paying attention to what it is doing to itself. 'Badger' is out of control: eating too much and eating its own vile shit. It is, quite literally "full of shit." For Mitchell and now for me, this poem seems to suggest that some people are not paying attention to what they are doing to themselves. They are, like 'badger', acting "out of control" and doing "ugly" things.

This poem, written as it is in Navajo, has as its audience Navajos. One Navajo poet who writes in Navajo (not Jim) has told me that his poetry is meant to encourage both non-Navajos and Navajos who do not know Navajo to learn Navajo (he has been reluctant to have me publish translations of his work for that reason); but that vision seems both radical (it was not a perspective I often heard) and utopian right now. Poetry in Navajo is still primarily for Navajos. Literacy in Navajo, however, is still relatively restricted among Navajos (see Spolsky 2002; Benally and Viri 2005; Webster 2009).

Thus, most Navajos come to this poem not as a text artifact but as an oral performance. Mitchell has pointed out that Jim does not always pronounce the velar fricative in the first line when he performs the poem, though all subsequent lines do include the expressive feature. The first line identifies 'badger' and the subsequent lines describe its actions. In such performances of the poem, then, it would appear that it is not 'badger' who is out of control, only its actions. Note that when one reads the poem on the page, the -x- is always present/available. In performance, it is optional. When I have seen Jim perform this poem, most notably in July 2001 in Window Rock to an audience of primarily Navajos (including Mitchell), Navajos in the audience laughed during it.* There is, indeed, something absurd about 'badger' acting in such an uncontrolled manner, becoming satiated from its own shit, its nostrils flaring. Here it is useful to remember, as Toelken and Scott (1981: 86) suggest, that for some Navajos, "any kind of extreme like . . . gluttony . . . is considered the kind of weakness that must be cured by ceremony, and is often in the meantime subject to laughter." Thus, it also appears that Jim is encouraging Navajos to think about their own actions, their own behavior—to reflect on the possibility that they too are acting without thinking, letting their bellies get too large; that, in Mitchell's words, "we don't know what we become."

Saad Aheełt'éego Diits'a'

Having provided the context for documenting the expressive use of the velar fricative in Navajo and a way to listen to Jim's poem, I now want to provide some ethnographic context for the poetic use of phonological iconicity and sound affinities in Jim's poem. We can broadly define this aesthetic practice as punning, or what some Navajos call *saad aheełt'éego diits'a'* 'words that resemble each other by sound'. As the Navajo form suggests, punning is based on homophony or phonological iconicity, where words sound alike. It has long been noted that among Navajos punning is a particularly appreciated way of speaking and form of verbal art (see Sapir 1932; W. W. Hill

---

* Because the poem was performed at Window Rock, which is the capital of the Navajo Nation, more than one Navajo has suggested that it evoked not just an image of Navajos who do not pay attention to what they are doing to themselves but also, specifically, an image of Navajo politics and politicians. The irony that Jim is now vice president of the Navajo Nation is not lost on Mitchell or other Navajos that Mitchell and I have discussed this poem with.

1943; Kluckhohn and Leighton 1962; Cisneros et al. 2006; Webster 2009, 2010a, b; for comparative purposes see Liebe-Harkort 1979; Samuels 2001, 2004a). Elsewhere (Webster 2009, 2010a), I have described the punning practices of a number of Navajo poets and nonpoets alike. Rather than give a series of Navajo puns, here I would like to discuss one interlingual pun in particular that speaks to the ways that Navajo verbal art based on phonolog-ical iconicity can be erased by a Western fixation on semantico-referential meanings. I will then provide two further examples of Jim using punning in his poetry and an example from the work of Luci Tapahonso as well.

One day in April 2001, a Navajo consultant and I are driving across the Navajo Nation. We drive past several signs for a Christian revival meeting. My Navajo companion asks me why Anglo-Christians, especially mission-aries, are overly focused on trees. I am at a loss for a response. My Navajo consultant then states that Anglo-Christians are always talking about *gad* 'juniper tree, cedar tree'. Here the pun arises from the homophony between *gad* and *God* [gáad]. This is an interlingual pun (Webster 2010a). Interlin-gual puns, puns that challenge the fixity of the boundaries of languages, are, following Kathryn Woolard (1998), bivalent, that is, they potentially sit uneasily in two linguistic codes. Note that the quickness of puns—their now-you-see-it-now-you-don't quality—is rooted in the always-present possibility of misrecognizing a pun as not a pun (on "quickness" see Calvino 1988). The interlingual punning by Navajos that I described in chapter 1, in the context of the boarding-school recitation of the Pledge of Allegiance, was predicated precisely on the same bivalency, the possibility of mis-recognizing Navajo as English. Navajos took the chance that teachers and matrons would hear not a pun but acquiescence.

Navajo linguist Ellavina Perkins (personal communication, 2009) has told me that the pun between *gad* and *God* has been around "for a while." Indeed, in Ethel Wallis's (1968) biography of the Protestant missionary linguist Faye Edgerton, we find Wallis claiming that some Navajos were "puzzled" by God's name, thinking the term was either *gad* 'juniper tree, cedar tree' (Wallis identifies it as a "cedar tree") or the onomatopoeic *gaagi* (*gáagii*) 'crow'. Indeed, Wallis claims that "when Christmas came and a tall cedar tree was gaily decorated and set in front of the church, The People [Navajos] concluded he [God] must be a plant" (6). For the Protestant mis-sionaries, the Navajos are unrepentant "literalists." Note that the interlingual pun is most decidedly not meant to be taken "literally." It works because of phonological iconicity, not literalism. It is verbal play based on sound that subverts semantic meanings as stable.

I would argue that Wallis's account betrays the missionaries' hyperfixation with reference and literalism (see Samuels 2006; Nevins 2010). Indeed, Wallis (1968: 6) notes that the "native" Navajo term for 'God' had too many "pagan" connotations. As it happens, the "native" term for 'God' that Wallis is talking about is *Diyin 'Ayói 'Át'éii* (*diyin* 'holy', *'ayói* 'exceedingly', *'át'éii* 'that which is'), which was actually coined by Catholic missionaries in consultation with Navajos (Bodo 1998: 4). It is an early example of a neologism. The term is "native" only insofar as it is in Navajo. Perhaps the "paganism" the Protestant biographer Wallis was alluding to was the "paganism" of Catholicism?

Be that as it may, I am suspicious of the supposed confusion on Navajos' part about "God" being a "tree"; I doubt that it is the straightforward confusion Wallis describes it as. From my experiences, it seems more likely to be an instance of playful punning and of putting naïve missionaries on. We can think of such forms of punning as mischievous grammars. Navajos that I know enjoy the straight-faced put-on, testing outsiders' threshold of gullibility. Like the Anglo anthropologists described by Américo Paredes (1977), who took Mexican American put-ons as straightforward description because they matched certain (negative) received assumptions about those Mexican Americans, the missionaries may have misrecognized speech play as straightforward confusion on the part of Navajos because it fit their expectations of Navajos being "primitive" and "childlike." The possibility that Navajos might have been playfully challenging the missionaries' assertions of authority and knowledge seems to have been utterly missed. Indeed, Navajo verbal art, based on phonological iconicity, is erased by a Western fascination and obsession with literalism.

As noted above, these punning practices, based on phonological iconicity, can also be found in contemporary written Navajo poetry. Both Laura Tohe and Luci Tapahonso have used homophony and punning in their poetry (Webster 2009: 211–12). Jim uses this poetic device in other poems besides the one discussed above. For example, in the following poem, also from *saad*, the first word can be heard at least two different ways, which creates a complex understanding of the poem (see Webster 2006b):

na'asts'ǫǫsí
ts'ǫǫs, ts'ǫǫs
yiits'a'go
iíts'ǫ́ǫ́z
(Jim 1995: 37)

mouse
suck, suck
sounding
kiss
(Webster 2006b: 39)

The first line, *na'asts'ǫǫsí*, is the conventional term in Navajo for 'mouse'. It can be morphologically analyzed as 'the one who goes about sucking'. It is based on the ideophonic (sound-symbolic) verb stem *-ts'ǫǫs* 'to suck, to kiss'. Not all Navajos I have spoken with, however, have been able to analyze it into its constituent parts. The independent ideophone is then used in reduplicated form in line 2 of the poem. The third line's use of the verb of sounding *yiits'a'* (plus the relative enclitic *-go*) is the conventional way to acknowledge that what has just been said is an ideophone (see Webster 2009). That line is also implicated in the consonance—the repeated use of /ts'/—that tumbles through the poem. The last line is semantically ambiguous. It can mean something akin to either 'kiss', 'suck', or 'perform a sucking ceremony'. The sucking ceremony is a curative ritual in traditional Navajo beliefs where a Navajo medicine man ritually sucks out an object that is causing harm to a patient.

Now the first line—*na'asts'ǫǫsí*—is homophonous with *náá'ásts'ǫǫs* 'to perform a sucking ceremony again' (semiliterative *náá-* 'again' + *'asts'ǫǫs* 'to suck, to kiss, to perform a sucking ceremony'). Given, as Jim explained to me in June 2001, that the mouse is an "omen of evil, the spirit of death" in "traditional" Navajo beliefs, and is now associated with the deadly hantavirus, the poem—through the initial homophony—takes on a rather ominous reading. Another way to translate the poem, then, is:

sucking again
suck, suck
sounding
a sucking ceremony is performed

There is, actually, yet another reading of this poem—a reading that led one Navajo teacher I know to not use this poem in her class because she was concerned about what some parents might say. Indeed, one Navajo consultant, with whom I was discussing some of Jim's poetry in a coffee shop in Farmington in 2008, made the following commentary:

This is one another prurient
ya know
so ya know the whole realm of observation
within the Navajo was very open
but ya know [looks around coffee shop]
everything got kinda strange after a while
NOW we're very sensitive

The coffee shop where we were conversing was filled with Anglo costum-
ers. My consultant appeared to be the only Navajo in the place. Here he
nicely encapsulated the history of Anglo-Navajo relations with the phrase
"everything got kinda strange after a while." And it is this sensitivity that
the Navajo teacher that I spoke with regarding Jim's poetry was concerned
about. It is sensitivity to the reactions of potential non-Navajo overhearers
that I will return to in the conclusion of this book.

Jim (2010) describes how another poem, which he wrote for the 250th-
anniversary celebration of Princeton University (Jim is an alum), plays with
the homophony or phonological iconicity between *ni* 'you' and *ni'* 'earth'.
Navajo poet Sherwin Bitsui has told me that one of the reasons he enjoys
Jim's poetry is because it is "ambiguous." The punning provides multiple
potential ways of imagining a poem, rather than forcing a singular interpretation. Punning is an important feature of Navajo poetics and ways of
speaking. It can be found in everyday conversations and in the poetry of
contemporary Navajo poets. Such poetic practices are based on phonological iconicity and not on a narrow semantico-referentialist view of language.

Jim is not the only poet to use punning in this way. Here we can look
briefly at the work of Luci Tapahonso. In the final stanza of Tapahonso's
(2008: 70) poem "Náneeskaadí" (which means 'tortilla' or 'the one that was
patted into a circle') there is a rumination that plays on the phonological
iconicity and semantic linking between *na'* 'here' and *ná(-)*, a form discussed below. Here is the final stanza.

"Na'. Here." As in "Na' k'ad yiłwoł. Here, now go run along."
"Ná. For you."
"Díí na'iishłaa. I made this for you."
"Na', díí ná iishłaa. Here, I made this for you."
"Ná 'ahéésh kad. I slapped this dough into shape for you."
"Díí náníínsííł kaad. This warm circle of dough is spread out for you."
"K'ad la'. There. Łikanish? Is it good?"
(Tapahonso 2008: 70)

Ná as an independent form has a sense of 'for you', as in the second line of the poem. *Ná-* as a prefix can mean, among other things, 'around in a circle', 'up', and something to do with 'smoke'. *Ná-* is also the sound that begins the word for 'tortilla', *náneeskaadí*, which supplies the poem's title—though the prefix there appears to be in fact *náni-* 'into a circle' or 'repeatedly do', which becomes *nánee-*. The word can be parsed as *nánee-* + the *si-* perfective (here reduced to *s-*) + the very productive (and according to some Navajo consultants onomatopoeic) verb stem *-kaad* 'to slap, to pat, to extend, to spread out, flatness, space' and the nominalizing enclitic *-í*. In the poem, Tapahonso appears to evoke the sense of *ná* 'for you' within *náneeskaadí* through the homophony between *ná* and *ná-*. One makes tortillas *for someone* (in the poem, the narrator's husband). This is similar to the felt echo, discussed in chapter 1, between *nihi-* 'our' and *nihi-* the terminative prefix.

The use of punning also resonates with the Navajo ethos of *t'áá bí bee bóholnííh* 'it's up to her/him to decide' described at the beginning of this chapter. As Lamphere (1977: 38–41) notes, this is an expression of Navajo views on autonomy. Individuals have the right to make their own decisions. Puns, like the "indirect" forms of requests Lamphere describes (57), reinforce an individual's autonomy by relying on "ambiguity." In form, then, rather than forcing a singular interpretation, they act as an invitation into imaginative processes. As some Navajos have indicated to me, overtly explaining something implies the listener does not have the proper mental capacity to discern something on their own. It is an infringement of the autonomy of the listener, with the added assumption that the listener is not capable of imagining autonomously. Puns are displays of verbal dexterity, but also invitations issued to the imaginative capacities of the listener/reader.

Finally, there is a sense among some Navajos that the creativity and strength found in contemporary poetry that is written and performed in Navajo should be understood as a *refinding* of prior utterances and forms—forms and utterances that were "put down" by the deities for Navajos to use. Like sacred mountains, the Navajo language is part of a larger category of *diné bá niilyáii* 'things that were created/set down for the Navajo'. In this view, the Navajo language is a "living language" or *saad niilyá*, to be treated with respect (see Peterson and Webster 2013). "Poems," as Jim explained to me, "grow just like people and in that situation the language becomes a way to explore, to discover, to create, to celebrate, and ultimately to live." I might add that Jim does not claim to consciously come up with all of the associations that are to be found in what he writes. As Jim explained to me in February 2001 (RLJ = Rex Lee Jim; AKW = Anthony K. Webster):

RLJ: Do I think through all these things I'm talking about when I write? Absolutely not. [laughter] It's more than enough to keep me from writing.

AKW: When do they come to you? After you've written it?

RLJ: When you ask me the questions. [laughter] No, I think they are all at play at a certain level that you're not aware of, but later on when you written it, you think about it, "yeah, I know and this is why I'm doing it" and then you say, "oh okay, to make it a little bit more satirical, or bit more strong, or more political, or whatever, and then I'm going change this word so it connect with this specific, this other set of stories."

Conclusions

In this chapter, I have attempted to give an interpretation of the use of the expressive feature -*x*- in a poem written in Navajo by Rex Lee Jim. The first thing to note is that the -*x*- is an expressive option. The words with the velar fricative are unmarked Navajo words without it. The use of the expressive feature is a creative and poetic choice by Jim.* I believe that in making that choice, Jim is suggesting something about the ways to understand this poem. I have argued that the -*x*- indicates an affective stance toward the character and actions depicted in the poem. This stance is reinforced by the repeated use of -*x*-, not alone but in combination with -*ch*-, creating a consonant cluster that is phonologically iconic with the consonant cluster in *hóchxǫ'* 'ugly, disorderly, out of control'. The affective stance that emerges in this poem, then, is not just "augmentative" or "depreciative," it expresses the attitude that 'badger' lacks control over its actions. 'Badger' is not paying attention to what it is doing. The distinction between control and lack of control is important in Navajo, both linguistically, in that there are verb stems that differentiate between doing something in a "controlled" manner and in a "noncontrolled" manner, and culturally, in that a premium is placed on acting in a controlled manner and much ritual is associated with restoring order to things that are disorderly (see Reichard [1950] 1963; Witherspoon

---

* I would note that this Navajo expressive device is an example of what Woodbury (1998) calls a "form-dependent expression." For a comparable discussion of an expressive feature found in poetry (here Gaelic poetry) and the importance of such features to local expressive practices see Dorian 2002.

1977). I would note, however, that this is one interpretation of the poem, developed in conversations between Mitchell and myself. Neither of us would presume to argue that it is the only interpretation. Also, while I have focused on one poem, Jim also uses the optional velar fricative in other poems in *saad* (1995) as well as in his other books of poetry (1989, 1998). I do not want to get into a discussion of these poems here, but it appears to me that Jim is using the velar fricative in them for similar expressive purposes.* When one reads or hears any poem in Navajo by Jim, I would suggest—echoing Jim—that it is important to be attentive to what sounds are highlighted in that poem; and to listen, then, for what other words those sounds may evoke. Mitchell's command of Navajo and his own interest in the importance of the sounds of the language are, obviously, the crucial component for the interpretation presented here. I would add that this discussion of the poetic use of the velar fricative and consonantal rhyme and of its interpretation by Mitchell suggests the creative agency both in the production and reception of poetic forms (see Kroskrity 2010). This is at the heart of a Navajo ethnoliterary criticism.

I also suggested that some linguists and linguistic anthropologists (among others) have not been overly concerned with the expressive features of languages. In fact, there has been a tendency to ignore such features because they do not aid "semantico-referential" meaning. We saw, for example, that Hoijer (1974; Sapir and Hoijer 1967) did not indicate the velar fricative even in verb stems where the -*x*- always occurs (-*tsxas*) or almost always occurs (-*chxą'*). An examination of Sapir and Hoijer's (1942) texts for evidence of the uses of the velar fricative would be misleading at best, because Sapir and Hoijer did not record that feature in their texts. Imagine, as is sometimes the case, that those texts were the only evidence of an Indigenous language in use. Such texts would then reproduce a Western fascination with reference at the expense of local feelingfully expressive features. The kind of ethnopoetic work that Hymes (1979) developed based on Sapir's Takelma materials is here impossible. Sapir and Hoijer (1942) erased the expressive use of the velar fricative. That is an ongoing tendency in Navajo-language materials. The use of -*x*- as an expressive feature indicating "augmentation," "intensity," or "depreciation" is not directly discussed in Irvy

---

* I also note that Luci Tapahonso (1987: 31) uses the form *nachxąągo* 'pouting' in one of her poems. This verb stem -*chxą'* 'bad, ugly, spoil, pout', which also occurs in the poetry of Jim (1995: 41), normally occurs with the velar fricative, as discussed above. To pout in the Navajo sense is to show a lack of control.

Goossen's (1995) *Diné Bizaad: Speak, Read, Write Navajo* (but there is at least an implicit suggestion that -*x*- indicates "intensity": xiv). Likewise, there appears to be no explicit discussion of the use of -*x*- as an expressive feature in Evangeline Parsons Yazzie and Margaret Speas's (2007) *Diné Bizaad Bínáhoo'aah: Rediscovering the Navajo Language*. Both of these are important Navajo-language textbooks, but neither discusses the use of the velar fricative as an expressive feature in Navajo. Mitchell, who has been a longtime Navajo-language instructor, has told me that he does not get to -*x*- when he is teaching Navajo. One Navajo-language teacher with whom I discussed some of Jim's poetry in 2001 went so far as to say that Jim had misspelled some of the words with the velar fricative. Kroskrity (2012a: 151) describes such practices and orientations toward narrative forms as "narrative discriminations" and uses this phrase to evoke the dual force of aesthetics and the political (see also Bourdieu 1986). Such narrative discriminations are clearly not only an aesthetic consideration but also fully implicated in the politics of Western educational regimes of knowledge that devalue presentational forms in favor of the banally semantico-referential (see K. Basso 1991: 74).

I also placed Jim's use of phonological iconicity in this poem within a larger context of Navajo ways of speaking and aesthetics. The aesthetic I examined is one based on implicit punning or *saad aheełt'éego diits'a'*. Such creative uses of homophony are part of the "interwovenness" of Navajo, the ways that patterns of use of features of language evoke and interanimate other aspects of language in use (see Woodbury 1998).* But such aesthetic and poetic practices do not occur outside of social and political realities. Here again it is useful to think of narrative discriminations (Kroskrity 2012a). As the pun between *gad* and *God* suggests, narrative discriminations that erase an aesthetic practice based on phonological iconicity

---

* For Woodbury (1998), interwovenness is one part of a larger pattern of "form-dependent expression." Form-dependent expressions are based "on a perception of non-arbitrariness in the relationship between form and function" (257). Iconicity and indexicality would be the most obvious examples of this. Punning is another example. Note that interlingual puns—not only intralingual puns—are form-dependent expressions. The linguistic forms involved are deeply implicated in the expressive economy of local groupness, but with a twist, because they are interwoven *across languages* through phonological iconicity. It is this twining of linguistic forms across languages and their expression of local groupness that are threatened by the current language shift on the Navajo Nation (see Webster 2010b). The language situation among Navajos is and has been one of heteroglossia; interlingual puns are one product of that heteroglossic context (see also Webster 2009, 2010a; Peterson and Webster 2013; Field 2009).

or punning have been a recurring theme in the Navajo context. As we have seen in this book, Euro-American outsiders and their institutions (schools and missions) have continually misrecognized or devalued Navajo poetic and aesthetic practices, from expressive features to puns to ideophones to Navajo English (see also Webster 2009). Such uses of language, which run the very real danger of being marginalized, erased, and/or ridiculed, I have been calling here intimate grammars.

There is an irony here, of course. The Western fixation on literalism obscures the poetic uses of punning in the Western canon. William Shakespeare, an icon of Western literary imaginings, often used puns in his works (see P. Parker 1996, 2009). Likewise, Jim and I had a number of conversations in 2000 and 2001 in which Jim talked of his admiration for the work of Edmund Spenser. Spenser is also known for his punning (Maley 2001). However, as Sherzer (2002) and Samuels (2004b) have noted, punning in contemporary Euro-American society is not highly valued (see also Bauman and Briggs 2003). One can see this as a curious oversight of what Lawrence Levine (1988) describes as the process of elevating Shakespeare in the cultural hierarchy of the United States. While Shakespeare may have gone from "lowbrow" to "highbrow," punning did not similarly become a valued aesthetic practice. In fact, there is a tradition in Shakespeare scholarship of apologizing for Shakespeare's use of puns (see Johnson [1765] 1968). Punning is still highly valued among many Navajos that I have worked with over the years. Jim's use of punning links intertextually to a Navajo poetic tradition of punning, but it also links intertextually to the punning practices of authors like Spenser and Shakespeare. If Jim's poem highlights an aesthetic feature of Navajo verbal art, it also chastises the devaluing of an aesthetic feature in English.

Hymes (2003: 42) once noted, "we tend to forget that the usual way of writing languages on the page is one that implies, or, one might say, conceals, linguistic information." Echoing this, I would suggest that as the Navajo language becomes standardized in a written form that is not attentive to expressive forms, some Navajos may not realize that inserting the -x- is an expressive option, or they may find that such expressive features, as a result of not being indicated in writing, have been devalued. Mitchell noted that today, "people use x without thinking." One day, Navajos may see words that normally are produced and written with the velar fricative, like *łitsxo* 'orange, dirty yellow', as fixed and conventionalized, merely "how one spells that word"—with any alternation fixed as a minimal pair for semantico-referential meaning, like *łitso* 'yellow' and *łitsxo* 'orange'—and not as

bearers of a productive expressive feature.* In fact, I have been told by some
Navajo consultants that *łitsxo* means *only* 'orange'. One Navajo-English
dictionary sold at Diné College (both Tsaile and Shiprock campuses) does
indeed list *łitsxo* as meaning only 'orange' (Parnwell and Yellowhair 1989:
104), thus obscuring the expressive use of -*x*- to indicate 'dirty yellow'
and creating a false equivalence between languages. We can think of this
process as the *vocabularization* of language, where languages are reduced
to interchangeable labels for the world (see Meek 2010). Concomitantly,
some Navajos may agree with the teacher that I talked to in 2001 and see
the insertion of the velar fricative in other words (like *bichx̨į́h*) as a mistake.
Spelling standards, however, hinder us when we look at Jim's poem (or the
poetry of John Clare or William Blake). As Char Peery (2012: 114) argues,
"Young's documentation of Navajo helped to create a standardized register
for use in political and educational institutions, helped to teach and model
the federal government's concept of the ideal modern Navajo citizen, and
attempted to create a Navajo public sphere modeled on the American public
sphere" (see also Webster 2014). As a part of this modernizing vision of
Navajo, expressive features were not overly valued. This is, however, not
an inherent problem of literacy but rather of a particular modernist vision
of literacy that promotes a referentialist view of language at the expense
of expressive features (see Tedlock 1983). This is an especially important
point given the language shift now occurring from Navajo to various forms
of Englishes (see Benally and Viri 2005; Webster 2010b). Jim's poem is a
promotion of, a calling of attention to, the poetic work that the velar fricative
can do in Navajo. Here I would echo the concerns of Woodbury (1998)
and Nancy Dorian (2002) about the importance of appreciating *the local
aesthetics* of expressive forms in use.

Mitchell once explained to me—in critiquing the way some linguists
and anthropologists approached Navajo—that "the validity of Navajo is

---

* For another example, one can insert the velar fricative into *łichíí'* 'it is red' to make *łichxíí'*
'really dark red'. And in a piece on color terminology in Navajo, Herbert Landar, Susan Ervin,
and Arnold Horowitz (1960) provide examples of the use of the velar fricative in relation to
color terms and illness. In describing the "common cold," three of their Navajo consultants
describe the mucus as being *łitsxo* 'nasty yoo' (*yoo* is Landar, Ervin, and Horowitz's term for
"yellow-orange"), with the velar fricative (381). Later on, the authors provide the transcript
of a medical interview between a doctor, a Navajo interpreter, and a Navajo patient (381–82).
Twice the patient describes his mucus as *łitsxo*, which, again, Landar, Ervin, and Horowitz
gloss as 'nasty yoo' (382). As they note, "the -*x*- gives the stem -*cxo* augmentative-pejorative
meaning, and has been rendered as 'nasty'" (381; in the authors' orthography, <c> corresponds
to contemporary <ts>).

in its sounds, not in the neat things it does." Mitchell, I believe, is suggesting that a phonic view of Navajo takes precedence over a Westernized semantic view of language (see Reichard [1950] 1963; McAllester 1980; Frisbie 1980). Navajo is from this perspective a language of sound and it is this *acoustemology* (Feld 1996) that makes real—validates—the language as a language that does something, that creates and enacts (Frisbie 1980; McAllester 1980; Reichard [1950] 1963). This is the "sound power" of Navajo that was first described by Reichard (1944: 51). Language—as a sounded phenomenon—is a creative force in the world. Jim's poetry, which is intimately concerned with the sounds of Navajo and the ways such sounds echo and reverberate, evoking affinities, stands as a testament that the validity of Navajo is in its sounds. Understanding Jim's poem means not just understanding the semantico-referential meanings behind the words but also catching a glimpse of the expressive meaning of the use of -*x*- as an optional poetic device, a device Jim chose to use in this poem. It means listening for potential ambiguities and sound affinities evoked through phonological iconicity. It means recognizing Jim's voice, or as some Navajos are fond of saying, "really listening" (see chapter 4). Expressive features like -*x*- may, as Mitchell once told me, be hard for "white people" to understand. More poignantly, they may be hard for those Navajos who have been educated in Euro-American institutions to understand. This lack of understanding may, of course, be predicated on a Western language ideology overly focused on semantico-referential meanings to the exclusion of the expressive and affective features of languages (see Bauman and Briggs 2003; Samuels 2004a). As Mitchell noted, Jim's use of the -*x*- is "very descriptive" and helps in "giving a picture" to those who hear or read this poem. Mitchell also noted that Jim's poem "is very strong" because it inspires continuing thought. Those are some of the qualities of an aesthetically pleasing Navajo poem; such a poem evokes an image for the listener or reader to ponder. Poetry— like all language—is not just, then, *about* the world, it is *of* the world; and being of the world it holds the possibility to change the world. For those who are willing and able to listen, Jim's poem suggests a strong moral statement about how one may have become disorderly, out of control, or, in a word, *hóchxǫ'* in their actions and thoughts. The strength of this poem is in the ways that it can elicit recognition of "what we have become." And, perhaps, begin the twin and twined processes of restoration and of beauty.

Conclusion

Study to be quiet
—IZAAK WALTON, *THE COMPLEAT ANGLER*

November 12, 2009. Blackhorse Mitchell has come to Southern Illinois University at Carbondale at my invitation to perform for the University's "Native American Heritage Month" program. Such performances are emblematic displays of Nativeness, Indianness, and Navajoness; I have analyzed such a performance by Laura Tohe from 2006 in the introduction and in previous work (Webster 2009). Mitchell, like Tohe, begins with a story that highlights outsider ways of misrecognizing Navajo practices—here, their ways of speaking. It also plays on expectations that outsiders have about Navajos. It is an opening gesture by Mitchell to shake the audience from their expectations about Navajos and to encourage them to listen before they jump to conclusions. Below is a transcript of the story that he told that night.

NOW, I just wanted to
tell you some things
about
the things that I run across.
There was a joke.
There's always this thing about the reservation.
And look at the government calling an Indian reservation as a zoo.
My concept is a zoo.
And I been asked why I think of the reservation as a zoo is because
when tourists are coming from back east or west
going to an Indian land
especially my biggest reservation that I live on
people like to take pictures of

164

a Navajo
like me herding sheep.
Or either outside of a trading post looking very Indianish.
And all these things
and I'll always think,
I always go to the zoo,
I take my camera,
I'll take the first animal or monkey
sitting on the tree
and I'll take these pictures
and I picture so-called reservation as a zoo
because that's what people do
when they come on the reservation.

And that kinda takes me back [clears throat]
and the kinda things that
the cultural difference
is that there was a time when
two couple were coming back from the west.
They were driving along
and
right on the I-40 they took the wrong turn
and they got onto a reservation
Indian reservation
and they got to a small community
and there was hardly anything going for miles
and they come to this community
and there was a big banner that goes across the highway
and it says "powwow"
with a arrow pointing in the southern direction.
And so they said,
the lady that was sitting on the side
asked her husband if sh he could make the turn
to see what that powwow was all about.
So the old man makes the turn
and they got to this little gym,
like this auditorium, [points to auditorium]
and there was noise in there
and the Indians were dancing. (AHEM)

So the lady goes in there
and finds a little aisle like this every seat was taken
and says sees that there was only one chair
close to the dancing.
Where all the feathers and plumes, and jingles,
dancing was going on and so she sat right behind two guys,
two Indian guys
and they were joking,
slapping one another,
telling a story.
And
knowing in the dominant culture you don't eavesdrop,
but she could listen to what these two guys were laughing about,
this, that, and the other guy
slapped the other guy on the back
and said "LISTEN
you have to remember the spelling.
Mmmm."
So the other guy was listening and he says,
"Remember mmm.
It starts with M,
mmm."
And then he also says,
"Next, I come,
directly after that happen is two asses comes together
and I come again.
Two asses comes together again,
and I come again,
P twice
and for the last time
I come."
He said
this old lady tapped him on the back
and said,
"You should be ashamed of yourself,
you shouldn't talk about
such things
in a public place."
So the two turned around to see it
who was talking

and there was this Anglo lady sitting there.
So he slapped
his friend
and said,
"Listen,
I'm trying to get this man
to learn how to spell
Mississippi."

There are a number of things going on in this richly evocative performance. Here I want to only make a few comments as a way of working
toward themes developed throughout this book. The first thing I want to
observe is that unlike at the Tohe performance presented at the beginning
of this book, here there was very little laughter after the story was told. One
explanation for this could be that Laura Tohe simply told her humorous
story better or that her story was in some sense funnier. Notice, though,
that Mitchell frames his narrative as a "joke," thus inviting laughter, while
Tohe framed her narrative as a "poem," which seems less likely to invite
laughter (though see Webster 2009). As a matter of fact, I have seen Mitchell
tell this story to a primarily Navajo audience and it has played much better.
Navajos laughed at the antics of the lady and her husband. Here, however,
with the preliminary discussion of the Navajo Nation as a zoo—this is a
common enough comment, which I have heard from several Navajos I have
known—there may be recognition by the audience that they are the tourists
at this "zoo." Mitchell locates the story on the border between the "Indian
reservation" and the setting in Carbondale when he makes the connection—
through gesture—between the "gym" where the powwow takes place and
the "auditorium" where he is performing. Like the "Midwestern tourists"
from Tohe's story, Mitchell indexically links the audience with the story
world. This may have been uncomfortable for some in the audience (though
such recognition did not stop audience members from laughing when Tohe
performed her poem). Some of that uncomfortableness may come from
Mitchell's use of the word *zoo*. He and other poets I have worked with have
emphasized that one goal of their poetry is to show to non-Navajos that
they are "human beings." The "zoo" reference here reminds the audience
that Navajos are not always seen as coeval human beings. There is also
the comment by Mitchell that the Anglo lady is clearly violating her own
cultural norms when she engages in "eavesdropping." Note, as well, that
these norms do not merely reflect a "cultural difference" between Anglo and
Navajo culture, because the two cultures are unequally related. The Anglo

lady comes from the "dominant culture." This is a cultural difference with ramifications that are based on unequal power relations.

Another factor may be that the topic—the intertwining of sex and language in the story—violated the expectations of the audience about the ways a Navajo performer should act. The audience consisted of parents and their children and the topic challenged certain white middle-class values (see Povinelli 2002). The pun between *asses* and *esses* (that is, the letter *s*) also seems to have failed for many in the audience. They could only hear *asses* as body parts and not as a letter of the alphabet. So while the humorous story is about an "eavesdropping" Anglo-American lady misrecognizing what the two Indian men are talking about and then jumping to conclusions based on certain biased expectations about Indian men, the audience in Carbondale may have not recognized that this was a humorous story based on puns, or the story may not have fit with their expectation of the kind of performance they were going to get from this Navajo performer, or both. In any case, the only person that can be heard laughing on the recording is me.

Thinking about *why* this story is told, at the beginning of this performance by this Navajo performer, also helps us flesh out some of the social work that he was trying to accomplish with this story. Mitchell—while well known on the Navajo Nation in certain areas—is quite conscious of the fact that he speaks in what is often labeled "Navajo English." He and I have had a number of conversations about this over the years. This includes him once humorously offering to help me learn Navajo if I helped him learn "correct" English. He was, through this story, asking the audience to listen to what he was saying and not judge him—as he knows he has been judged—based on the variety of English that he speaks. His explanation to me of why the story did not evoke laughter was that the audience did not understand him.

I think he is right, but not exactly in the way he might have meant. Tohe's story satisfied certain audience expectations about Navajos. The Midwesterners misrecognized a Navajo practice as equivalent to an idealized American patriarchal practice (namely, wives are supposedly subservient to their husbands). In doing so, the story critiques the misrecognition of Navajo practices but also critiques the very logic of this notion of the subservient wife in American life. Most in the audience were probably sympathetic to that critique. On the other hand, Mitchell's story challenges non-Navajo views about Navajos and "the English language." For many people in this country, there is an assumption that there is an "English language" that both is homogeneous and has correct and incorrect forms (based on some assumption concerning the "rules" of "grammar"). Audience members were inclined to acknowledge that American patriarchy is misguided, but they were not as willing to license the use of varieties of English at variance with their notions of "standard" English. Like the discussion in chapter 3, Mitchell had challenged them to think more broadly about languages and ways of speaking. He was not critiquing the Indian men and their ways of speaking; he was critiquing the listener who thought she knew better. Some in the audience may not have found that critique particularly compelling, though some surely did. The United States is largely a country that uses linguistic differences as a proxy for various forms of discrimination, intentional or not (Lippi-Green 1997; Haviland 2003; J. Hill 2008). Furthermore, Mitchell's own English was a variety of Navajo English and not a more "articulate" (in the racialized sense of Alim and Smitherman 2012) variety of English. Indeed, the shift in the variety of English came not when the performer voiced the words of the Indian men, but rather when he performed the voice of the eavesdropping lady. He performed that night in the ways of speaking that were satisfying to him. And that, I should note, was in his Navajo English. In the end, Mitchell did not accommodate his English to the expectations of the audience, he encouraged the audience to listen and respect his English. And, over the course of the night's performance, many did.

Both this performance and Tohe's performance from the introduction are reminiscent of what Keith Basso (1979) described as Western Apaches' "portraits of the whiteman." As Basso describes them, these are "statements by Apaches for Apaches that are about Apaches and the kinds of dealings they have with Anglo-Americans" (16). Like the examples described by Basso, Tohe and Mitchell present models of proper behavior by way of using the figure of the "white person" as a model of how not to act. Like the Western Apache portraits, the characters of the "white person" are based on the kinds of people that Navajos regularly encounter and interact with (here tourists). Tourists, through these performances, are recognizable as significant others for Navajos (see Sutton 2008). Unlike the portraits described by Basso, though, these performances are done in the presence of white people. For Basso, Western Apache portraits are ways of critiquing Apaches who may behave in non-Apache ways. For the Navajo poets, the portraits are a way of critiquing non-Navajo behaviors and assumptions about Navajos, but also of laying the groundwork for future encounters between audience members (as potential tourists) and Navajos. It is here that the risk of such performances—as a cultural critique—becomes most apparent. These portraits of tourist encounters, performed before potential tourists, are a dangerous attempt to correct outside assumptions about Navajos, dangerous because they run the risk of offending those potential tourists. The humor of the stories is meant to mitigate the challenge to outsider assumptions of privileged knowledge. But as with the portraits described by Basso, there is danger for Navajo poets in such stories: the risk of offending the audience. Tourism is an important component of the economy on the Navajo Nation and the tribe markets itself as a tourist destination. Nevertheless, many Navajo poets do engage in such portraits of tourist encounters in an attempt to make future real encounters less painful for Navajos—because they hope to make the world more just.

I have intentionally framed this book with two examples of Navajos depicting the misrecognition of semiotic practices—the order in which Navajo men and women walk and the ways that Navajos speak their Englishes—to highlight the saliency of such forms of misrecognition for Navajos. It is an issue that many Navajo poets are acutely aware of and their poetry resonates with it. Some of the social work of the stories is about offering non-Navajo audiences the opportunity to listen and to hear what Navajos are saying. To reflect, that is, on the expectations that they bring to poetry performances by Navajos. It doesn't always work, and questions about "shamans" and the "ancient Navajo writing system" seen on *The X-Files* still occur. One Navajo poet that I talked with about this said that there are times when the "ridiculousness" of the questions can be taxing. Some audience members, he went on to note, only want the "sacred," and audience expectations can make one feel like an "object" and not a human being. When such questions arise, Navajo poets—and Navajos more generally—are confronted with ordeals of languages (E. Basso 2009): Maintain imagined civility. Speak in a way that satisfies dominant cultural expectations. Paint the painting that satisfies tourists' expectations. These are the questions and issues that confront Navajos and that, through expressive and creative forms like poetry, they attempt to say something about and possibly change as well. We cannot understand contemporary Navajo poetry without some sense of the ways that Navajo poets have negotiated and come to terms—however imperfectly or fleetingly—with their own ordeals of languages.

Identifying expectations and forms of misrecognition—both of ourselves and of others—are, for me anyway, one of the central and perduring goals of anthropology. This was the lesson of Franz Boas's (1889) early paper concerning "alternating sounds." Identifying expectations and forms of misrecognition was also the goal of Benjamin Whorf's (1956) concern with linguistic relativity. This book has been about identifying expectations (often based on racist stereotypes) and forms of misrecognition in the ways that

Navajo poets and poetry have been approached. It has been about trying to listen to what Navajos have been trying to tell me over the course of the last decade plus, in conversations, poetry, and poetry performances. The key, for me as an anthropologist, is always to be found in and through ethnography. I won't claim to know exactly what Navajos have been trying to tell me, but I hope to have provided enough context—enough ethnography—to allow for a glimpse of what I imagine they've been trying to say. I have, at times, been a slow learner. I am surprised (disappointed?) at how long it took me to recognize that Mitchell's use of *ugly* was not based on my Midwestern aesthetic sensibilities, but was rather a moral evaluation about lack of control and disorder (*hóchxǫ'*). But that's the power of misrecognition. I was sure that I recognized and hence understood his use of *ugly*. Was sure that it was an English word and that there was only one English. I knew these things were false, and yet I fell into the easy grooves of expectations. Whorf (1956: 244) made this point years ago when he noted that "it is the 'plainest' English which contains the greatest number of unconscious assumptions about nature." Coming to such reflexive forms of recognition, as I have argued throughout this book, requires repeated acts of listening. And that, as Izaak Walton long ago suggested, means studying to be quiet.

But, and let me end with this point and a bit of ethnography, the twin senses of *intimate grammars* for me have to do with the ways that linguistic and expressive forms can be devalued and marginalized, on the one hand, but on the other hand with the ways that linguistic and expressive forms become satisfying in some measure to speakers and listeners. There is another audience here. This is an audience that engages in imaginative acts of recognition and communion. And this audience is composed of Navajos. Navajos who read Mitchell's *Miracle Hill* (2004) and hear the voice of their parents. Navajos who hear or read portions of Tohe's *No Parole Today* (1999) and recognize themselves or their parents or grandparents in its boarding-school context. Navajos who read or hear Mitchell's "Beauty of Navajoland" or Rex Lee Jim's poetry and are inspired to think about the ugliness that surrounds them and the ways that beauty (*hózhǫ́*) might be restored. To recognize, that is, what they have become and what they are becoming. There is pleasure here as well. There is aesthetic delight. Navajo poetry is aesthetically pleasing and there is value in that, as I have tried to describe in chapters 4 and 5. One reason why some Navajo poets are writing poetry is to help restore *hózhǫ́*. There are other reasons. There is the historical-memory work that Tohe has engaged in. Another reason is that they find such expressive practices as poetry to be satisfying and enjoyable. And still more. And none of them have to be mutually exclusive. That's poetry. Poetry, like a good pun, is ambiguous and has multiple potential interpretations. Poetry, again like a good pun, should inspire reflection and thought. Poems, like puns, are invitations for imaginative acts. My goal in this book has been to reflect on such poetry and some of the kinds of social work it does. Such reflection is and should be an open-ended and continual process—a process of ongoing reflection, imagining, and listening.

Now the ethnographic fragment: I am riding in the car of a Navajo friend and I have just purchased a couple of bottles of Dasani bottled water (one for him and one for me). When my friend asks me why I drink "porcupine water," there are a number of things going on. One thing that may be going on is his recognition that I drink a fair amount of bottled water, partly based on a concern about water quality on the Navajo Nation. Another thing that is going on is that moment of mutual recognition when I reply, "*dahsání*,"and my friend smiles in acknowledgment that I have gotten the pun. *Dahsání* 'porcupine' is an interlingual pun on Dasani bottled water. It's a good pun and we both know it. Years later, today, as I write this in 2014, I cannot look at *Dasani* and not hear the echo of *dahsání*.

References

Aberle, David. 1961. "Navaho." In *Matrilineal Kinship*, edited by David Schneider and Kathleen Gough, 96–201. Berkeley: University of California Press.

Adams, David Wallace. 1997. *Education for Extinction: American Indians and the Boarding School Experience 1875–1928*. Lawrence: Kansas University Press.

Agha, Asif. 2003. "The Social Life of Cultural Value." *Language and Communication* 23:231–73.

Alim, Samy, and Geneva Smitherman. 2012. *Articulate While Black*. Oxford: Oxford University Press.

Allen, Krista. 2012. "Diné Worker Fired for Speaking Navajo." *Navajo Times*, May 10, A1, A3.

Allen, T. D. 1963. *Navahos Have Five Fingers*. Norman: University of Oklahoma Press.

———. 1967. "Please Read Loose." Introduction to *Miracle Hill*, by Emerson Blackhorse Mitchell and T. D. Allen, vii–xvi. Norman: University of Oklahoma Press.

———. 1972. "Emerson Blackhorse 'Barney' Mitchell." In *Whispering Wind*, edited by Terry Allen, 91. Garden City, NY: Doubleday.

———, ed. 1969–74. *Arrow*. 6 vols. Pacific Grove, CA: Pacific Grove Press.

Ashley, Rutherford. 2001. *Heart Vision 2000*. Window Rock, AZ: Cool Runnings.

———. 2013. *A Navajo Scrapbook*. N.p.: Indigenous Quill.

Bailey, Flora. 1942. "Navaho Motor Habits." *American Anthropologist* 44 (2): 210–34.

Bakhtin, Mikhail. 1981. *The Dialogic Imagination*. Austin: University of Texas Press.

———. 1986. *Speech Genres and Other Late Essays*. Austin: University of Texas at Austin.

Ball, Jessica, and B. May Bernhardt. 2008. "First Nations English Dialects in Canada: Implications for Speech-Language Pathology." *Clinical Linguistics and Phonetics* 22 (8): 570–88.

Bartelt, H. Guillermo. 1981. "Some Observations on Navajo English." *Papers in Linguistics* 14 (3): 377–85.

———. 1982. "Rhetorical Redundancy in Apachean English Interlanguage." In *Essays in Native American English*, edited by H. Guillermo Bartelt, Susan Penfield-Jasper, and Bates Hoffer, 157–72. San Antonio: Trinity University Press.

———. 1983. "Mode and Aspect Transfer in Navajo and Western Apache English Narrative Technique." *International Review of Applied Linguistics* 21:104–24.

———. 2001. *Socio- and Stylolinguistic Perspectives on American Indian English Texts*. Lewiston, NY: Edwin Mellen Press.

Basso, Ellen. 2009. "Ordeals of Language." In *Culture, Rhetoric, and the Vicissitudes of Life*, edited by Michael Carrithers, 121–37. New York: Berghahn Books.

Basso, Keith. 1979. *Portraits of "the Whiteman": Linguistic Play and Cultural Symbols Among the Western Apache*. Cambridge: Cambridge University Press.

———. 1991. *Western Apache Language and Culture*. Tucson: University of Arizona Press.

———. 1996. *Wisdom Sits in Places*. Albuquerque: University of New Mexico Press.

Bauman, Richard. 1984. *Verbal Art as Performance*. Chicago: Waveland Press.

———. 1992. "Contextualization, Tradition, and the Dialogue of Genres: Icelandic Legends of the Kraftaskáld." In *Rethinking Context*, edited by Alessandro Duranti and Charles Goodwin, 125–45. Cambridge: Cambridge University Press.

———, and Charles Briggs. 2003. *Voices of Modernity: Language Ideologies and the Politics of Inequality*. Cambridge: Cambridge University Press.

———, and Joel Sherzer, eds. (1974) 1989. *Explorations in the Ethnography of Speaking*. London: Cambridge University Press.

Becker, Alton. 1995. *Beyond Translation*. Ann Arbor: University of Michigan Press.

Belin, Esther. 1999. *From the Belly of My Beauty*. Tucson: University of Arizona Press.

———. 2002. "First Woman." In *Sister Nations*, edited by Heid Erdrich and Laura Tohe, 8–9. St. Paul: Minnesota Historical Society Press.

———. 2007. "Contemporary Navajo Writers' Relevance to Navajo Society." *Wicazo Sa Review* 22 (1): 69–76.

———. 2009. "Conference Man." *Sentence: A Journal of Prose Poetics* 7:118–19.

Benally, AnCita, and Denis Viri. 2005. "*Diné Bizaad* (Navajo Language) at a Crossroads: Extinction or Renewal." *Bilingual Research Journal* 29 (1): 85–108.

Berman, Judith. 1992. "Oolachan-Woman's Robe: Fish, Blankets, Masks, and Meaning in Boas's Kwakw'ala Texts." In *On the Translation of Native American Literatures*, edited by Brian Swann, 125–62. Washington, DC: Smithsonian.

Bird, Dani, and Toben Mintz. 2010. *Discovering Speech, Words, and Mind*. Malden, MA: Wiley-Blackwell.

Bitsui, Sherwin. 2003. *Shapeshift*. Tucson: University of Arizona Press.

Blommaert, Jan. 2005. *Discourse*. Cambridge: Cambridge University Press.

———. 2006. "Ethnopoetics as Functional Reconstruction: Dell Hymes' Narrative View of the World." *Functions of Language* 13 (2): 255–75.

Boas, Franz. 1889. "On Alternating Sounds." *American Anthropologist* 2:47–53.

Bodo, Fr. Murray. 1998. *Tales of an Endishodi: Father Berard Haile and the Navajos, 1900–1960s*. Albuquerque: University of New Mexico Press.

Bolinger, Dwight. 1940. "Word Affinities." *American Speech* 15 (1): 62–73.

Bourdieu, Pierre. 1986. *Distinction*. Cambridge, MA: Harvard University Press.

Brandt, Rose, ed. 1937. *The Colored Land: A Navajo Indian Book*. New York: Charles Scribner's Sons.

Brill de Ramírez, Susan. 1999. *Contemporary American Indian Literatures and the Oral Tradition*. Tucson: University of Arizona Press.

———. 2007. *Native American Life-History Narratives: Colonial and Postcolonial Navajo Ethnography*. Albuquerque: University of New Mexico Press.

Brugge, Doug, Timothy Benally, and Esther Yazzie-Lewis. 2007. *The Navajo People and Uranium Mining*. Albuquerque: University of New Mexico Press.

Bsumek, Erika. 2008. *Indian-Made: Navajo Culture in the Marketplace, 1868–1940*. Lawrence: University of Kansas Press.

Bunte, Pamela. 2002. "Verbal Artistry in Southern Paiute Narratives: Reduplication as a Stylistic Process." *Journal of Linguistic Anthropology* 12 (1): 3–33.

Bunten, Alexis. 2008. "Sharing Culture or Selling Out? Developing the Commodified Persona in the Heritage Industry." *American Ethnologist* 35 (3): 380–95.

Burke, Kenneth. 1968. *Counter-statements*. Berkeley: University of California Press.

Calvino, Italo. 1988. *Six Memos for the Next Millennium*. New York: Vintage Press.

Caton, Steve. 1990. *"Peaks of Yemen I Summon": Poetry as Cultural Practice in a North Yemeni Tribe*. Berkeley: University of California Press.

Cavanaugh, Jillian. 2009. *Living Memory: The Social Aesthetics of Language in a Northern Italian Town*. Malden, MA: Wiley-Blackwell.

Chafe, Wallace. 1998. "Polysynthetic Puns." In *Studies in American Indian Languages: Description and Theory*, edited by Leanne Hinton and Pamela Munro, 87–89. Berkeley: University of California Press.

Chee, Norla. 2001. *Cedar Smoke on Abalone Mountain*. Los Angeles: University of California, Los Angeles.

Cisneros, Ruth, Joey Alexanian, Jalon Begay, and Megan Goldberg. 2006. "The Language of Humor: Navajo." In *Proceedings from the Ninth Workshop on American Indigenous Languages*, edited by Lea Harper. Santa Barbara Papers in Linguistics 18. Santa Barbara: Department of Linguistics, University of California, Santa Barbara. http://www.linguistics.ucsb.edu/research/santa-barbara-papers.

Collins, James. 1987. "Reported Speech in Navajo Myth Narratives." In *Linguistic Action*, edited by Jef Verschueren, 69–85. Norwood, NJ: Ablex.

———, and Richard Blot. 2003. *Literacy and Literacies: Text, Power, and Identity*. Cambridge: Cambridge University Press.

Cook, Eung-Do, and Keren Rice. 1989. Introduction to *Athapaskan Linguistics: Current Perspectives on a Language Family*, edited by Eung-Do Cook and Keren Rice, 1–61. Berlin: Mouton de Gruyter.

Craig, Vincent. 1998. *Yer' Jus' Somehow: Recorded Live at San Juan College*. Mutton Man Productions, compact disc.

Cruikshank, Julie. 1998. *The Social Life of Stories*. Lincoln: University of Nebraska Press.

———. 2005. *Do Glaciers Listen? Local Knowledge, Colonial Encounters, and Social Imagination*. Vancouver: University of British Columbia Press.

Davis, Jeffrey, and Samuel Supalla. 1995. "A Sociolinguistic Description of Sign Language Use in a Navajo Family." In *Sociolinguistics in Deaf Communities*, edited by Ceil Lucas, 77–108. Washington, DC: Gallaudet University Press.

Debenport, Erin. 2011. "As the Rez Turns: Anomalies Within and Beyond the Boundaries of a Pueblo Community." *American Indian Culture and Research Journal* 35 (2): 87–109.

———. 2012. "Continuous Perfectibility: Pueblo Propriety and the Consequences of Literacy." *Journal of Linguistic Anthropology* 22 (3): 201–19.

Deloria, Philip. 2004. *Indians in Unexpected Places*. Lawrence: University Press of Kansas.

———. 2011. "On Leaking Languages and Categorical Imperatives." *American Indian Culture and Research Journal* 35 (2): 173–81.

Denetdale, Jennifer Nez. 2007. *Reclaiming Diné History: The Legacies of Navajo Chief Manuelito and Juanita*. Tucson: University of Arizona Press.

Deyhle, Donna. 1992. "Constructing Failure and Maintaining Cultural Identity: Navajo and Ute School Leavers." *Journal of American Indian Education* 31 (2): 24–47.

———. 2009. *Reflections in a Place: Connected Lives of Navajo Women*. Tucson: University of Arizona Press.

Dick, Galena Sells, and Teresa McCarty. 1997. "Reclaiming Navajo." In *Indigenous Literacies in the Americas*, edited by Nancy Hornberger, 69–92. Berlin: Mouton de Gruyter.

Dilworth, Leah. 1996. *Imagining Indians in the Southwest: Persistent Visions of a Primitive Past*. Washington, DC: Smithsonian Press.

Dinwoodie, David. 2007. "'He Expects We Would Be Off from His Lands': Reported Speech-Events in Tsilhqut'in Contact History." *Anthropological Linguistics* 49 (1): 1–26.

Dorian, Nancy. 2002. "Commentary: Broadening the Rhetorical and Descriptive Horizons of Endangered-Language Linguistics." *Journal of Linguistic Anthropology* 12 (2): 134–40.

Emerson, Gloria. 1971. "The Poetry of Gloria Emerson." *Indian Historian* 4 (2): 8–9.

———. 1972. "Slayers of the Children." *Indian Historian* 5 (1): 18–19.

Enfield, Nick. 2001. "'Lip-Pointing': A Discussion of Form and Function with Reference to Data from Laos." *Gesture* 1 (2): 185–212.

Evans, Nicholas. 2010. *Dying Words: Endangered Languages and What They Have to Tell Us*. Malden, MA: Wiley-Blackwell.

Fabian, Johannes. 1983. *Time and the Other: How Anthropology Makes Its Object*. New York: Columbia University Press.

Falk, Julia. 1999. *Women, Language, and Linguistics: Three American Stories from the First Half of the Twentieth Century*. London: Routledge.

Faltz, Leonard M. 1998. *The Navajo Verb: A Grammar for Students and Scholars*. Albuquerque: University of New Mexico Press.

Farella, John. 1984. *The Main Stalk: A Synthesis of Navajo Philosophy*. Tucson: University of Arizona Press.

Farnell, Brenda. 1995. *Do You See What I Mean?: Plains Indian Sign Talk and the Embodiment of Action*. Austin: University of Texas Press.

———. 2004. "The Fancy Dance of Racializing Discourse." *Journal of Sport and Social Issues* 28 (1): 30–55.

Faudree, Paja. 2013. *Singing for the Dead: The Politics of Indigenous Revival in Mexico*. Durham, NC: Duke University Press.

Feld, Steven. 1988. "Aesthetics as Iconicity of Style, or 'Lift-Up-Over Sounding': Getting into the Kaluli Groove." *Yearbook for Traditional Music* 20:74–113.

———. 1996. "Waterfalls of Song: An Acoustemology of Place Resounding in Bosavi, Papua New Guinea." In *Senses of Place*, edited by Steven Feld and Keith Basso, 91–135. Santa Fe: School of American Research Press.

Fernald, Theodore, and Paul Platero. 2000. *The Athabaskan Languages*. Oxford: Oxford University Press.

Field, Margaret. 1998. "Politeness and Indirection in Navajo Directives." *Southwest Journal of Linguistics* 17 (2): 23–33.

———. 2001. "Triadic Directives in Navajo Language Socialization." *Language in Society* 30:249–63.

———. 2009. "Changing Navajo Language Ideologies and Changing Language Use." In *Native American Language Ideologies: Beliefs, Practices, and Struggles in Indian Country*, edited by Paul Kroskrity and Margaret Field, 31–47. Tucson: University of Arizona Press.

———, and Taft Blackhorse Jr. 2002. "The Dual Role of Metonymy in Navajo Prayer." *Anthropological Linguistics* 44 (3): 217–30.

Fixico, Donald. 2004. "Federal and State Policies and American Indians." In *A Companion to American Indian History*, edited by Philip Deloria and Neal Salisbury, 379–96. Malden, MA: Blackwell.

Foster, Susan, Gloria Singer, Lucy Benally, Theresa Boone, and Ann Beck. 1989. "Describing the Language of Navajo Children." *Journal of Navajo Education* 7 (1): 13–17.

Francisco, Nia. 1977. "táchééh." *College English* 39 (3): 346–47.

———. 1994. *Carried Away by the Black River*. Farmington, NM: Yoo-Hoo Press.

Friedrich, Paul. 1979. "The Symbol and Its Relative Non-arbitrariness." In *Language, Context, and the Imagination*, edited by Anwar Dil, 1–61. Stanford: Stanford University Press.

———. 1986. *The Language Parallax*. Austin: University of Texas Press.

———. 2006. "Maximizing Ethnopoetics: Fine-Tuning Anthropological Experience." In *Language, Culture, and Society*, edited by Christine Jourdan and Kevin Tuite, 207–28. Cambridge: Cambridge University Press.

Frisbie, Charlotte. 1980. "Vocables in Navajo Ceremonial Music." *Ethnomusicology* 24 (3): 347–92.

Gill, Sam. 1987. *Mother Earth*. Chicago: University of Chicago Press.

Goossen, Irvy. 1995. *Diné Bizaad: Speak, Read, Write Navajo*. Flagstaff, AZ: Salina Bookshelf.

Graham, Laura. 2002. "How Should an Indian Speak?" In *Indigenous Movements, Self-Representations, and the State in Latin America*, edited by Kay Warren and Jean Jackson, 181–228. Austin: University of Texas Press.

Greenfeld, Philip. 2001. "Escape from Albuquerque: An Apache Memorate." *American Indian Culture and Research Journal* 25 (3): 47–71.

Haas, Mary. 1951. "Interlingual Word Taboos." *American Anthropologist* 53:338–44.

Haile, Fr. Berard. 1947. *Prayerstick Cutting in a Five Night Navaho Ceremonial of the Male Branch of the Shooting Way*. Chicago: University of Chicago Press.

Hanks, William. 1999. *Intertexts*. New York: Rowman and Littlefield.

Harkin, Michael. 2000. "Sacred Places, Scarred Spaces." *Wicazo Sa Review* 15 (1): 49–70.

———. 2004. "Thirteen Ways of Looking at a Landscape." In *Coming Ashore*, edited by Marie Mauzé, Michael Harkin, and Sergei Kan, 385–406. Lincoln: University of Nebraska Press.

Harrison, K. David. 2007. *When Languages Die: The Extinction of the World's Languages and the Erosion of Human Knowledge*. London: Oxford University Press.

Harvey, Gina. 1974. "Dormitory English: Implications for Teachers." In *Southwest Areal Studies*, edited by Garland Bills, 283–91. San Diego: San Diego State University.

———. 1976. "Some Observations About Red English and Standard English in the Classroom." In *Studies in Southwestern Indian English*, edited by William Leap, 223–33. San Antonio: Trinity University Press.

Hastings, Adi, and Paul Manning. 2004. "Introduction: Acts of Alterity." *Language and Communication* 24:291–311.

Haviland, John. 2003. "Ideologies of Language: Some Reflections on Language and US Law." *American Anthropologist* 105 (4): 764–74.

Herzfeld, Michael. 1997. *Cultural Intimacy*. New York: Routledge.

Hill, Jane. 2002. "Expert Rhetorics in Advocacy for Endangered Languages: Who Is Listening, and What Do They Hear?" *Journal of Linguistic Anthropology* 12 (2): 119–33.

———. 2008. *The Everyday Language of White Racism*. Malden, MA: Wiley-Blackwell.

———, and Ofelia Zepeda. 1998. "Tohono O'odham (Papago) Plurals." *Anthropological Linguistics* 40 (1): 1–42.

———. 1999. "Language, Gender, and Biology: Pulmonic Ingressive Airstream in Women's Speech in Tohono O'odham." *Southwest Journal of Linguistics* 18 (1): 15–41.

Hill, W. W. 1943. *Navajo Humor*. Menasha, WI: George Banta.

———, and Dorothy Hill. 1945. "Navaho Coyote Tales and Their Position in the Southern Athabaskan Group." *Journal of American Folklore* 58 (203): 317–43.

Hirschfelder, Arlene, and Beverly Singer, eds. 1992. *Rising Voices: Writings of Young Native Americans*. New York: Ivy Books.

Hoijer, Harry. 1974. *A Navajo Lexicon*. Berkeley: University of California Press.

Holm, Agnes, and Wayne Holm. 1995. "Navajo Language Education: Retrospect and Prospects." *Bilingual Research Journal* 19 (1): 141–67.

———, Wayne Holm, and Bernard Spolsky. 1971. *English Loan Words in the Speech of Six-Year-Old Navajo Children*. Navajo Reading Study Progress Report 16. Albuquerque: University of New Mexico.

Hopper, Paul. 1987. "Emergent Grammar." *Berkeley Linguistics Society* 13:139–57.

Horoshko, Sonja. 2008. "Tribute to Resistance: An Exhibition Showcases Desert Rock Opposition." *Four Corners Free Press* 5 (11): 16–17.

House, Deborah. 2002. *Language Shift Among the Navajos*. Tucson: University of Arizona Press.

Hymes, Dell. 1960. "Phonological Aspects of Style: Some English Sonnets." In *Style in Language*, edited by Thomas Sebeok, 109–31. Cambridge, MA: Massachusetts Institute of Technology Press.

———. 1965. "Some North Pacific Coast Poems: A Problem in Anthropological Philology." *American Anthropologist* 67 (2): 316–41.

———. 1974. *Foundations in Sociolinguistics*. Philadelphia: University of Pennsylvania Press.

———. 1979. "How to Talk Like a Bear in Takelma." *International Journal of American Linguistics* 45 (2): 101–6.

———. 1981. *In Vain I Tried to Tell You*. Philadelphia: University of Pennsylvania Press.

———. 1987a. "Tonkawa Poetics: John Rush Buffalo's 'Coyote and Eagle's Daughter.'" In *Native American Discourse: Poetics and Rhetoric*, edited by Joel Sherzer and Anthony Woodbury, 17–61. Cambridge: Cambridge University Press.

———. 1987b. "A Pattern of Verbal Irony in Chinookan." *International Journal of the Sociology of Language* 65:97–110.

———. 1996a. *Ethnography, Linguistics, Narrative Inequality: Toward an Understanding of Voice*. Bristol, PA: Taylor and Francis.

———. 1996b. "Consonant Symbolism in Kathlamet and Shoalwater Chinook." *University of Oregon Anthropological Papers* 52:163–71.

———. 1998. *Reading Takelma Texts*. Bloomington, IN: Trickster Press.

———. 2000. "Sung Epic and Native American Ethnopoetics." In *Textualization of Oral Epics*, edited by Lauri Honko, 291–342. Berlin: Mouton de Gruyter.

———. 2003. *Now I Know Only That Far*. Lincoln: University of Nebraska Press.

Inoue, Miyako. 2006. *Vicarious Language*. Berkeley: University of California Press.

Irvine, Judith. 1990. "Registering Affect: Heteroglossia in the Linguistic Expression of Emotion." In *Language and the Politics of Emotion*, edited by Lila Abu-Lughod and Catherine Lutz, 126–61. Cambridge: Cambridge University Press.

———, and Susan Gal. 2000. "Language Ideology and Linguistic Differentiation." In *Regimes of Language*, edited by Paul Kroskrity, 35–83. Santa Fe: School of American Research.

Iverson, Peter. 1998. *"We Are Still Here": American Indians in the Twentieth Century*. Wheeling, IL: Harlan Davidson.

———. 2002. *Diné: A History of the Navajos*. Albuquerque: University of New Mexico Press.

Jakobson, Roman. 1960. "Closing Statement: Linguistics and Poetics." In *Style in Language*, edited by Thomas Sebeok, 350–77. Cambridge, MA: Massachusetts Institute of Technology Press.

Jim, Rex Lee. 1989. *Áhí Ni' Nikisheegiizh*. Princeton, NJ: Princeton Collections of Western Americana.

———. 1995. *saad*. Princeton, NJ: Princeton Collections of Western Americana.

———. 1998. *Dúchas Táá Kóó Diné*. Beal Feirste, Ireland: Au Clochan.

———. 2010. "Video: Poems by Rex Lee Jim '86." *Princeton Alumni Weekly* video, 4:52, November 3. http://paw.princeton.edu/issues/2010/11/03/pages/8440/index.xml.

Johnson, Samuel. (1765) 1968. "Preface to Shakespeare." In *The Yale Edition of the Works of Samuel Johnson, Volume VII: Johnson on Shakespeare*, edited by Arthur Sherbo, 74. New Haven, CT: Yale University Press.

Johnstone, Barbara. 1996. *The Linguistic Individual*. Oxford: Oxford University Press.

Kamper, David. 2010. *The Work of Sovereignty: Tribal Labor Relations and Self-Determination at the Navajo Nation*. Santa Fe: School of Advanced Research Press.

Katanski, Amelia. 2005. *Learning to Write "Indian": The Boarding-School Experience and American Indian Literature*. Norman: University of Oklahoma Press.

Kluckhohn, Clyde. 1949. "The Philosophy of the Navaho Indians." In *Ideological Differences and World Order*, edited by F. S. C. Northrop, 356–84. New Haven, CT: Yale University Press.

——— , and Dorothea Leighton. 1962. *The Navajo*. New York: Doubleday.

Krakoff, Sarah. 2008. "Healing the West with Taxes: The Navajo Nation and the Enactment of Sovereignty." In *Remedies for a New West*, edited by Patricia Nelson Limerick, Andrew Cowell, and Sharon Collinge, 27–46. Tucson: University of Arizona Press.

Kroskrity, Paul. 1993. *Language, History, and Identity: Ethnolinguistic Studies of the Arizona Tewa*. Tucson: University of Arizona Press.

——— . 2004. "Language Ideologies." In *A Companion to Linguistic Anthropology*, edited by Alessandro Duranti, 496–517. Malden, MA: Blackwell.

——— . 2009. "Embodying the Reversal of Language Shift: Agency, Incorporation, Language Ideological Change in the Western Mono Community of Central California." In Kroskrity and Field 2009, 190–210.

——— . 2010. "The Art of Voice: Understanding the Arizona Tewa Inverse in Its Grammatical, Narrative, and Language-Ideological Contexts." *Anthropological Linguistics* 52 (1): 49–79.

——— . 2011. "All Intimate Grammars Leak: Reflections on 'Indian Languages in Unexpected Places.'" *American Indian Culture and Research Journal* 35 (2): 161–72.

——— . 2012a. "Growing with Stories: Ideologies of Storytelling and the Narrative Reproduction of Arizona Tewa Identities." In Kroskrity 2012b, 151–83.

——— , ed. 2012b. *Telling Stories in the Face of Danger: Narratives, Ideological Reproduction, and Language Endangerment in Native American Communities*. Norman: University of Oklahoma Press.

——— , and Margaret Field, eds. 2009. *Native American Language Ideologies: Beliefs, Practices, and Struggles in Indian Country*. Tucson: University of Arizona Press.

Lamphere, Louise. 1969. "Symbolic Elements in Navajo Ritual." *Southwestern Journal of Anthropology* 25:279–305.

——— . 1977. *To Run After Them: Cultural and Social Bases of Cooperation in a Navajo Community*. Tucson: University of Arizona Press.

Landar, Herbert, Susan Ervin, and Arnold Horowitz. 1960. "Navaho Color Categories." *Language* 36 (1): 368–92.

Lawlor, Mary. 2006. *Public Native America: Tribal Self-Representation in Museums, Powwows, and Casinos*. New Brunswick, NJ: Rutgers University Press.

Leap, William. 1993a. *American Indian English*. Salt Lake City: University of Utah Press.

——— . 1993b. "Written Navajo English: Texture, Construction, and Point of View." *Journal of Navajo Education* 11 (1): 41–48.

Leavitt, John. 2011. *Linguistic Relativities: Linguistic Diversity and Modern Thought*. Cambridge: Cambridge University Press.

Lee, Tiffany. 2007. "'If They Want Navajo to Be Learned, Then They Should Require It in All Schools': Navajo Teenagers' Experiences, Choices, and Demands Regarding Navajo Language." *Wicazo Sa Review* 22 (1): 7–33.

Leighton, Dorothea. 1968. "Review of *Miracle Hill: The Story of a Navaho Boy*." *American Anthropologist* 70 (3): 616.

Leonard, Wesley. 2011. "Challenging 'Extinction' Through Modern Miami Language Practices." *American Indian Culture and Research Journal* 35 (2): 135–60.

Levine, Lawrence. 1988. *Highbrow/Lowbrow*. Cambridge, MA: Harvard University Press.

Li, Charles. 1986. "Direct Speech and Indirect Speech: A Functional Study." In *Direct and Indirect Speech*, edited by Florian Coulmas, 29–45. Berlin: Mouton De Gruyter.

Liebe-Harkort, M. L. 1979. "Bilingualism and Language Mixing Among the White Mountain Apaches." *Folia Linguistica* 13 (3/4): 345–56.

Lippi-Green, Rosina. 1997. *English with an Accent: Language, Ideology and Discrimination in the United States*. London: Routledge.

Littlefield, Alice. 2004. "Education." In *A Companion to the Anthropology of American Indians*, edited by Thomas Biolsi, 321–37. Malden, MA: Blackwell.

Lomawaima, K. Tsianina. 1995. *They Called It Prairie Light: The Story of Chilocco Indian School*. Lincoln: University of Nebraska Press.

———, and Teresa McCarty. 2006. *To Remain an Indian*. New York: Teachers College Press.

Maley, Willy. 2001. "Spenser's Languages: Writing in the Ruins of English." In *The Cambridge Companion to Spenser*, edited by Andrew Hadfield, 162–79. Cambridge: Cambridge University Press.

Marcus, George, and Fred Myers. 1995. *The Traffic in Culture*. Berkeley: University of California Press.

McAllester, David. 1954. *Enemy Way Music: A Study of Social and Esthetic Values as Seen in Navajo Music*. Papers of the Peabody Museum of American Archaeology and Ethnology, Harvard University, vol. 41, no. 3. Cambridge, MA: Peabody Museum.

———. 1980. "The First Snake Song." In *Theory and Practice: Essays Presented to Gene Weltfish*, edited by Stanley Diamond, 1–27. New York: Mouton.

McCarty, Teresa. 2002. *A Place to Be Navajo*. Mahwah, NJ: Lawrence Erlbaum Associates.

———, Mary Eunice Romero-Little, and Ofelia Zepeda. 2008. "Indigenous Language Policies in Social Practice." In *Sustaining Linguistic Diversity*, edited by Kendall King, Natalie Schilling-Estes, Lyn Fogle, Jia Jackie Lou, and Barbara Soukup, 159–72. Washington, DC: Georgetown University Press.

McDonough, Joyce. 2003. *The Navajo Sound System*. Dordrecht, the Netherlands: Kluwer Academic Publishers.

———, and Valerie Wood. 2008. "The Stop Contrasts of the Athabaskan Languages." *Journal of Phonetics* 36 (3): 427–49.

McLaughlin, Daniel. 1992. *When Literacy Empowers: Navajo Language in Print*. Albuquerque: University of New Mexico Press.

M'Closkey, Kathy. 2002. *Swept Under the Rug: A Hidden History of Navajo Weaving*. Albuquerque: University of New Mexico Press.

Meek, Barbra. 2006. "And the Injun Goes 'How!': Representations of American Indian English in White Public Space." *Language in Society* 35:93–128.

———. 2010. *We Are Our Language: An Ethnography of Language Revitalization in a Northern Athabaskan Community*. Tucson: University of Arizona Press.

———. 2011. "Failing American Indian Languages." *American Indian Culture and Research Journal* 35 (2): 43–60.

———. 2014. "'She Can Do It in English Too': Acts of Intimacy and Boundary-Making in Language Revitalization." *Language and Communication* 38:73–82.

———, and Jacqueline Messing. 2007. "Framing Indigenous Languages as Secondary to Matrix Languages." *Anthropology and Education Quarterly* 38 (2): 99–118.

Mignolo, Walter. 1995. *The Darker Side of the Renaissance*. Ann Arbor: University of Michigan Press.

Milroy, James. 2001. "Language Ideologies and the Consequences of Standardization." *Journal of Sociolinguistics* 5 (4): 530–55.

Milroy, Lesley. 2000. "Britain and the United States: Two Nations Divided by the Same Language (and Different Language Ideologies)." *Journal of Linguistic Anthropology* 10 (1): 56–89.

Mitchell, Blackhorse. 1967. "The Drifting Lonely Seed." In *Miracle Hill*, by Emerson Blackhorse Mitchell and T. D. Allen, xiv–xv. Norman: University of Oklahoma Press.

———. 2004. *Miracle Hill*. Tucson: University of Arizona Press.

———. 2006. *Where Were You When I Was Single? Old-Time Sheepherder Songs*. Cool Runnings Music, compact disc.

———, and Anthony K. Webster. 2011. "'We Don't Know What We Become': Navajo Ethnopoetics and an Expressive Feature in a Poem by Rex Lee Jim." *Anthropological Linguistics* 53 (3): 259–86.

Mithlo, Nancy. 2008. *"Our Indian Princess": Subverting the Stereotype*. Santa Fe: School of Advanced Research Press.

Mithun, Marianne. 2008. "The Extension of Dependency Beyond the Sentence." *Language* 84 (1): 69–119.

Molina, Felipe, and Larry Evers. 1998. "Like This It Stays in Your Hands: Collaboration and Ethnopoetics." *Oral Tradition* 13 (1): 15–57.

Moore, Robert. 1993. "Performance Form and the Voices of Characters in Five Versions of the Wasco Coyote Cycle." In *Reflexive Language*, edited by John Lucy, 213–40. Cambridge: Cambridge University Press.

———. 2006. "Disappearing, Inc.: Glimpsing the Sublime in the Politics of Access to Endangered Languages." *Language and Communication* 26: 296–315.

———, Sari Pietikäinen, and Jan Blommaert. 2010. "Counting the Losses: Numbers as the Language of Language Endangerment." *Sociolinguistic Studies* 4 (1): 1–26.

Morgan, Mindy. 2009. *The Bearer of This Letter: Language Ideologies, Literacy Practices, and the Fort Belknap Indian Community*. Lincoln: University of Nebraska Press.

Morgan, William. 1949. *Coyote Tales*. Lawrence, KS: Bureau of Indian Affairs, Haskell Institute.

Muehlmann, Shaylih. 2008. "'Spread Your Ass Cheeks': And Other Things That Should Not Be Said in Indigenous Languages." *American Ethnologist* 35 (1): 34–48.

———. 2013. *Where the River Ends: Contested Indigeneity in the Mexican Colorado Delta*. Durham, NC: Duke University Press.

Myers, Fred. 2002. *Painting Culture: The Making of an Aboriginal High Art*. Durham, NC: Duke University Press.

———. ed. 2001. *The Empire of Things*. Santa Fe: School of American Research.

Nadasdy, Paul. 2005. "Transcending the Debate over the Ecologically Noble Indian: Indigenous Peoples and Environmentalism." *Ethnohistory* 52 (2): 291–331.

Nettle, Daniel, and Suzanne Romaine. 2000. *Vanishing Voices*. Oxford: Oxford University Press.

Neundorf, Alyse. 1983. *Áłchíní Bi Naaltsoostsoh: A Navajo/English Bilingual Dictionary*. Albuquerque: Native American Materials Development Center.

Nevins, Eleanor. 2004. "Learning to Listen: Confronting Two Meanings of Language Loss in the Contemporary White Mountain Apache Speech Community." *Journal of Linguistic Anthropology* 14 (2): 269–88.

———. 2010. "The Bible in Two Keys: Traditionalism and Evangelical Christianity on the Fort Apache Reservation." *Language and Communication* 30 (1): 19–32.

———. 2013. *Lessons from Fort Apache: Beyond Language Endangerment and Maintenance*. Malden: Wiley-Blackwell.

Nuckolls, Janis. 1996. *Sounds like Life: Sound-Symbolic Grammar, Performance, and Cognition in Pastaza Quechua*. London: Oxford University Press.

———. 1999. "The Case for Sound Symbolism." *Annual Review of Anthropology* 28:225–52.

———. 2006. "The Neglected Poetics of Ideophony." In *Language, Culture, and the Individual*, edited by Catherine O'Neil, Mary Scoggin, and Kevin Tuite, 39–50. Munich: Lincom.

———. 2010. *Lessons from a Quechua Strongwoman: Ideophony, Dialogue and Perspective*. Tucson: University of Arizona Press.

Paredes, Américo. 1977. "On Ethnographic Work Among Minority Groups: A Folklorist's Perspective." *New Scholar* 6:1–32.

Park, James. 2007. "Ethnogenesis or Neoindigenous Intelligentsia: Contemporary Mapuche-Huilliche Poetry." *Latin American Research Review* 42 (3): 15–42.

Parker, Patricia. 1996. *Shakespeare from the Margins: Language, Culture, Context*. Chicago: University of Chicago Press.

———. 2009. "Shakespeare's Sound Government: Sound Defects, Polyglot Sounds, and Sounding Out." *Oral Tradition* 24 (2): 359–72.

Parker, Robert Dale. 2003. *The Invention of Native American Literature*. Ithaca, NY: Cornell University Press.

Parnwell, E. C., and Marvin Yellowhair. 1989. *The New Oxford Picture Dictionary: English/Navajo Edition*. Oxford: Oxford University Press.

Peery, Char. 2012. "New Deal Navajo Linguistics: Language Ideology and Political Transformation." *Language and Communication* 32:114–123.

Peirce, C. S. 1956. *The Philosophy of Peirce: Selected Writings*. Edited by J. Buchler. London: Routledge Kegan and Paul.

Penfield, Susan. 1982. "Mohave English and Tribal Identity." In *Essays in Native American English*, edited by H. Guillermo Bartelt, Susan Penfield-Jasper, and Bates Hoffer, 23–31. San Antonio: Trinity University Press.

Perley, Bernard. 2011. *Defying Maliseet Language Death: Emergent Vitalities, Culture, and Identity in Eastern Canada*. Lincoln: University of Nebraska Press.

Peterson, Leighton C. 2006. "Technology, Ideology, and Emergent Communicative Practices Among the Navajo." PhD dissertation, University of Texas, Austin.

———. 2011. "'Reel Navajo': The Linguistic Creation of Indigenous Screen Memories." *American Indian Culture and Research Journal* 35 (2): 111–34.

———. 2013. "Reclaiming Diné Film: Visual Sovereignty and the Return of *Navajo Film Themselves*." *Visual Anthropology Review* 29 (1): 29–41.

———, and Anthony K. Webster. 2013. "Speech Play and Language Ideologies in Navajo Terminology Development." *Pragmatics* 23 (1): 93–116.

———, eds. 2011. "American Indian Languages in Unexpected Places." Special issue, *American Indian Culture and Research Journal* 35 (2).

Philips, Susan U. 1993. *The Invisible Culture*. Prospect Heights, IL: Waveland Press.

Platero, Paul. 2001. "Navajo Head Start Language Study." In *The Green Book of Language Revitalization in Practice*, edited by Leanne Hinton and Ken Hale, 87–97. San Diego: Academic Press.

Port, Robert, and Adam Leary. 2005. "Against Formal Phonology." *Language* 81 (4): 927–64.

Povinelli, Elizabeth. 2002. *The Cunning of Recognition: Indigenous Alterities and the Making of Australian Multiculturalism*. Durham, NC: Duke University Press.

———. 2006. "Intimate Grammars: Anthropological and Psychoanalytic Accounts of Language, Gender, and Desire." In *Language, Culture, and Society*, edited by Christine Jourdan and Kevin Tuite, 190–206. Cambridge: Cambridge University Press.

Reichard, Gladys. 1944. *Prayer: The Compulsive Word*. American Ethnological Society Monograph 7. Seattle: University of Washington Press.

———. 1948. "The Significance of Aspiration in Navaho." *International Journal of American Linguistics* 14:15–19.

———. (1950) 1963. *Navaho Religion: A Study of Symbolism*. New York: Bollingen Foundation.

———. 1951. *Navaho Grammar*. New York: J. J. Augustin.

Rice, Keren. 2001. "Learning as One Goes." In *Linguistic Fieldwork*, edited by Paul Newman and Martha Ratliff, 230–49. Cambridge: University of Cambridge Press.

Richland, Justin. 2007. *Arguing with Tradition: The Language of Law in Hopi Tribal Court*. Chicago: University of Chicago Press.

Rodríguez, Juan Luis, and Anthony K. Webster. 2012. "Ordeals of Language: Essays in Honor of Ellen Basso." *Journal of Anthropological Research* 68 (3): 305–14.

Rosaldo, Michelle. 1972. "Metaphors and Folk Classification." *Southwestern Journal of Anthropology* 28:83–98.

Rumsey, Alan. 2001. "*Tom Yaya Kange*: A Metrical Narrative Genre from the New Guinea Highlands." *Journal of Linguistic Anthropology* 11 (2): 193–239.

———. 2007. "Musical, Poetic, and Linguistic Form in *Tom Yaya* Sung Narratives from Papua New Guinea." *Anthropological Linguistics* 49 (3–4): 235–82.

Rushforth, Scott. 1992. "The Legitimation of Beliefs in a Hunter-Gatherer Society: Bearlake Athapaskan Knowledge and Authority." *American Ethnologist* 19 (3): 483–500.

———. 1994. "Political Resistance in a Contemporary Hunter-Gatherer Society: More About Bearlake Athapaskan Knowledge and Authority." *American Ethnologist* 21 (2): 335–52.

———, and James Chisholm. 1991. *Cultural Persistence*. Tucson: University of Arizona Press.

Samuels, David. 2001. "Indeterminacy and History in Britton Goode's Western Apache Placenames." *American Ethnologist* 28 (2): 277–302.

———. 2004a. *Putting a Song on Top of It*. Tucson: University of Arizona Press.

———. 2004b. "Language, Meaning, Modernity, and Doowop." *Semiotica* 149: 297–323.

———. 2006. "Bible Translation and Medicine Man Talk: Missionaries, Indexicality, and the 'Language Expert' on the San Carlos Apache Reservation." *Language in Society* 35 (4): 529–57.

Sapir, Edward. (1915) 1985. "Abnormal Types of Speech in Nootka." In *Selected Writings in Language, Culture, and Personality*, edited by David Mandelbaum, 179–96. Berkeley: University of California Press.

———. 1921. *Language*. New York: Harcourt, Brace.

———. 1925. "Sound Patterns in Language." *Language* 1: 37–51.

———. 1929a. "The Status of Linguistics as a Science." *Language* 5(4): 207–14.

———. 1929b. "A Study in Phonetic Symbolism." *Journal of Experimental Psychology* 12: 225–39.

———. 1932. "Two Navajo Puns." *Language* 8: 217–18.

———, and Harry Hoijer. 1942. *Navaho Texts*. Iowa City, IA: Linguistic Society of America.

———. 1967. *The Phonology and Morphology of the Navaho Language*. Linguistics 50. Berkeley: University of California Press.

Schaengold, Charlotte. 2003. "The Emergence of Bilingual Navajo: English and Navajo Languages in Contact Regardless of Everyone's Best Intentions." In *When Languages Collide*, edited by Brian Joseph, Johanna DeStefano, Neil Jacobs, and Ilse Lehiste, 235–54. Columbus: Ohio State University Press.

Scollon, Ronald, and Suzanne Scollon. 1981. *Narrative, Literacy, and Face in Interethnic Communication*. Norwood, NJ: Ablex.

Scott, James. 1990. *Domination and the Arts of Resistance*. New Haven, CT: Yale University Press.

Sherzer, Joel. 1983. *Kuna Ways of Speaking: An Ethnographic Perspective*. Austin: University of Texas Press.

———. 1987. "A Discourse-Centered Approach to Language and Culture." *American Anthropologist* 89:295–309.

———. 1989. "The Kuna Verb: A Study in the Interplay of Grammar, Discourse, and Style." In *General and Amerindian Ethnolinguistics*, edited by Mary Ritchie Key and Henry Hoenigswald, 261–77. Berlin: Mouton de Gruyter.

———. 1990. *Verbal Art in San Blas*. Cambridge: Cambridge University Press.

——. 2002. *Speech Play and Verbal Art*. Austin: University of Texas Press.

——, and Anthony Woodbury, eds. 1987. *Native American Discourse: Poetics and Rhetoric*. Cambridge: Cambridge University Press.

Shonerd, Henry. 1990. "Domesticating the Barbarous Tongue: Language Policy for the Navajo in Historical Perspective." *Language Problems and Language Planning* 14 (3): 193–208.

Shorter, David Delgado. 2009. *We Will Dance Our Truth: Yaqui History in Yoeme Performances*. Lincoln: University of Nebraska Press.

Sicoli, Mark. 2010. "Shifting Voices with Participant Roles: Voice Qualities and Speech Registers in Mesoamerica." *Language in Society* 39 (4): 521–53.

Silverstein, Michael. 1979. "Language Structure and Linguistic Ideology." In *The Elements*, edited by Paul Clyne, William Hanks, and Carol Hofbauer, 193–247. Chicago: Chicago Linguistic Society.

——. 1981. "The Limits of Awareness." Sociolinguistic Working Paper 84. Austin: Southwest Educational Development Laboratory.

——. 1985. "The Culture of Language in Chinookan Narrative Texts; or, On Saying That . . . in Chinook." In *Grammar Inside and Outside the Clause*, edited by Johanna Nichols and Anthony Woodbury, 132–71. London: Cambridge University Press.

——. 1994. "Relative Motivation in a Denotational and Indexical Sound Symbolism of Wasco-Wishram." In *Sound Symbolism*, edited by Leanne Hinton, Johanna Nichols, and John Ohala, 40–60. Cambridge: Cambridge University Press.

——. 2003. "The Whens and Wheres—as Well as Hows—of Ethnolinguistic Recognition." *Public Culture* 15 (3): 531–57.

Slate, Clay, Martha Jackson, and Tony Goldtooth. 1989. "Navajo Literacy in a Postsecondary Setting: Work in Progress at Navajo Community College." *Journal of Navajo Education* 7 (1): 10–12.

Spears, Arthur, and Leanne Hinton. 2010. "Languages and Speakers: An Introduction to African American English and Native American Languages." *Transforming Anthropology* 18 (1): 3–14.

Sperber, Dan, and Deidre Wilson. 1981. "Irony and the Use-Mention Distinction." In *Radical Pragmatics*, edited by Peter Cole, 295–318. New York: Academic Press.

Spicer, Edward. 1962. *Cycles of Conquest*. Tucson: University of Arizona Press.

Spolsky, Bernard. 2002. "Prospects for the Survival of the Navajo Language: A Reconsideration." *Anthropology and Education Quarterly* 33 (2): 139–62.

Stensland, Anna Lee. 1971. "American Indian Cultures: Promises, Problems and Possibilities." *English Journal* 60 (9): 1195–1200.

Suslak, Daniel. 2010. "Battered Spanish, Eloquent Mixe: Form and Function of Mixe Difrasismos." *Anthropological Linguistics* 52 (1): 80–103.

——. 2011. "Ayapan Echoes: Linguistic Persistence and Loss in Tabasco, Mexico." *American Anthropologist* 113 (4): 569–81.

Sutton, David. 2008. "Tradition and Modernity: Existential Memory Work on a Greek Island." *History and Memory* 20 (2): 84–105.

Tapahonso, Luci. 1987. *A Breeze Swept Through*. Albuquerque: West End Press.

——. 1995. Interview. *LINEbreak* (radio program), Buffalo, NY, October 12. http://writing.upenn.edu/pennsound/x/LINEbreak.html.

———. 1997. *Blue Horses Rush In*. Tucson: University of Arizona Press.

———. 2008. *A Radiant Curve*. Includes compact disc. Tucson: University of Arizona Press.

Tedlock, Dennis. 1983. *The Spoken Word and the Work of Interpretation*. Philadelphia: University of Pennsylvania Press.

———, and Bruce Mannheim, eds. 1995. *The Dialogic Emergence of Culture*. Urbana: University of Illinois Press.

Teller, Terry. n.d. *Talk in Navajo: Wherever U Are* (website). http://daybreak_warrior .angelfire.com.

Toelken, Barre. 1987. "Life and Death in Navajo Coyote Tales." In *Recovering the Word*, edited by Brian Swann and Arnold Krupat, 388–401. Berkeley: University of California Press.

———. 2003. *The Anguish of Snails*. Logan: Utah State University Press.

———, and Tacheeni Scott. 1981. "Poetic Retranslation and the 'Pretty Languages' of Yellowman." In *Traditional Literatures of the American Indians*, edited by Karl Kroeber, 65–116. Lincoln: University of Nebraska Press.

Tohe, Laura. 1986. *Making Friends with Water*. Omaha, NE: Nosila Press.

———. 1999. *No Parole Today*. Albuquerque: West End Press.

———. 2005. *Tséyi': Deep in the Rock*. Tucson: University of Arizona Press.

Trafzer, Clifford, Jean Keller, and Lorene Sisquoc, eds. 2006. *Boarding School Blues: Revisiting American Indian Educational Experiences*. Lincoln: University of Nebraska Press.

Urban, Greg. 1991. *A Discourse-Centered Approach to Culture*. Austin: University of Texas Press.

Urciuoli, Bonnie. 1996. *Exposing Prejudice*. Boulder, CO: Westview Press.

Voloshinov, V. N. 1986. *Marxism and the Philosophy of Language*. Cambridge, MA: Harvard University Press.

Wall, Leon, and William Morgan. (1958) 1994. *Navajo-English Dictionary*. New York: Hippocrene Books.

Wallis, Ethel Emily. 1968. *God Speaks Navajo*. New York: Harper and Row.

Webster, Anthony. 2004. "Coyote Poems: Navajo Poetry, Intertextuality, and Language Choice." *American Indian Culture and Research Journal* 28 (4): 69–91.

———. 2006a. "From *Hóyéé* to *Hajinei*: On Some of the Implications of Feelingful Iconicity and Orthography in Navajo Poetry." *Pragmatics* 16 (4): 535–49.

———. 2006b. "The Mouse That Sucked: On 'Translating' a Navajo Poem." *Studies in American Indian Literature* 18 (1): 37–49.

———. 2008a. "'Plaza'góó and Before He Can Respond . . .': Language Ideology, Bilingual Navajo, and Navajo Poetry." *Pragmatics* 18 (3): 511–41.

———. 2008b. "Running Again, Roasting Again, Touching Again: On Repetition, Heightened Affective Expressivity, and the Utility of Linguaculture in Navajo and Beyond." *Journal of American Folklore* 121 (482): 441–72.

———. 2009. *Explorations in Navajo Poetry and Poetics*. Albuquerque: University of New Mexico Press.

———. 2010a. "A Note on Navajo Interlingual Puns." *International Journal of American Linguistics* 76 (2): 289–98.

———. 2010b. "On Intimate Grammars: With Examples from Navajo English, Navlish, and Navajo." *Journal of Anthropological Research* 66 (2): 187–208.

———. 2010c. "'Still, She Didn't See What I Was Trying to Say': Towards a History of Framing Navajo English in Navajo Written Poetry." *World Englishes* 29 (1): 75–96.

———. 2012a. "'Don't Talk About It': Navajo Poets and Their Ordeals of Language." *Journal of Anthropological Research* 68 (3): 399–414.

———. 2012b. "'To Give an Imagination to the Listener': Replicating Proper Ways of Speaking in and Through Contemporary Navajo Poetry." In *Telling Stories in the Face of Danger: Language Renewal in Native American Communities*, edited by Paul Kroskrity, 205–27. Norman: University of Oklahoma Press.

———. 2014. "DIF'G'OŊE and Semiotic Calquing: A Signography of the Linguistic Landscape of the Navajo Nation." *Journal of Anthropological Research* 70 (3): 385–410.

———, and Leighton C. Peterson. 2011. "Introduction: American Indian Languages in Unexpected Places." *American Indian Culture and Research Journal* 35 (2): 1–18.

Wee, Lionel. 2005. "Intra-language Discrimination and Linguistic Human Rights: The Case of Singlish." *Applied Linguistics* 26 (1): 48–69.

Wheeler, Lesley. 2008. *Voicing American Poetry: Sound and Performance from the 1920s to the Present*. Ithaca, NY: Cornell University Press.

Whorf, Benjamin. 1956. *Language, Thought, and Reality*. Edited by John Carroll. Cambridge, MA: Massachusetts Institute of Technology Press.

Williams, Raymond. 1977. *Marxism and Literature*. Oxford: Oxford University Press.

Witherspoon, Gary. 1977. *Language and Art in the Navajo Universe*. Ann Arbor: University of Michigan Press.

Woodbury, Anthony. 1985. "The Functions of Rhetorical Structure: A Study of Central Alaskan Yupik Eskimo Discourse." *Language in Society* 14:153–90.

———. 1987. "Meaningful Phonological Processes: A Consideration of Central Alaskan Yupik Eskimo Prosody." *Language* 63 (4): 685–740.

———. 1998. "Documenting Rhetorical, Aesthetic, and Expressive Loss in Language Shift." In *Endangered Languages*, edited by Lenore Grenoble and Lindsay Whaley, 234–58. Cambridge: Cambridge University Press.

Woolard, Kathryn. 1998. "Simultaneity and Bivalency as Strategies in Bilingualism." *Journal of Linguistic Anthropology* 8 (1): 3–29.

Wyman, Leland. 1970. *Blessingway*. Tucson: University of Arizona Press.

Yazzie, Evangeline Parsons, and Margaret Speas. 2007. *Diné Bizaad Bínáhoo'aah: Rediscovering the Navajo Language*. Flagstaff, AZ: Salina Bookshelf.

Yazzie, Venaya. 2008. "Uranium Monsters Once More Approach?" *Navajo Times*, Feb. 21, A6.

Young, Robert. 1970. "The Rise of the Navajo Tribe." In *Plural Society in the Southwest*, edited by Edward Spicer and Raymond Thompson, 167–237. Albuquerque: University of New Mexico Press.

———, and William Morgan. 1943. *The Navaho Language: The Elements of Navaho Grammar with a Dictionary in Two Parts Containing Basic Vocabularies of Navaho and English*. Phoenix: Education Division, U.S. Indian Service.

———. 1987. *The Navajo Language.* Albuquerque: University of New Mexico Press.

———. 1991. *Colloquial Navajo: A Dictionary.* New York: Hippocrene Books.

———. 1992. *Analytical Lexicon of Navajo.* With the assistance of Sally Midgette. Albuquerque: University of New Mexico Press.

Yurth, Cindy. 2009. "Tongue Tied: Navajo Men Say They're Not Allowed to Speak Native Language at Work." *Navajo Times,* April 23: A1, A3.

Zachary, Mary-Kathryn. 2005. "More Than the Law: Perspectives on an English-Only Case in Navajo Country." *Labor Law Journal* 56 (1): 5–29.

Zentella, Ana Celia. 2002. "Latin@ Languages and Identities." In *Latinos: Remaking America,* edited by Marcelo Suárez-Orozco and Mariela Páez, 321–38. Berkeley: University of California Press.

———. 2003. "'José, Can You See?' Latin@ Responses to Racist Discourse." In *Bilingual Aesthetics,* edited by Doris Sommer, 51–66. New York: Palgrave Press.

Zolbrod, Paul. 1984. *Diné Bahane.* Albuquerque: University of New Mexico Press.

———. 2004. Foreword to *Miracle Hill,* by Blackhorse Mitchell, xi–xxiv. Tucson: University of Arizona Press.

Index

About the Author

Anthony K. Webster is a linguistic anthropologist and associate professor in the Department of Anthropology at the University of Texas at Austin. He is the author of *Explorations in Navajo Poetry and Poetics* (2009, University of New Mexico Press) as well as numerous articles on Navajo language, ethnopoetics, and culture in journals such as the *Journal of Linguistic Anthropology*, *Language in Society*, *Anthropological Linguistics*, the *Journal of Anthropological Research*, the *International Journal of American Linguistics*, and the *Journal of Folklore Research*. His research focuses on the interrelationships between language, imagination, poetics, and the individual and cultural.